# THE SOCIAL STUDY OF JUDAISM

Program in Judaic Studies
Brown University
BROWN JUDAIC STUDIES
Edited by
Jacob Neusner,
Wendell S. Dietrich, Ernest S. Frerichs, William Scott Green,
Calvin Goldscheider, David Hirsch, Alan Zuckerman

**Project Editors (Project)**

David Blumenthal, Emory University (Approaches to Medieval Judaism)
William Brinner (Approaches to Judaism and Islam)
Ernest S. Frerichs, Brown University (Dissertations and Monographs)
Lenn Evan Goodman, University of Hawaii (Studies in Medieval Judaism)
William Scott Green, University of Rochester (Approaches to Ancient Judaism)
Norbert Samuelson, Temple University (Jewish Philosophy)
Jonathan Z. Smith, University of Chicago (Studia Philonica)

Number 160
THE SOCIAL STUDY OF JUDAISM
Essays and Reflections
*Volume One*

by
Jacob Neusner

# THE SOCIAL STUDY OF JUDAISM
## Essays and Reflections
### *Volume One*

by
Jacob Neusner

Scholars Press
Atlanta, Georgia

# THE SOCIAL STUDY OF JUDAISM
## Essays and Reflections
### *Volume One*

© 1988
Brown University

**Library of Congress Cataloging in Publication Data**

Neusner, Jacob, 1932-
  The social study of Judaism.

  (Brown Judaic studies ; no. 160)
  Includes index.
  1. Rabbinical literature--History and criticism.
2. Sociology, Jewish. I. Title. II. Series.
BM496.5.N482    1988      296.3'87      88-33664
ISBN  1-55540-306-9 (v. 1 : alk. paper)

Printed in the United States of America
on acid-free paper

For
My friend, colleague, ally, and co-worker
on the National Council on the Arts

## SENATOR ROBERT JOHNSON

FLORIDA STATE SENATE

HE BRINGS TO DISCOURSE ON PUBLIC POLICY IN THE ARTS
THE EFFECTIVE POLITICIAN'S RESPECT FOR THE PLEDGED WORD,
THE WORKING POLITICIAN'S COMMITMENT TO
NEGOTIATION AND GIVE AND TAKE,
AND THE LIFE-LONG POLITICIAN'S DEVOTION TO
THE PUBLIC INTEREST.

HE GIVES HIS PROFESSION AND HIS CALLING A GOOD NAME.

I VALUE HIS INSIGHT AND POWER OF APPLIED REASON AND
PRACTICAL LOGIC, RESPECT HIS GIFTS TO THE ARTS THROUGH
THE ENDOWMENT,
BUT ABOVE ALL, PRIZE AND APPRECIATE HIS FRIENDSHIP.

# Contents

# Preface

The social study of Judaism addresses the way in which a Judaism sets forth its conception of the social order. Systems of thought concerning the social order work out a cogent picture, self-evidently true for those who make them up, of *how* things are correctly to be sorted out and fitted together, of *why* things are done in one way, rather than in some other, and of *who* they are that do and understand matters in this particular way. These systems of thought then are composed of three elements: ethics, ethos, ethnos, that is, world-view, way of life, and an account of the social entity at hand. Such systems need not fall into the category of religion or invariably be held to form religions, and it is the fact that not all religions set forth accounts of the social order. But when, as has often been the case, people invoke God as the foundation for their world-view, maintaining that their way of life corresponds to what God wants of them, projecting their social entity in a particular relationship to God, then we have a system that is, as a matter of fact. And when, finally, a religious system appeals as an important part of its authoritative literature or canon to the Hebrew Scriptures of ancient Israel or "Old Testament," we have a Judaism. This book addresses the social scientific setting for the academic study of religion, with special reference to the three principal components of a the program of a social system, politics, economics, and philosophy. My most current work has called me to study the economics, politics, and philosophy of the Judaic systems in their successive unfolding in late antiquity. Let me set this present project forth. I have undertaken the development of the field of the political economy of religion, exemplified through the case of Judaism in its classical age.

This is a book of essays meant to explain and illustrate through free-standing essays a large project that I have undertaken. It also serves, at Chapter Eight, to supplement a major study with additional sources. In the scholarly initiative partially represented here, I propose to describe Judaism as a social system, hence the title, "the social study of Judaism." In doing so, I carry forward my sustained interest in the systemic study of religion, exemplified by Judaism. That is to say, reading a text in its context and as a statement of a larger matrix of meaning, I propose to ask larger questions of systemic description of a religious system represented by the particular text and its encompassing canon. Here, in particular, I take up the initial systemic statement of the paramount of Judaism of all time, which is the Mishnah, the first document of the Judaism of the dual Torah beyond Scripture. When we ask that a religious composition such as the Mishnah speak to a society with a message of the *is* and the *ought* and with a meaning for the everyday, we focus on the power of that system to hold the whole together: the society the system addresses, the individuals who compose the society, the ordinary lives they lead, in ascending order of consequence. And that system then forms a whole and well composed structure. All this in the case of a Judaism appeals not only to voluntary agreement but to the utilization of force, hence to politics, and that is what makes the politics of Judaism an important example in the study of the social foundations of a religion, any religion. These form the principal concerns of my effort to study Judaism as a social system.

No one should imagine that all religions set forth social systems and so may be subjected to social study, that is to say, description, analysis, interpretation of a social system of a religious character. Quite to the contrary, for the Judaisms and Christianities of late antiquity no political systems of comparable dimension and equivalent outreach parallel to that of the Mishnah come to hand. If the late antique religions of Israel, the several Judaisms and Christianities, yield no counterpart to the politics of the Judaism of the Mishnah, then how are we to identify any context for theoretical inquiry? And where are we to find that counterpart political system that makes possible comparison and contrast, hence the interpretation of what we have in hand in the context of other systematic statements on the same subject and in the same topical context? In theory any politics will do. For politics – the legitimate exercise of violence, the disposition of power, the determination of who gets to tell whom what to do, why, and with what outcome – by definition is ubiquitous. Wherever two or more are assembled in an on-going social entity, one tells the other what to do, and the other submits or concurs; a theory of power therefore operates. And with the gathering of more than a few, the social entity – community, people, village, class, or other classification of social entity – sets forth and sustains enduring structures and on-going systems of public policy that, in the aggregate, form a politics.

In this book, as in others of its classification, I address specialists in fields other than the study of Judaism, or in other aspects of Judaic or

Jewish Studies than the study of Judaism in late antiquity. I systematically set forth, in books of essays, results that seem to me accessible to a wider readership than is likely to study my sustained and detailed presentation of method and results. That accounts for the character of the work and also for the selections of chapters within it; all of the chapters are meant to be read individually, and there is no sustained argument.

In Chapter One I set forth my larger theory of what I wish to study about religion, which accounts for the entire research program beginning here. Chapters Two and Three define what I mean by a Judaism, and also make very clear which Judaism I treat here, what sources of that Judaism are under discussion, and why that Judaism defines an important social system for sustained analytical study. There is a slight overlap between Chapters Two and Three, because these are meant to be read individually and were written separately. But the level of generalization at Chapter Two serves to place one Judaism into the context of a variety of Judaisms, and the level of particularization at Chapter Three then explains in considerable detail the reason that the methods I have devised have been shaped by the data at hand. Chapters Four and Five go over two important questions of the economics of Judaism. Chapter Four began as a lecture at Connecticut College. Chapter Five sets forth the three major themes of the economics of Judaism. The chapter summarizes the principal parts of my *Economics of Judaism.*

Chapter Six then defines the entire project concerning politics. It is a preliminary statement of the method of my book, *The Politics of Judaism. The Initial Structure and System,* which is presently in progress. Chapter Seven takes up the most difficult question, which is how to discern, in a philosophy set forth as a law-code, a substrate of myth. Since the Mishnah contains no mythic materials, e.g., narratives that explain how and why things are the way they are, truths set forth in the form of a teleology, how are we to proceed? The chapter explains the method that I devised for the entire politics project, since the same data that told me where and how to uncover the Judaic political myth brought me to a variety of other fundamental topics. Chapter Eight is meant as a supplement to *The Politics of Judaism.* In connection with that work, I of course drew together a vast quantity of pertinent data. When I found that much of the data bore no important consequences for my systemic analysis, being thematically relevant but systemically inert, I organized it as a set of supplements for the chapters of that book. The materials are provided here mainly for reference; I do not anticipate that readers will find the presentation engaging in its own terms. In all, two chapters, the one on distributive economics, the other on political myth, form sizable representations of the larger project and also present the results I think of widest interest outside of the field of the study of Judaism. The other chapters define the subject and method and explain what I think I am doing. Closely related to politics, economics, and philosophy, in the study of any religion's social system are science and technology. My earlier discussion of science in Judaism in its formative age is summarized here, since the papers at hand, read along with my "Why No Science in Judaism?" form a response to the program of intellectual inquiry devised by Max Weber. "Why No Capitalism in Judaism?" strikes me as a question with such an ineffably obvious answer that I have not found it necessary to provide the answer in a sustained way.

I conceive this project of social study to form a chapter in the study of the rise of Western civilization to world dominance. Just as Weber understood the issue, why has the West defined the world, so I want to explain in what ways Judaism has formed a Western religion, and in what ways it has not. Just as Weber asked questions of comparison and contrast in finding out what is particular and what common, so I want to find points of commonality and difference. At issue in academic debate in the next half century will be the place of the West in the world. Since, as a matter of fact, everywhere in the world, people aspire to those material advantages that flow, uniquely I think, from the modes of social organization that the West has devised – the West's economics, its science and technology, and also – let us say it straight out – its politics and also its philosophy as modes of thought and inquiry, I think it is time to stop apologizing and start analyzing what has made Western civilization the world-defining power that it has become. When Weber asked why no capitalism in India, China, or Judaism, he opened, in that exemplary manner, a much broader set of questions. When, nowadays, people rightly want to find a place, in the study of civilization that the academy sustains, for Africa, Asia, peoples indigenous to every region and land, we all need to frame a global program of thought and reflection. And if we are not merely to rehearse the facts of this one and that one, we shall require modes of comparison and in particular the comparative study of rationalities.

Hence sustaining questions, applying to all areas because of their ubiquitous relevance, why this, not that? have to come to definition. And since the simple fact of world civilization is that the West has now defined the world's economy, politics, and philosophy, and since all social systems measure themselves by Western civilization in its capacity to afford to large masses of people both the goods of material wealth and the services of political power, the indicative traits of the West demand close study. These are, I think, in politics, mass distribution of power in political structures and systems, in economics, capitalism, and in philosophy, the modes of thought and inquiry we call scientific. That explains how I have now undertaken to revise the entire program of the study of the Jews and Judaism. And, it is self-evident, what I mean to do is provide a model for others to follow in the study of all other social entities and their social systems. So the stakes in this scholarly program of mine are as high as I can make them.

As is clear, I plan a sequence of three sets of three studies, on the philosophy, politics, and economics of Judaism in the three stages of its initial development, the system of the Mishnah (ca. A.D. 200), the system represented by the Talmud of the Land of Israel and closely-allied writings such as Genesis Rabbah and Leviticus Rabbah (ca. A.D. 400), and the system adumbrated by the Talmud of Babylonia and its closest affines (ca. A.D. 600). These nine books then will allow both synchronic pictures of the successive Judaisms as these came to expression in the designated periods and places, and also diachronic pictures of the interrelationships among those same successive Judaisms. It is a somewhat complex project, but I think worth attempting. The nine planned books are of course underway, so it is not premature to announce the plan and to set forth initial results.

These first results pertain to two of the three principal components of what I conceive to be any theoretical system of the social order. Among the three, philosophy (world-view, ethics), politics (social entity, ethnos), and economics (way of life, ethos), I take up the second and the third. My next range of inquiry will confront the first of the three. The organization of the book is simple. I begin by defining the document I propose to analyze, explaining why it is important, and setting forth the premises and method of inquiry. Then I turn to free-standing papers on economics. Most of these papers are original here; some revise chapters of *Economics of Judaism,* for the interest of readers not likely to turn to the complete exposition there. The free-standing papers on politics include original ones as well as reprises of what is offered in *Politics of Judaism.*

Clearly, this work flows from a long sequence of earlier studies and carries forward ideas and problems that have occupied me in inquiries of a quite different order. Prior publications of mine relevant to this program are as follows:

*Judaism. The Evidence of the Mishnah.* Chicago: University of Chicago Press, 1981. *Choice,* "Outstanding academic book list," 1982-83. Paperback edition: 1984. Second printing, 1985. Third printing, 1986. Second edition, augmented: Atlanta: Scholars Press for Brown Judaic Studies, 1987.

*Judaism in Society: The Evidence of the Yerushalmi. Toward the Natural History of a Religion.* Chicago: The University of Chicago Press, 1983. *Choice,* "Outstanding Academic Book List," 1984-85.

*Death and Birth of Judaism. The Impact of Christianity, Secularism, and the Holocaust on Jewish Faith.* New York: Basic Books, 1987.

*Self-Fulfilling Prophecy: Exile and Return in the History of Judaism.* Boston: Beacon Press, 1987.

*Judaism and its Social Metaphors. Israel in the History of Jewish Thought.* New York: Cambridge University Press, 1988.

*The Making of the Mind of Judaism.* Atlanta: Scholars Press for Brown Judaic Studies, 1987.

*The Economics of Judaism. The Initial Statement.* Chicago: The University of Chicago Press, 1989.

*The Formation of the Jewish Intellect. Making Connections and Drawing Conclusions in the Traditional System of Judaism.* Atlanta: Scholars Press for Brown Judaic Studies, 1988.

*The Politics of Judaism. The Initial Structure and System.* In Press, 1990.

Editor: *Take Judaism, for Example. Studies toward the Comparison of Religions.* Chicago: University of Chicago Press, 1983.

*First Principles of Systemic Analysis. The Case of Judaism in the History of Religion.* Lanham: University Press of America, 1988. *Studies in Judaism* series.

*The Systemic Analysis of Judaism.* Atlanta: Scholars Press for Brown Judaic Studies, 1988.

*The Ecology of Religion: From Writing to Religion in the Study of Judaism.* Nashville: Abingdon, 1989.

*Understanding Seeking Faith. Essays on the Case of Judaism.* Volume Two. *Literature, Religion, and the Social Study of Judaism.* Atlanta: Scholars Press for Brown Judaic Studies, 1987.

*Understanding Seeking Faith. Essays on the Case of Judaism.* Volume Three. *Society, History, and the Political and Philosophical Uses of Judaism.* Atlanta: Scholars Press for Brown Judaic Studies, 1988.

*A Religion of Pots and Pans? Modes of Philosophical and Theological Discourse in Ancient Judaism. Essays and a Program.* Atlanta: Scholars Press for Brown Judaic Studies, 1988.

Editor: *Social Foundations of Judaism. Case-Studies of Religion and Society in Classical and Modern Times.* Edited with Calvin Goldscheider. Englewood Cliffs: Prentice Hall, 1989.

Many of these papers emerged in conversations with my colleague, teacher, and friend, Professor Calvin Goldscheider, and benefited also from discussions with his wife, Francis K. Goldscheider, both Professors of Sociology at Brown University. I discussed and planned this project, as I do all of my books of essays and many other things as well, with Professor William Scott Green, University of Rochester. To Professors Ernest S. Frerichs and Wendell S. Dietrich I express my on-going thanks for companionship of a highly enlightening sort; I learn more than, at times, they think they are teaching (or imagine I am hearing). I call attention to the excellent craftsmanship of Joshua Bell, Verbatim Word Processing, Inc., who carefully and conscientiously prepared the camera-ready copy of this book, as of so many other books of mine. I appreciate the extra effort and intelligence he invests in my books for Scholars Press/Brown Judaic Studies.

JACOB NEUSNER

Program in Judaic Studies
Brown University
Providence, Rhode Island

# PROLOGUE

# 1

## The Political Economy of Religion: Explaining a Field of Learning

My field of study is religion, and the shape of my method finds outline and definition in that academic subject. Now religions form social worlds and do so through the power of their rational thought, that is, their capacity to explain data in a (to an authorship) self-evidently valid way. The framers of religious documents answer urgent questions, framed in society and politics to be sure, in a manner deemed self-evidently valid by those addressed by the authorships at hand. For at stake in my *oeuvre*, now in print in more than two hundred books of various classifications and serving diverse purposes and audiences, are striking examples of how people in writing explain to themselves who they are as a social entity. Religion as a powerful force in human society and culture is realized in society, not only or mainly theology; religion works through the social entity that embodies that religion. Religions form social entities – "churches" or "peoples" or "holy nations" or monasteries or communities – that, in the concrete, constitute the "us," as against "the nations" or merely "them." And religions carefully explain, in deeds and in words, who that "us" is – and they do it every day. To see religion in this way is to take religion seriously as a way of realizing, in classic documents, a large conception of the world. But how do we describe, analyze and interpret a religion, and how do we relate the contents of a religion to its context? These issues of method are worked out through the reading of texts, and, I underline, through taking seriously and in their own terms the particularity and specificity of texts.

The formative writings of a particular Judaism serve as an example of how such work might be done. My *oeuvre* has concerned exemplary classics of Judaism and how they form a cogent statement. These

3

classical writings, produced from the first to the seventh centuries A.D., form the canon of a particular statement of Judaism, the Judaism of the dual Torah, oral and written. That canon defined Judaism in both Christendom and Islam from the seventh century to the present. The circumstances of its formation, in the beginnings of Western civilization, the issues important to its framers, the kind of writings they produced, the modes of mediating change and responding to crisis – these form the center of interest. To expound my method for systemic description, analysis, and interpretation on the basis of written evidence, I wrote this book. But the larger context in which my method has taken shape requires explanation in its own terms. That is what I propose to explain concerning my *oeuvre*, now three decades in the making.

To undertake systemic analysis on the strength of written evidence, I have systemically reread the classic documents of the Judaism that took shape in the first through sixth centuries A.D. and that has predominated since then, the Judaism of the dual Torah. These documents – the Mishnah, Midrash-compilations, the two Talmuds – represent the collective statement and consensus of authorships (none is credibly assigned to a single author and all are preserved because they are deemed canonical and authoritative) and show us how those authorships proposed to make a statement to their situation – and, I argue, upon the human condition. What I want to do is in three stages. First, I place a document on display in its own terms, examining the text in particular and in its full particularity and immediacy. Here I want to describe the text from three perspectives: rhetoric, logic, and topic (the standard program of literary criticism in the age at hand). Reading documents one by one represents a new approach in this field. Ordinarily, people have composed studies by citing sayings attributed to diverse authorities without regard to the place in which these sayings occur. They have assumed that the sayings really were said by those to whom they are attributed, and, in consequence, the generative category is not the document but the named authority. But if we do not assume that the documentary lines are irrelevant and that the attributions are everywhere to be taken at face value, then the point of origin – the document – defines the categorical imperative, the starting point of all study.

Second, I seek to move from the text to that larger context suggested by the traits of rhetoric, logic, and topic. Here I want to compare one text to others of its class and ask how these recurrent points of emphasis, those critical issues and generative tensions, draw attention from the limits of the text to the social world that the text's authorship proposed to address. Here too the notion that a document exhibits traits particular to itself is new with my work, although, overall, some have episodically noted traits of rhetoric distinctive to a given document, and, on the surface, differences as to topic – observed but not explained – have been noted. Hence the movement from text to context and how it is effected represents a fresh initiative on my part.

Finally, so far as I can, I want to find my way outward toward the matrix in which a variety of texts find their place. In this third stage I want to move from the world of intellectuals to the world they proposed to shape and create. That inquiry defines as its generative question how the social world formed by the texts as a whole proposes to define and respond to a powerful and urgent question, that is, I want to read the canonical writings as response to critical and urgent questions. Relating documents to their larger political settings is not a commonplace, and, moreover, doing so in detail – with attention to the traits of logic, rhetoric, and topic – is still less familiar.

That brings us to the systemic approach to the reading of the formative documents of Judaism, which I have invented. Spelling it out is not difficult. Writings such as those we read have been selected by the framers of a religious system, and, read all together, those writings are deemed to make a cogent and important statement of that system, hence the category, "canonical writings." I call that encompassing, canonical picture a "system," when it is composed of three necessary components: an account of a world-view, a prescription of a corresponding way of life, and a definition of the social entity that finds definition in the one and description in the other. When those three fundamental components fit together, they sustain one another in explaining the whole of a social order, hence constituting the theoretical account of a system. Systems defined in this way work out a cogent picture, for those who make them up, of *how* things are correctly to be sorted out and fitted together, of *why* things are done in one way, rather than in some other, and of *who* they are that do and understand matters in this particular way. When, as is commonly the case, people invoke God as the foundation for their world-view, maintaining that their way of life corresponds to what God wants of them, projecting their social entity in a particular relationship to God, then we have a religious system. When, finally, a religious system appeals as an important part of its authoritative literature or canon to the Hebrew Scriptures of ancient Israel or "Old Testament, we have a Judaism.

I recognize that in moving beyond specific texts into the larger world-view they join to present, I may be thought to cross the border from the humanistic study of classical texts to the anthropological reading of those same texts. I therefore emphasize that I take most seriously the particularity and specificity of each document, its program, its aesthetics, its logic. I do not propose to commit upon a classic writing an act of reductionism, reading a work of humanistic meaning merely as a sociological artifact. And, further, as between Weber and his critics, I take my place with Weber in maintaining that ideas constitute, in their context and circumstance, what sociologists call independent variables, not only responding to issues of society, but framing and giving definition to those larger issues. In this way I make a stand, in the systemic reading of the classic writings of Judaism in its formative age, with those who insist upon the ultimate rationality of discourse.

The movement from text to context and matrix is signalled by use of the word "system." For reading a text in its context and as a statement of a larger matrix of meaning, I propose to ask larger questions of systemic description of a religious system represented by the particular text and its encompassing canon. Colleagues who work on issues of religion and society will find familiar the program I am trying to work out. But, I underline, the success of that program is measured by its power to make the texts into documents of general intelligibility for the humanities, to read the text at hand in such a way as to understand its statement within, and of, the human condition. That seems to me not only the opposite of reductionism but also a profoundly rationalist mode of inquiry.

Systems begin in the social entity, whether one or two persons or two hundred or ten thousand – there and not in their canonical writings, which come only afterward, or even in their politics. The social group, however, formed, frames the system, the system then defines its canon within, and addresses its politics to the larger setting, the *polis* without. We describe systems from their end products, the writings. But we have then to work our way back from canon to system, not to imagine either that the canon is the system, or that the canon creates the system. The canonical writings speak, in particular, to those who can hear, that is, to the members of the community, who, on account of that perspicacity of hearing, constitute the social entity or systemic community. The community then comprises that social group the system of which is recapitulated by the selected canon. The group's exegesis of the canon in terms of the everyday imparts to the system the power to sustain the community in a reciprocal and self-nourishing process. The community through its exegesis then imposes continuity and unity on whatever is in its canon.

While, therefore, we cannot account for the origin of a successful system, we can explain its power to persist. It is a symbolic transaction, as I said just now, in which social change comes to expression in symbol-change. That symbolic transaction, specifically, takes place in its exegesis of the systemic canon, which, in literary terms, constitutes the social entity's statement of itself So, once more, the texts recapitulate the system. The system does not recapitulate the texts. The system comes before the texts and defines the canon. The exegesis of the canon then forms that on-going social action that sustains the whole. A system does not recapitulate its texts, it selects and orders them. A religious system imputes to them as a whole cogency, one to the next, that their original authorships have not expressed in and through the parts, and through them a religious system expresses its deepest logic, *and it also frames that just fit that joins system to circumstance.*

The whole works its way out through exegesis, and the history of any religious system – that is to say, the history of religion writ small – is the exegesis of its exegesis. And the first rule of the exegesis of systems is the simplest, and the one with which I conclude: *the system does not recapitulate the canon. The canon recapitulates the system.* The system forms a statement of a social entity, specifying its world view and way of life in such a way that, to the participants in the system, the whole makes sound sense, beyond argument. So in the beginning are not words of inner and intrinsic affinity, but (as Philo would want us to say) the Word: the transitive logic, the system, all together, all at once, complete, whole, finished – the word awaiting only that labor of exposition and articulation that the faithful, for centuries to come, will lavish at the altar of the faith. A religious system therefore presents a fact not of history but of immediacy, of the social present.

The issue of why a system originates and survives, if it does, or fails, if it does, by itself proves impertinent to the analysis of a system but of course necessary to our interpretation of it. A system on its own is like a language. A language forms an example of language if it produces communication through rules of syntax and verbal arrangement. That paradigm serves full well however many people speak the language, or however long the language serves. Two people who understand each other form a language-community, even, or especially, if no one understands them. So too by definition religions address the living, constitute societies, frame and compose cultures. For however long, at whatever moment in historic time, a religious system always grows up in the perpetual present, an artifact of its day, whether today or a long-ago time. The only appropriate tense for a religious system is the present. A religious system always *is*, whatever it was, whatever it will be. Why so? Because its traits address a condition of humanity in society, a circumstance of an hour – however brief or protracted the hour and the circumstance.

When we ask that a religious composition speak to a society with a message of the *is* and the *ought* and with a meaning for the everyday, we focus on the power of that system to hold the whole together: the society the system addresses, the individuals who compose the society, the ordinary lives they lead, in ascending order of consequence.  And that system then forms a whole and well composed structure.  Yes, the structure stands somewhere, and, indeed, the place where it stands will secure for the system either an extended or an ephemeral span of life.  But the system, for however long it lasts, serves.  And that focus on the eternal present justifies my interest in analyzing why a system works (the urgent agenda of issues it successfully solves for those for whom it solves those problems) when it does, and why it ceases to work (loses self-evidence, is bereft of its "Israel," for example) when it no longer works.  The phrase, the *history* of a *system*, presents us with an oxymoron.  Systems endure – and their classic texts with them – in that eternal present that they create.  They evoke precedent, they do not have a history.  A system relates to context, but, as I have stressed, exists in an enduring moment (which, to be sure, changes all the time).  We capture the system in a moment, the worm consumes it an hour later.  That is the way of mortality, whether for us one by one, in all mortality, or for the works of humanity in society.  But systemic analysis and interpretation requires us to ask questions of history and comparison, not merely description of structure and cogency.  So in this exercise we undertake first description, that is, the text, then analysis, that is, the context, and finally, interpretation, that is, the matrix, in which a system has its being.

Let me now specify the discipline within which my method is meant to find its place.  It is the history of religion, and my special area, history of Judaism in its formative period, the first six centuries A.D.  I am trying to find out how to describe a Judaism in a manner consonant with the historical character of the evidence, therefore in the synchronic context of society and politics, and not solely or mainly in the diachronic context of theology which, until now, has defined matters.  The inherited descriptions of the Judaism of the dual Torah (or merely "Judaism") have treated as uniform the whole corpus of writing called "the Oral Torah."  The time and place of the authorship of a document played no role in our use of the allegations, as to fact, of the writers of that document.  All documents have ordinarily been treated as part of a single coherent whole, so that anything we find in any writing held to be canonical might be cited as evidence of views on a given doctrinal or legal, or ethical topic.  "Judaism" then was described by applying to all of the canonical writings the categories found imperative, e.g., beliefs about God, life after death, revelation, and the like. So far as historical circumstance played a role in that description, it was assumed that everything in any document applied pretty much to all cases, and historical facts derived from sayings and stories pretty much as the former were cited and the latter told.

Prior to the present time, ignoring the limits of documents, therefore the definitive power of historical context and social circumstance, all books on "Judaism" or "classical," "Rabbinic," "Talmudic" Judaism, have promiscuously cited all writings deemed canonical in constructing pictures of the theology or law of that Judaism, severally and jointly, so telling us about Judaism, all at once and in the aggregate. That approach has lost all standing in the study of Christianity of the same time and place, for all scholars of the history of Christianity understand the diversity and contextual differentiation exhibited by the classical Christian writers. But, by contrast, ignoring the documentary origin of statements, the received pictures of Judaism have presented as uniform and unitary theological and legal facts that originated each in its own document, that is to say, in its distinctive time and place, and each as part of a documentary context, possibly also of a distinct system of its own. I had of course corrected that error by insisting that each of those documents be read in its own terms, as a statement – if it constituted such a statement – *of* a Judaism, or, at least, *to* and so in behalf of, a Judaism. I maintained that each theological and legal fact was to be interpreted, to begin with, in relationship to the other theological and legal facts among which it found its original location.

The result of that reading of documents as whole but discrete statements, as I believe we can readily demonstrate defined their original character, is in such works as *Judaism: The Evidence of the Mishnah, Judaism and Society: The Evidence of the Yerushalmi, Judaism and Scripture: The Evidence of Leviticus Rabbah,* as well as *Judaism and Story: The Evidence of The Fathers According to Rabbi Nathan.* At the conclusion of that work, for reasons spelled out in its own logic, I stated that the documentary approach had carried me as far as it could. I reached an impasse for a simple reason. Through the documentary approach I did not have the means of reading the whole all together and all at once. The description, analysis, and interpretation of a religious system, however, require us to see the whole in its entirety, and I had not gained such an encompassing perception. That is why I recognized that I had come to the end of the line, although further exercises in documentary description, analysis, and interpretation and systemic reading of documents assuredly will enrich and expand, as well as correct, the picture I have achieved in the incipient phase of the work.

I have worked on describing each in its own terms and context the principal documents of the Judaism of the dual Torah. I have further undertaken a set of comparative studies of two or more documents, showing the points in common as well as the contrasts between and among them. This protracted work is represented by systematic accounts of the Mishnah, tractate Avot, the Tosefta, Sifra, Sifré to Numbers, the Yerushalmi, Genesis Rabbah, Leviticus Rabbah, Pesiqta deRab Kahana, The Fathers According to Rabbi Nathan, the Bavli, Pesiqta Rabbati, and various other writings (listed presently). In all of this work I have proposed to examine one by one and then in groups of like writings the main components of the dual Torah. I wished to place each into its own setting and so attempt to trace the unfolding of the dual Torah in its historical manifestation. In the later stages of the work, I attempted to address the question of how some, or even all, of the particular documents formed a general statement. I wanted to know where and how documents combined to constitute one Torah of the dual Torah of Sinai.

Time and again I concluded that while two or more documents did intersect, the literature as a whole is made up of distinct sets of documents, and these sets over the bulk of their surfaces do not as a matter of fact intersect at all. The upshot was that while I could show interrelationships among, for example, Genesis Rabbah, Leviticus Rabbah, Pesiqta deRab Kahana, and Pesiqta Rabbati, or among Sifra and the two Sifrés, I could not demonstrate that all of these writings pursued in common one plan, defining literary, redactional, and logical traits of cogent discourse, or even one program, comprising a single theological or legal inquiry. Quite to the contrary, each set of writings demonstrably limits itself to its distinctive plan and program and not to cohere with any other set. And the entirety of the literature most certainly cannot be demonstrated to form that one whole Torah, part of the still larger Torah of Sinai, that constitutes the Judaism of the dual Torah.

Having begun with the smallest whole units of the oral Torah, the received documents, and moved onward to the recognition of the somewhat larger groups comprised by those documents, I reached an impasse. On the basis of literary evidence – shared units of discourse, shared rhetorical and logical modes of cogent statement, for example – I came to the conclusion that a different approach to the definition of the whole, viewed all together and all at once, was now required. Seeing the whole all together and all at once demanded a different approach. But – and I state with heavy emphasis: *it has to be one that takes full account of the processes of formation and grants full recognition to issues of circumstance and context, the layers and levels of completed statements.* That is what I propose to accomplish in the exercise of systemic analysis, which the seminar is meant to illustrate and carry forward. My explanation of the movement from text, to context, to matrix, now takes on, I believe, more concrete meaning.

It may help to specify current work. I am trying to find out how to describe that "Judaism" beyond the specific texts – now beyond the text and the context and toward the matrix of all of the canonical texts – that each document takes for granted but no document spells out. And that research inquiry brings me to the matter of category-formation, which, in this context, requires me to specify the categorical imperative in the description of a Judaism. As I see it, there are three components of any Judaism, deriving their definition from the systemic model with which I began: world-view, way of life, social entity. As is clear, "Israel" forms the social entity. The documents at hand, as I shall show, demand that we focus upon that same matter. So the category comes to me both from the theoretical framework I have devised, but also from the inductive reading of the sources as I have now read the bulk of them. Two further categories that will occupy my attention in time to come may be stated in Judaic and also in abstract theoretical terms. The Judaic category, God "in our image" corresponds to the theoretical component of the world-view, and the Judaic category of the human being "after our likeness" corresponds – though not so self-evidently – to the theoretical component of the way of life. The correspondence will strike the reader as a simple one, when we recall that, in any Judaism, "we" are what "we" do. To all Judaic systems known to me, one's everyday way of life forms a definitive element in the system, and if we wish to know how a Judaic system at its foundations defines its way of life, we do well to translate the details of the here and the now into the portrait of humanity "after our likeness." I have now spelled out in my studies the systemic social entity and the systemic world-view in, respectively, *"Israel": Judaism and its Social Metaphors* (Cambridge: Cambridge University Press, 1988), and *The Incarnation of God. The Character of Divinity in Formative Judaism* (Philadelphia: Fortress Press, 1988). My account of the systemic way of life in due course will be *In Our Image: Judaism and its Anthropological Metaphors* (not andropological!). My sense is that the planned study is full of self-evident propositions, which is why I have been reluctant to carry it out. What these studies set forth, then, are the systemic social entity, world-view, and, in the anthropology, way of life.

To explain these two works and the anticipated completion of the project: I therefore determined to pursue through the formative documents, as I had traced the stages of their unfolding, the formation and function of the principal systemic components of the world-view of the Judaism at hand. Since any Judaism will make a statement concerning world-view, way of life, and social entity or "Israel," I see three choices and plan to work on all three of them. "World-view" begins with heaven, not earth, since that is the world, up there, upon which Judaic sages fix their gaze. So I wrote a work on the personality of God, "in our image." "Social entity" of course requires us to examine "Israel." As to "way of life," I see that category as representing, in a Judaic system, the systemic theory of humanity or anthropology. I identify as anthropological the metaphors through which the authorships of the documents of the dual Torah speak in concrete terms of that abstraction treated as a thing when we speak of "way of life." The seminar will work on these three matters and how we may learn to identify appropriate data and critically – in the correct social and historical context – to describe, analyze, and interpret those data.

This brings us to the book at hand. To place this book into its context, I wish to specify the field of learning in which I wish to participate – indeed, which I hope to help renovate. It is the study of the political economy of religion. Let me now explain what I mean by that field and how in this book and in the others of its series on economics and philosophy I wish to join in its work: the study of political economy with special attention to religion. Let us begin with the a simple statement of the premise concerning the character of religion on which my work is constructed.

Religion as a powerful force in human society and culture is realized in society, not only or mainly theology; religion works through the social entity that embodies that religion. Religions form social entities – appealing for social metaphors of hierarchization to such entities as "churches" or "peoples" or "holy nations" or "monasteries" or "communities" or classes of castes of persons – that, in the concrete, constitute the "us," as against "the nations" or merely "them." And religions carefully explain, in deeds and in words, who that "us" is – and through designing the social order, religions attempt to realize that explanation. That viewpoint on the nature of religion accounts for the questions raised here and in related studies of mine, present and projected, all together concerning the politics, philosophy, and economics of a Judaism in its nascent stage, then in its median, and third in its final and classic stages and statements as well: a three-dimensional analysis of the unfolding of a sustaining social vision and design for the society of Judaism.

Political economy joins the study of the institutions of the management of power we know as the politics of a society with the analysis of the disposition of scarce resources we know as economics. In prior ages, the ideas that governed collective life and conduct, that is, political ideas, encompassed issues of material life generally deemed economic, and in the interstices and interplay of both politics and economics, large-scale conceptions of the public interest and of society took shape. Aristotle's *Politics*, which is the model of a political economy, pays ample attention to economics in the setting of politics, and, in the case of Aristotle, what the system says about economics forms a chapter within the larger statement of the system as a whole. And that is the point at which religion becomes a matter of acute interest. For religious systems may make statements not only about matters we identify as theology but also about economics and political behavior.

If, as is commonly said, religions are, and are today studied as, modes of making social worlds, that language very commonly veils considerable uncertainty about what we wish to know about the "making of a social world" that a religion proposes to accomplish (and may actually effect). In any event one universal criterion for the differentiation and classification of religious systems is whether or not a religious system addresses, encompasses within its system, the realm of political economy. Some do, some do not. Christianity in late antiquity had virtually nothing to say about economics and cannot be said to have affected political economy at all, while in medieval times, with its encounter with Aristotle in particular, Christianity in the West worked out a political economy that predominated until the eighteenth century, when politics went its way, and economics became disembedded from the political world. It is perfectly self-evident that, from antiquity, Judaism, and from its beginning in early medieval times, Islam, have taken as critical the issues of political economy and have assumed a powerful role in the organization of politics and the management of economics. And other religious systems do as well. That is why the political economy of religions, how it is to be described, analyzed, and interpreted, forms a central concern for anyone interested in how humanity in the past, and the world today, sort out the issues of public policy for politics and economics alike.

Not only so, but until World War I, considerable interest attached to generalizations about political economy of religion. The field does not have to be invented, only renewed and reworked in light of things we have learned about religion and about the academic study of religion. For one major example, Weber's *Protestant Ethic and the Spirit of Capitalism* was only a chapter in public discussion, alongside Sombart's work on the theory that capitalism arose not from the Protestants but from the Jews. Weber worked on China, India, and ancient Israel as well, asking about the relationships between religious belief and the conduct of political economy, that is, rational economic action within a defined political framework of power relationships, all read against the backdrop of beliefs about "the sacred" or other religious concerns. So we may say that the political economy of religions is an old subject. But it has to be reworked, since we now realize that belief systems of religion form only one part of the whole, and not, as even Weber posited, the centerpiece of interest. Since Weber we have learned much about religion and how to study religion, but we have not pursued Weber's questions. And that is why, through the reengagement with political economy as a dimension of religious systems and their construction of societies and world-views, I have undertaken to renew a discipline that, well over half a century ago, proved its worth.

But political economy of religion assuredly requires renewal, and available work guides only as to goal, but not as to method, and that is for two reasons. First, because none of the inherited work accomplished the useful description of the religions under study. The ways in which religions were described have vastly changed. My work on systemic description, analysis, and interpretation of religions, focused on Judaism, shows in the contrast with Weber's *Ancient Judaism* that we have made many steps forward since that time and has rendered utterly obsolete every word in Weber's book on the same subject. Second, because, in point of fact, while the issues of political economy in relationship to religion retain their urgency, in Islam, Christendom, and the worlds of India and Southeast Asia, for example, so that we cannot speak of Latin America without its Liberation Theology, a vast statement upon issues of political economy, systematic and critical work is virtually unknown. In the range of theory and accurate description, analysis, and interpretation of the political economy of a religious world, and in the comparison of the political economy of one religious system with that of another, so far as I know, scholarship in the study of religion has fallen silent. And yet, as we now recognize, there is simply no coping with the world today without the intellectual tools for understanding religion, not as a theory of another world, but as a power and force in the shaping of this world. Events in Iran and Afghanistan, as to Islam, Azerbaijan and Armenia as to Islam and Christianity, Latin America and Poland, as to Roman Catholic Christianity, the State of Israel and the USA, as to Judaism, only illustrate that simple fact that most (though not all) of humanity does what it does by reason of religious conviction. And since public policy falls silent before that fact, it is time to reenter discourse with issues long dormant on the relationship between religious systems and the world of politics and of economics.

I use as my case the Judaism of late antiquity, because that is one religious system that did, indeed, develop a large-scale conception of political economy, that is to say, that is a religious system that made its encompassing statement, also, through what it had to say about the household as the irreducible unit of production, about the market and its role in rationing scarce goods, and about wealth and its relationship to money (and to land, as a matter of fact). In this regard, that Judaism carried forward in a way, so far as I know unique in ancient times the systematic thought of Aristotle, the only figure in antiquity who had anything important to say about economics. The system of that Judaism, further, paid ample attention also to the disposition of issues and institutions of power we know as political science, once again, a remarkable labor of large-scale social thought. The study, therefore, of the political economy of ancient Judaism, beginning in the law-codes and other writings of that Judaism, seems to me a promising area in which to develop the intellectual tools – points of inquiry, modes of thought – that will serve as a useful model in studying the political economy of Buddhism or of Islam, each in its varieties and rich diversity, as well as of Christianities of medieval and modern times. It goes without saying that the reading of the law for other than legal theory, so far as the study of antiquity is concerned, also is not a commonplace inquiry.

My own preparation for this work began with my study of the logical structures – that is to say, in Weber's language, the rationalities – of the writings of ancient Judaism, yielding *The Making of the Mind of Judaism. The Formative Age* and *The Formation of the Jewish Intellect.* When I finished *Formation*, I turned to economics, which is now *The Economics of Judaism: The Initial Statement.* Reading for this work and conversations with colleagues here have broadened my conception and made me realize that Aristotle is the model for this system as a whole, combining as he did the issues of the material sustenance of society and the political organization of society, and, of course, exercising a sustaining influence nearly down to the eighteenth century Physiocrats, founders of economics as we now know it. It was with my study of Plato and Aristotle in the setting of economics, as I looked for the affinities and influences on the thought of the writers of the formative documents of Judaism, that my notion of the "re-founding" of political economy of religion as a subfield of the academic study of religion came up. And that brings us to this and the next planned studies of the initial system, *The Politics of Judaism* and, to come, *The Philosophy of Judaism.* When this systematic account of the economics, politics, and philosophy embedded in the initial system have been completed, I shall turn to the next system, connected to, but not continuous or wholly symmetrical with the first, which is the system of the Talmuds of the Land of Israel and Babylonia and related writings. Although meant to be read on its own, this work therefore forms part of a tripartite inquiry into the social foundations of Judaism, which I conceive to be philosophy, politics, and economics. That tripartite grid, moreover, in due course will be joined by two further grids, so that in the end a three-dimensional picture of the initial social system of Judaism ought to emerge. The other two stages in the triplet-grid are defined by the middle and then final stages in which the Judaism under study came to formation and expression.

Since by a religion, e.g., a Judaism, I mean the account of a world-view, way of life, and social entity, that all together takes up an urgent question and sets forth a self-evidently valid answer, I translate my generative categories into social scientific ones. These then are, for way of life, economics; world-view, philosophy; and social entity, politics. Hence a picture of the social foundations of Judaism is defined by the philosophy, politics, and economics set forth in the writings identified as canonical by a given system, a Judaism. In my *Economics of Judaism. The Initial Statement* (Chicago: University of Chicago Press, 1989) I explain why the same system-builders also resorted to economics to make their systemic statement, and in work to follow this one, the *Philosophy of Judaism*, I shall lay out the philosophical system on which the entire composition rests. I plan to build my account on a set of monographs on how discrete philosophical issues are investigated and discussed by the framers of the Mishnah.

These three inquiries set forth only the initial system of Judaism, the one to which the Mishnah attests. But that Judaism in many important ways hardly turned out wholly symmetrical with the final system of Judaism that emerged from the formative age and defined matters to the present day. The economics, politics, and philosophy of the initial formation of Judaism set the agenda and formed the court of appeal. But successors and continuators picked and chose, and, it follows, they framed a fresh definition for the social foundations of the world they proposed to invent. The philosophy, politics, and economics of the next phase in the formation of Judaism, seen on their own but also in relationship with the initial theories, will therefore demand sustained description, analysis, and interpretation. That explains why, as I said just now, in work that lies beyond, I plan to show how the initial system was revised and adapted by later system-makers. What is at stake, in all, is how intellectuals defined the rationalities of Judaism as a social composition: a theory of the society of Israel, the holy people of God.

This work on the successive rationalities of an unfolding Judaism is meant to answer for Judaism those questions that the coming renewal of the inquiry into the history and comparative study of religion will certainly address.  In providing the example of the initial politics of a particular Judaism, I mean to continue a discussion by proposing a new set of possibilities for examination by a field the rebirth of which is foresee.  For the twenty-first century will see a world in which otherness demands explanation, and in which diverse rationalities will impose the necessity for renewed inquiry into what people think is normal and right and true – and why, therefore they may tell one another what to do, which is to say, an inquiry into the political systems and structures put forth by religion.

In setting forth the initial politics of Judaism, moreover, I need hardly remind the reader, we cannot claim to know the sources of Judaic political thought or action, either among sages of the third century, who received the Mishnah, or, all the more so, in the twenty-first century.  The Mishnah and its Judaism are not on everybody's tongue, except for isolated circles, where people do not ask questions about rationality and the comparison of rationalities.  Accordingly, as for the issues set forth here, people can hardly be expected even to recognize the name of the document.  What we contemplate – to repeat – is only the work of mind and imagination of a small group of religious intellectuals, who, as I said, set forth to make up a world, and did.  True enough, their design laid out the foundations of the Judaism that proved paramount and, over time, definitive.  But their systemic boundaries, in particular the political ones, turn out to rest on foundations laid out in a wholly asymmetrical relationship with the outlines of the politics that ultimate came to full realization among the Jews and in their governments and administrations, from the third century onward.  In many aspects we follow the map for ways not taken.

But, as a matter of fact, on the journey people did undertake, they thought that they were following this very map.  And, in a way, they did.  But it was not the way they thought, and it did not lead to where they imagined they would end up.  In tracing their steps, in the systems that were built, asymmetrically to be sure, on the foundations of the initial system, in time to come, in time to come we shall understand what happened and why.  For the one thing of which we may be certain is that, when religions set out to form politics and invent a state, in the end they never come up with what at the outset they propose to set forth.  That is to say, religions make worlds, but not always, indeed, not very often, the ones they wanted or ever ha in mind.  If I had to explain that odd fact of the human encounter with the divine, I would invoke God's infinite capacity for laughter.  But why explain the world above, when the task at hand is simply to describe the plan and the program to begin with founded in, and formative of, this world of ours.  And that is what in this book and its companions I am trying to accomplish.

To conclude this account, let me turn to undergraduate education, for, I maintain, one important concern of all methods worked out for the academy is the impact of scholarship on undergraduate education.  In our shared work, we did not neglect that consideration.  In my *oeuvre* I see two important results for the teaching of religion as an academic subject.  First, I am trying to learn how to read a text in such a way as to highlight the human situation addressed by an authorship.  If I can do so, I can show undergraduates of diverse origin what this text has to say to people in general, not only to Jews (of a quite specific order) in particular.   In other words, my entire enterprise is aimed at a humanistic and academic reading of classics of Judaism, yet with full regard for their specific statements to their own world.  People wrote these books as a way of asking and answering questions we can locate and understand – that is my premise – and when we can find those shared and human dimensions of documents, we can relate classic writings to a world we understand and share.  That imputes a common rationality to diverse authorships and ages – theirs and ours – and, I believe, expresses the fundamental position of the academic humanities.

The second lesson draws us from text to context.  Treating a religion in its social setting, as something a group of people do together, rather than as a set of beliefs and opinions, prepares colleagues to make sense of a real world of ethnicity and political beliefs formed on the foundation of religious origins.  Indeed, if colleagues do not understand that religion constitutes one of the formative forces in the world today, they will not be able to cope with the future.  But how to see precisely the ways in which religious forms social worlds?  In the small case of Judaism, a set of interesting examples is set forth.  Here they see that diverse Judaic systems responded to pressing social and political questions by setting forth cogent and (to the believers) self-evidently valid answers.  That is one important aspect of the world-creating power of religion, and one nicely illuminated in the formation of Judaic systems.

The more critical academic issue should be specified.  We are living in an age in which the old humanities are joined by new ones; women's studies (in their humanistic mode), black studies, Jewish studies, and a broad variety of other subjects enter the curriculum.  The universities require them, because we now know that the humanities encompass a world beyond the European, religions in addition to the Christian, for instance. But how are we to make our own and academic what appears at first encounter to be alien and incomprehensible? One solution accepts as special and particular the new humanities, treating as general and normal the old ones. Hence – in the settlement accepted by some – Jews teach Jewish things to Jews, and form a segregated intellectual community within the larger academic world. But I think that the subject-matter at hand is too urgent and important – and altogether too interesting – to be left to the proprietors or to be permitted to be segregated. To deprive interested colleagues and students of access to the rich human experience and expression contained within the cultural artifacts of hitherto excluded parts of humanity diminishes the academic program and misrepresents the condition of humanity. But how to afford access to what is strange and perceived as abnormal is not readily explained. I have spent nearly thirty years trying to find appropriate access for colleagues and students alike to one of the new humanities. In the terms of Judaic studies I have insisted that the ghetto walls, once down, may not be reconstructed in the community of intellect. And, in that same framework, I have spent my life trying to explore the dimensions of a world without walls. That is the context in which the entire program now spelled out finds its shape and motivation. Now to the bibliography itself.

Part One

# IDENTIFYING A JUDAISM

# 2

## Defining a Judaism

A religious system that appeals to the Hebrew Scriptures or Old Testament in setting forth a world-view and describing a way of life addressed to a particular "Israel" comprises a Judaism. While every Judaism known in history has appealed to the Old Testament, any definition of a single normative Judaism requires theological judgments that rest upon conviction. Description, rather than conviction, begins in the recognition of the variety of Judaic systems known not only in today's world, but also in the past. For diverse Judaisms have flourished over time, from the completion of the Pentateuch, the five books of Moses, in ca. 500 B.C., to our own day. All of them have identified "Israel," meaning God's holy people, and all have appealed to passages of Scripture, particularly the Pentateuch, for justification for the respective systems that they have set forth. The symbolic system of each Judaism, however, rests upon a system particular to itself. One Judaism may appeal for its generative symbol to "the Torah," meaning not only the Five Books of Moses but a much larger heritage of divine revelation in the media of both writing and oral formulation and transmission. Another Judaism may identify as its principal mode of expression a way of life centered upon cultic holiness realized within the community, as with the Essenes in general, and the Qumran Essenes in particular. The symbol of that Judaism will be not the Torah but the table at which everyday food was consumed in a state of cultic cleanness. A third Judaism, Orthodoxy of the Zionist sort, in our own time, may utilize the Messiah-theme and identify the formation of a Jewish state with the beginning of the attainment of the Messianic age.

These and other examples of Judaisms point both to the diversity of the religious systems that identify themselves as "Judaism" but also to commonalities among them. These are, first, appeal to Scripture (but each to its own florilegium of verses as prooftexts for pre-selected propositions); second, address to "Israel" (but each with its own identification of its devotees with "Israel" or, at least, "the true Israel"); and, third, a program of concrete actions in the workaday world for the realization of the faith (but every Judaism has its own notion of the essential or required actions). The theological definition of Judaism yields only diversity, therefore, and a comparison of ideas about God or the definition of the Torah held among several Judaisms would yield equivalent diversity (just as comparisons among Christianities' Christologies or ecclesiologies presents considerable points of disagreement). Defining all Judaisms within a single structure, rather than through a search for common points of theology, by contrast, produces a clear picture of shared and fundamental traits.

When we state in general terms the pentateuchal story, which is shared among all Judaisms, we find ourselves retelling in the setting of mythical ancestors the experience of exile and return, alienation and redemption, that actually characterized the Jews' history from the destruction of the temple of Jerusalem in 586 B.C. to the return to Jerusalem (Zion) and the rebuilding of the temple about a century and a half later. While not all Jews were sent by the conquerors, the Babylonians, into exile in 586, and among those who did go away, still fewer came back from 540 onward, when the new masters of the Middle East, the Iranians under Cyrus of the Persian dynasty, the compilers of the Pentateuch treated as normative the experience of being sent away from the land and returning to the land, hence, exile and redemption. Thus Abraham was commanded to leave Ur of the Chaldees, in the general vicinity of the Babylonia to which the exiles had been sent, and to wander to the land. His "children" (within the theory of "Israel" as one big family) gained the land but lost it to Egypt; then underwent wanderings in the desert until they regained the land. The land was held not permanently and as a settled fact of life but only on condition of obeying God's Torah, meaning, revelation, including law for the conduct of everyday life, and so living up to the covenant made by God with successive progenitors of "Israel." This pentateuchal story set forth the stipulative quality of possession of the land and treated the life of the people, Israel, as subject to qualifications and conditions, not as a given. Setting forth both the conditionality of Israel's existence but also the promise of reward for obedience to God's covenant, the Pentateuch laid out a fundamental structure which, thereafter, defined the generative experience of all Judaisms. Each would both set forth an account of its "Israel" that treated the given as subject to conditions, but also defined those conditions that would provide security and resolve doubt. A Judaism, in general, therefore both provoked resentment and doubt, but also resolved the doubt and provided remission for resentment, and that fundamental structural pattern, expressed as (in political and this-worldly terms) exile and redemption, characterizes every known Judaism.

But among Judaisms, a single one predominated from late antiquity to modern times and remains a powerful influence among Jews even today, and that is the Judaism that finds its definitive statement in the myth that, when Moses received the Torah, revelation, from God at Mount Sinai, God gave the Torah through two media, writing and also memory. The written Torah of this Judaism of the dual Torah is represented by Scripture or the Old Testament. The other Torah, formulated orally and transmitted only in memory, was handed on for many generations, from Moses down to the great sages of the early centuries of the Common Era (C.E.=A.D.), when it finally reached writing in documents produced by sages, who bore the honorific title, "rabbi," "my lord." This kind of Judaism bears several titles, one, rabbinic, because of the character of its leadership, another, Talmudic, because of its principal document, and, for theological reasons, "classical" or "normative," as indeed became the fact from the promulgation of the Talmud onward. Talmudic Judaism may best be traced through the unfolding of its writings, therefore, because it was in writing, in study in academies, through the teaching of holy men (in contemporary times, women as well) qualified for saintliness by learning, specifically, mastery of the Torah through discipleship, that that Judaism took shape. Just as one may write the history of Roman Catholic Christianity by tracing the story of the papacy, though that history would not be complete, and the history of Protestant Christianity through telling the story of the Bible in the world since the Reformation, so the history of the Judaism of the dual Torah takes shape in the tale of its holy books.

Among these, the first to reach closure was the Mishnah, an account, in the form of a law-code, of the holy life of "Israel," in the household and in the temple, in the family and in the village, to be compared to Plato's *Republic* and Aristotle's *Politics* as a picture of an ideal polity. The Mishnah came to conclusion in ca. A.D. 200, after about a century of sustained composition among successive generations of sages. While some of its materials go back into the first centuries, and basic facts even to scriptural times, the fundamental statement of the document as a whole is worked out as a complete and self-contained system, a cogent philosophy, not as the result of a sedimentary process of tradition. The emphasis of the Mishnah's philosophy stresses stability, order, the self-contained and stationary character of society, position, wealth and resources, all things in their proper place and under their proper name, reminiscent of the priestly account of creation in Genesis 1:1-2:4. Since, in the preceding century, with the destruction of the second temple in A.D. 70, the defeat of a major rebellion against Rome, then at the height of its power, in A.D. 132-135, and the disruption of the life of the Jews in their land ("Israel" in the "land of Israel," in theological terms), the people had known chaos, the document described the opposite of the everyday reality. Obedience to its design for the life of its "Israel" then promised what its authorship deemed critical.

If the Mishnah came forth as a utopian design in response to an existential crisis, however, it soon was turned into something quite different, namely, the constitution, along with Scripture, for the life of the Jews wherever they lived, not only in the Land of Israel but also in Babylonia, and for the here and now, not only for the time, envisaged by the Mishnah's authorship and therefore subjected to ample legislation, when the temple would be rebuilt. For the Mishnah was adopted as the basic law code of administration and government by the Jewish ethnarch of Palestine, which is to say, the patriarch of Israel in the Land of Israel, and many of the sages of the Mishnah's schools were employed as his clerks and administrators. Consequently a document only partially addressing the everyday life, in its divisions devoted to family affairs and civil law, but largely focused upon the temple and its cult, in its divisions concerning the conduct of the cult in everyday circumstances (the fifth division, Holy Things), on festivals (the second division, Appointed Times), and in regard to cultic cleanness (the sixth division, Purities), was reformed. The exegesis of the Mishnah now focused upon only part of its contents. The systemic study and application of those parts of the contents of the Mishnah pertinent to the everyday life of Israel in the Land of Israel in ca. A. D. 400 yielded a systematic restatement, known as the Talmud of the Land of Israel ("Yerushalmi"), and, in ca. A.D. 600, the counterpart for the Jews in Babylonia was the Talmud of Babylonia ("Bavli"). Of these two Talmuds, the latter, became paramount and authoritative and through its sustained exegesis and application under nearly all circumstances and in every age defined the Judaism of the dual Torah, that is to say, Judaism, from its time to our own. For even today all Judaisms, Reform, Orthodox, Conservative, Reconstructionist, appeal to the Bavli and related writings as the foundation-document for all else, while, of course, differing on points of interpretation and even the weight and authority of that writing and the other documents that appeal to it.

The Judaism of the dual Torah, appealing as it did to Scripture as much as to the Mishnah, in the time following the closure of the Mishnah took up certain books of Scripture and read them in light of its larger systemic interests. That reading yielded two classifications of scriptural exegesis, called, in Hebrew, Midrash. The first involved the rereading of legal passages of the books of Exodus, Leviticus, Numbers, and Deuteronomy, with an eye to discovering the connections, especially the harmonies, between the laws of the Mishnah and the statements of Scripture. The point is repeatedly made that the rules of the Mishnah are not autonomous, resting only upon reason, but depend upon their origin in divine revelation in written form, that is, Scripture. Sifra, to Leviticus, Sifré, to Numbers, and another Sifré, to Deuteronomy, repeatedly make that single point. Mekhilta, to Exodus, stands apart from these documents but in its program and polemic is coherent with them. The second classification of scriptural exegesis encompasses compilations of scriptural exegeses that concern historical and social laws, as distinct from the everyday rules for the workaday world that the Mishnah sets forth. These documents of scriptural exegesis provide a theology for Israel's life in history and beyond, identifying those social rules and historical points of regularity that will guide Israel through time. They cover Genesis, in Genesis Rabbah, Leviticus, in Leviticus Rabbah, and other writings as well. Yet other compilations of scriptural exegeses cover the synagogue liturgy, particularly the lections for special occasions, and deliver messages on the same themes. In these ways the writings of the Oral Torah, in relationship to the Written Torah, form that "one whole Torah of Moses, our lord," that sets forth the definitive and exhaustive statement of Judaism.

That Judaism of the dual Torah from the seventh century onward flourished within Christendom and Islam. Its success in both worlds derived from its capacity to explain, for the Jews, the condition of the Israel that they unanimously concurred they constituted. The dual Torah explained the present and accounted for a worthwhile future. In the context of Christianity it addressed the Christian *défi* of Israel, with its claim that the Messiah had already come and "Israel after the flesh" had had its redemption when the second temple was built; that "Israel" was now another Israel, after the spirit; that history focused not upon holy Israel but upon Jesus Christ. The answer of the dual Torah, from its documents in the fourth century (the Yerushalmi) onward, was that the Messiah would come when Israel obeyed the Torah; that Israel after the flesh was the true and only family of Abraham, Isaac, and Jacob; and that what happened in all of history responded to the moral condition of Israel and God's judgment of Israel. Islam, later on, posed a less acute, because less specific, challenge, since it did not claim to supersede, but only to succeed and form the seal of, the revelation of God to Moses (and Jesus). The subordination of Israel to Islam found ample explanation in the apologia already composed in response to the triumph of Christianity in the time of Constantine, in the fourth century.    That is why the Judaism of the dual Torah prevailed from Morocco to India, from France to Hungary and Roumania, Lithuania, Poland, and the Ukraine, and from Algeria to England, in medieval times, and throughout the places in the Western hemisphere, Africa,  and in Australasia, to which Jews migrated in the nineteenth and twentieth centuries.    In Europe and North America producing variations and varieties in the forms of Reform Judaism, Orthodoxy, Conservative Judaism, and the like, that single Judaism, appealing to its well-defined canon of writings, absorbing within itself an extraordinarily varied range of spiritual impulses, mystical and philosophical alike, predominated, and, so far as Jews seek to work out a religious system for the explanation of their existence as a social group, defines Judaism today.    Evidence for that fact derives from the character of heresies in medieval and modern times.    In every instance, the heresy denied a principle critical to the Judaism of the dual Torah, or affirmed a belief denied by it.    An example of the former is Karaism, from the ninth century, which denied the belief that there was an oral, as well as a written, Torah revealed at Sinai, and of the latter, Sabbateanism, in the seventeenth and eighteenth centuries, which affirmed that the Messiah had come and was not an observer of the laws of the Torah at all.    The first important Judaic system to stand wholly outside of the symbolic system and mythic structure of the Judaism of the dual Torah is the Judaism of Holocaust and Redemption, which has taken shape since 1967, and the influence of which is presently considerable; but no one now knows the future history of that Judaism.    Now to turn to the Judaism of the Mishnah in particular.

# 3

## The Judaism of the Mishnah

A Judaism is a religious system that appeals for authority to the Hebrew Scriptures or Old Testament in setting forth a way of life and a world-view for a social entity, "Israel." By "Judaism" here, however, among the many Judaic systems produced over time I refer to a particular one. It is the Judaic religious system that appealed to the myth of the Torah, or divine revelation, in two media, written and oral, which is called "the one whole Torah (that is, revelation by God) to Moses, our rabbi." Together the written Torah and the oral Torah form the foundation-document of the Judaism considered here. Accordingly the Hebrew Scriptures, in this Judaism called "the written Torah," were joined to another Torah preserved in the medium of memory. Hence we may call this particular Judaism, "the Judaism of the dual Torah." Within this mythic account of the holy writings of the canon, the Mishnah, is identified as the first piece of writing that transcribed the originally-oral part of the Torah. Between the mosaic of writings compiled in ca. 450 B.C. by Ezra and identified as the Pentateuch (with the remaining writings as well) and the Mishnah of ca. A.D. 200, this Judaism identified no writings that formed part of this Torah. But after the Mishnah, there would be a great many writings accepted as canonical, that is to say, as part of the Torah revealed by God to our lord (rabbenu) Moses at Mount Sinai.[1] The

---

[1]These fall into two categories, compilations of exegeses and amplifications of the Mishnah, and equivalent documents serving Scripture, that is to say, the oral and the written forms of the Torah, respectively. The former comprise, among other writings, the Tosefta, the Talmud of the Land of Israel, and the Talmud of Babylonia, and the latter, Sifra, to Leviticus, Sifré to Numbers, another Sifré, to Deuteronomy, Mekhilta attributed to R. Ishmael, Genesis Rabbah, Leviticus Rabbah, Pesiqta deRab Kahana, and other compilations, all completed between the third and the seventh centuries A.D.

Mishnah therefore is important because, with the Hebrew Scriptures, it formed the foundation of the Judaism paramount from that time to the present.

Up to now I have used as though they were commonplace certain formulations that are not necessarily accessible to readers, for instance, not Judaism but *"a"* Judaism, not "a religion" but "a religious *system.*" These shifts in terminology permit more precise and accurate identification of our subject and avoid needless errors in conception. There has not been a single, unitary, internally harmonious Judaism, from the beginning to the present. Hence I have invented the conception of "a Judaism." This permits identification of coherent data and makes it unnecessary to form theological judgments of authenticity or truth in addressing conflicting data. The alternative is to try to harmonize the Judaism of the Dead Sea Scrolls with the Judaism of the Mishnah, but these scarcely intersect. "Religion" covers many things. "A religious system" refers to religion within society and addresses only the identifiable traits of society and culture defined here. Let me expand on what I mean by *a* Judaism and a religious *system.*

A religious system is an account, appealing to supernatural origin or authority, of the shared life of a social entity, composed of a way of life and a world-view, that is, the [1] ethos and [2] ethics of [3] an ethnos, studied, in the terms of social science, as the [1] philosophy, [2] economics, and [3] politics of a religion.[2] Such a social entity (which may also constitute a political entity, e.g., a state with access to legitimate violence to secure its goals) may be made up of any number of

---

[2]As I explained in Chapter One, this book of essays falls into a larger systematic effort to describe the politics, philosophy, and economics – hence the social system – of a Judaism. In fact, it is to be a triplet of descriptions, the economics, politics, and philosophy, of the Judaism of the dual Torah in the first, intermediate, and final stages of the formation of that Judaism, I hope nine books in all. Since these stages interrelate, both diachronically and synchronically, the analysis proves somewhat complex. And, it must be added, the diachronic measure is not only taken by showing how a later formation has found its own definitions of matters, but how a later formation has realized in itself conceptions or principles implicit or hidden within an earlier one. For no one can maintain that the Mishnah's inner tensions and generative logic have reached full exposure only within the formulations of the Mishnah itself. What we find later on can be shown to bring to the surface results of premises, resolutions of tensions, contained even at the outset. So the three-dimensional, nine part, inquiry of which this book forms the second stage, yields a rich variety of theoretical initiatives indeed.

persons, and it may last for any length of time, for an hour to an epoch.[3] The power of as religious system is to hold the social entity together: the society the system addresses, the individuals who compose the society, the ordinary lives they lead, in ascending order of consequence. That system then forms a whole and well composed structure.[4] Systems endure in that eternal present that they create. They evoke precedent, they do not have a history. A system relates to context, but exists in an enduring moment.

Moving along down on the same path to define a Judaism, we now see a Judaism as a religious system comprising a theory of the social entity, the "Israel,"[5] constituted by the group of Jews who sustain that

---

[3]No criterion of age or of longevity pertains. For how long does a system have to survive to be classified as a system? A system that meets the definition at hand – world-view, complemented by a way of life, addressed to a clearly denoted Israel – however long it lasts constitutes a system. The reason is that a religious system presents a fact not of history but of immediacy, of the social present. The issue of term of survival by itself proves impertinent to the analysis of a system. A system is like a language. A language forms an example of language if it produces communication through rules of syntax and verbal arrangement. That paradigm serves full well however many people speak the language, or however long the language serves. Two people who understand each other form a language-community, even, or especially, if no one understands them. For however long, at whatever moment in historic time, a religious system always grows up in the perpetual present, an artifact of its day, whether today or a long-ago time. The only appropriate tense for a religious system is the present. A religious system always *is*, whatever it was, whatever it will be. Why so? Because its traits address a condition of humanity in society, a circumstance of an hour – however brief or protracted the hour and the circumstance.

[4]So the phrase, the *history* of a *system*, presents us with an oxymoron.

[5]I put "Israel" into quotation marks to underline that the word can stand for a variety of types of social entities, and that an "Israel" will form a component of a Judaism and bear the systemic message of that Judaism. I have laid out these matters on their own in my *Judaism and its Social Metaphors* (Cambridge: Cambridge University Press, 1988). The question of the social entity of a religious system is not primary in the present work, though I should imagine that the politics of a Judaism will play an important role in bearing the systemic judgment upon its Israel. I hope, therefore, in future reflection to make sense of the relationship between the politics of this particular Judaism and its "Israel." But we are still at the stage of laying out the principal components of the system, viewed as a social system and therefore read as an account of social science: systematic learning about society. That accounts for my tripartite program: economics, politics, philosophy, a full picture of the social theory of a religious system.

Judaism; a way of life characteristic of, perhaps distinctive to, that group of Jews; and a world-view that accounts for the group's forming a distinctive social entity and explains those indicative traits that define the entity. Within this definition, I see the formation of the system of a Judaism in three aspects: [1] the context of the social entity or group that constituted Judaism, corresponding to the ethnos, [2] the components of the canon of that group, that is, of the literary analysis of Judaism as displayed in its sacred writings, the writings as they emerge at a particular time and place, corresponding to the ethos, and [3] of the system of questions and answers that served that group of Jews in conducting its everyday affairs, corresponding to the ethics. That context finds definition in the encompassing society, by contrast to which the distinctive social entity sees itself as different.

The encompassing world constitutes the framework within which a given Judaism takes shape, and I call this "the ecology" of a Judaism. The social entity in the case of a Judaism always appeals to "Israel" and calls itself (an, or the only,) "Israel. Within the framework of a program to describe the social foundations of a Judaism, the principal points of inquiry are readily defined. I see the politics as a concrete and material statement of the social entity of the system; the economics as the equally practical expression of its way of life; and the philosophy, of course, as the agenda through which the prevailing world-view addresses concrete and urgent questions of mind.[6]

Since I claim to know the difference between one Judaism and another, I have now to explain how we may tell Judaisms apart. For people may well want to ask, are Judaisms not continuous with one another, forming a linear system through time as (at the very least) one begets the next? And even though exhibiting difference, do all Judaism(s) not in the end appeal to a single set of beliefs that make of the many things one thing? The answer to these questions formed as description, not as theology, is negative. Theology begins with the

---

[6]My work on the philosophy of this same Judaism will take a somewhat different form; it must rest on a series of monographs on specific philosophical problems as I think these problems make their appearance in the epiphenomenological discourse of the Mishnah. Only then can the projected *The Philosophy of Judaism* take its place beside *The Economics of Judaism* and *The Politics of Judaism*. Then, as is self-evident, I shall have to proceed to the politics, philosophy, and economics of the Judaism that comes to systemic expression in the Talmud of the Land of Israel and closely associated writings, and, finally, to the same categories of systemic construction as these are worked out in the final and classical statement of the Judaism of the dual Torah, the one in the Talmud of Babylonia and its associated writings. These form the three planes at which the conceptional cube divides.

conception of a single Judaism, attested by a single canon. But description yields different results. In the concrete facts of history, we find no justification for the classification of all data within a single harmonious and linear system, not *a* Judaism but (the only) Judaism. By diachronic measure we have no single Judaism any more than at any one moment, the synchronic dimension marks the bounds, everywhere, of the one and only Judaism, universally acknowledged and practiced. Therefore the fundamental error in the study of any Judaism is to treat all Judaisms as one (that is, as that one or as heresies). There is not now, and never has been, a linear and incremental history of one continuous Judaism, beginning, middle, end, for there has never been Judaism, only Judaisms. Whether we take the measure diachronically or synchronically, we come up with no single Judaism, continuing on through time and absorbing within itself all manner of differences. We undertake a long and fruitless task if we try (on a descriptive, not on a theological basis) to harmonize all matters of faith and religious practice regarded by Jews in all times and places as authoritative.

But what if we forego harmonization and instead claim to pick and choose the authentic from the unauthentic, or the normative from the aberrational? Then we abandon all claim to describe and instead evaluate as to truth, which is to say, we make theological judgments. In doing so we impose the judgment of what is merely one Judaism upon all Judaisms. Within the framework of description, analysis, and interpretation, theological judgments find no place. Indeed they upset the composition and composure of academic inquiry of a descriptive and analytical character. Accordingly, vast differences characteristic of elements of a single genus of religions, e.g., the genus Judaism, the species Judaisms, require not harmonization, let alone theological triage, but respectful attention. Each Judaism therefore is to be examined on its own, within the stages of its development as written sources attest to those stages. The natural history of Judaism(s) permits no other procedure than generalization out of speciation.

How to begin? When we identify Judaisms in one circumstance or period after another, we begin by trying to locate, in the larger group of Jews, those social entities that see themselves and are seen by others as distinct and bounded. The social entities of special interest are the ones that (in form accessible to us, e.g., writing) further present to themselves a clear account of who they are in distinction from all other Jews, and what they do that is different from what all other (and unsuitable) Jews do, as well as why they do what they do (and other Jews, as well as gentiles, do not). These, the indicative rules and the characteristic modes of exegesis and explanation, all together define their own, distinctive, even "unique" Judaism, just as the social entity commonly defines itself as the unique "Israel." For a Judaism addresses a social group, an Israel, with the claim that because that group constitutes not *an* Israel but (the only) Israel, people are to conduct themselves in one way, rather than in some other, and, it follows a principal issue of the system will be a theory of power, its institutionalization and utilization, that is to say, its structure and its system. So a Judaism, or a Judaic system, constitutes a clear and precise account of the source and rationalization of power in and through the life of a social group, the way of life and world-view of a group of Jews, however defined.

This stress on the multiplicity of Judaisms precipitates an obvious question. If there are only many Judaisms but has never been one Judaism, how can we speak of *Judaism* at all? Perhaps we deal with various species of the genus, religion, but not with species of the genus, Judaism.[7] As a matter of fact, all Judaisms from the formation of the Pentateuch in ca. 450 B.C. onward have recapitulated a single paradigmatic and definitive human experience, which each Judaism reworked in its own circumstance and context. That single paradigmatic experience to which all Judaisms, everywhere and under all conditions, refer is a political experience of exile and return, destruction and restoration of the state in the specified territory of that state.[8] So is formed the paradigm set forth by the Pentateuch in the myth of patriarchal Israel, gaining the land not unconditionally but contingently: politics as not a given but a gift.[9]

---

[7]That position of extreme nominalism is factually incorrect, as I shall now argue But the argument affords no comfort to the position of idealism that finds only one Judaism throughout, or that identifies in diverse Judaisms a single essential, or underlying Judaism. For reasons now spelled out, a position between nominalism and idealism proves descriptively entirely in order.

[8]Such a paradigm should impart to all Judaisms a political character, but it does not. Why the Mishnah's heirs and continuators persisted in encompassing within their systems a well-framed politics, while others among the Pentateuch's many heirs and continuators did not, I cannot say. But from the Mishnah to the nineteenth century, we have considerable difficulty in locating an essentially apolitical or non-political Judaism: a construction of a social entity, world-view, and way of life, with no interest whatever in the day-to-day uses of legitimate violence. Clearly, the nineteenth century's Judaisms, Reform, Historical or Conservative, and Orthodox, radically reframed the inherited pattern of a political religion.

[9]I treat the question of enlandisement in *Politics of Judaism*, Chapters Ten and Eleven, with the upshot in Chapter Twelve. In my view the premises of Aristotle's politics are profoundly locative, while those of the Mishnah's politics are wholly utopian. This is spelled out in due course. So far as the Mishnah's

The reason for this uniform paradigm among otherwise diverse Judaisms is simple. All Judaisms from the formation of the Pentateuch by Ezra in the aftermath of the return to Zion in the fifth century B.C. have identified the Torah or the Five Books of Moses as the written down statement of God's will for "Israel, the Jewish people" (which, as a matter of fact, every Judaism also identifies as its own social group). Specifically, all Judaisms in one way or another have sorted out whatever social experience their "Israels" proposed to explain by appeal to the tension of exile and the remission of return, and Judaisms in general appeal to the fixed paradigm of Israel's exile and return. That singular and indicative appeal formed an ecological fact for all Judaisms, as much as the Jews' minority status and utopian situation defined issues to be addressed by any Judaism. As a matter of fact that framing of events into the pattern at hand – exile and return, the paradigm for all Judaisms – represents an act of powerful imagination and interpretation. It is an experience that is invented, because no one person or group both went into "exile" and also "returned home." Diverse experiences have been sorted out, various persons have been chosen, and the whole has been worked into a system by those who selected history out of happenings, and models out of masses of persons. I say "selected," because no Jews after 586 actually experienced what in the aggregate Scripture says happened. None both went into exile and then came back to Jerusalem. So, to begin with, Scripture does not record a particular person's experience.

Let me state with emphasis the lesson people claimed to learn out of the events they had chosen for their history: *the life of the group is uncertain, subject to conditions and stipulations.* Nothing is set and given, all things are a gift and an act of grace, not coerced, not earned, but merely given freely: land and life itself. But what actually did happen in that uncertain world – exile but then restoration – marked the group as special, different, select. With the promulgation of the "Torah of Moses" under the sponsorship of Ezra, the Persians' viceroy, at ca. 450 B.C., all future Israels would then refer to that formative experience as it had been set down and preserved as the norm for Israel in the mythic terms of that "original" Israel, the Israel not of Genesis and Sinai and the end at the moment of entry into the promised land, but the "Israel" of the families that recorded as the rule and the norm

---

politics are properly characterized as applicable to no place in particular (though obviously, only to the Holy Land in general), they must be regarded as a step away from the deeply locative politics of Deuteronomy, but, of course, well within the entirely utopian politics of Leviticus.

the story of both the exile and the return.  In that minority genealogy, that story of exile and return, alienation and remission, imposed on the received stories of pre-exilic Israel and adumbrated time and again in the Five Books of Moses and addressed by the framers of that document in their work over all, we find that paradigmatic statement in which every Judaism, from then to now, found its structure and deep syntax of social existence, the grammar of its intelligible message.

I dwell on this matter because the myth of exile and return or of resentment and remission took a political form.  It spoke, in particular, of the destruction of not only a Temple but the state and government that that Temple had realized.  Ezra (and therefore Moses) used legitimate coercion and violence, and so the Judaism he framed, and all Judaisms that appealed to his writing and paradigm, by definition constituted politics as well.  That experience (in theological terms) rehearsed the conditional moral existence of sin and punishment, suffering and atonement and reconciliation, and (in social terms) the uncertain and always conditional national destiny of disintegration and renewal of the group viewed as a political entity: a society properly able to coerce, even through violence, conformity to its calling. That political moment captured within the Five Books of Moses, that is to say, the judgment of the generation of the return to Zion, led by Ezra, about what it conceives to have been its extraordinary experience of exile and return would inform the attitude and viewpoint of all the Judaisms and all the Israels beyond.  Accordingly, we identify as a fact of the diachronic ecology of all Judaisms that generative and definitive moment precisely as all Judaisms have done, that is, by looking into that same Scripture.  All Judaisms identify the Torah or the Five Books of Moses as the written down statement of God's will for Israel, the Jewish people (which, as a matter of fact, every Judaism also identifies as its own social group).

Why not appeal, for an explanation for the fact that Judaisms would fall into the classification of political religions, to Moses, instead of to Ezra?  Or even to Abraham for that matter?  I suppose that on the surface, we should specify that formative and definitive moment, recapitulated by all Judaisms, with the story of Creation down to Abraham and the beginning of his family, the children of Abraham, Isaac and Jacob.  Or perhaps we are advised to make our way to Sinai and hold that that original point of definition descends from heaven. But allowing ourselves merely to retell the story deprives us of the required insight.  Recapitulating the story of the religion does not help us understand the religion.  Identifying the point of origin of the story, by contrast, does.  For the story tells not what happened on the occasion to which the story refers (the creation of the world, for instance) but how (long afterward and for their own reasons) people want to portray themselves. The tale therefore recapitulates that resentment, that obsessive and troubling point of origin, that the group wishes to to explain, transcend, transform.

Every Judaism found as its task the recapitulation of the original Judaism: exile and return. And these formed, as a matter of fact, political categories: exile from statehood, marked by the person of the monarch; return to the capital of not only the cult but also the government, and return under political auspices at that, with Iranian troops to carry out the commands of the Jewish satrap. The psychological counterpart of the political taxon sustained the politics. It invoked resentment of circumstance and also the reconciliation with the human condition of a given "Israel." That is to say, each made its own distinctive statement of the generative and critical resentment contained within that questioning of the given, that deep understanding of the uncertain character of the existence of the group in its normal location and under circumstances of permanence that (so far as the Judaic group understood things) characterized the life of every other group but Israel. What for everyone else (so it seemed to the Judaisms addressed to the Israels through time) was a given for Israel was a gift. What all the nations knew as how things *must* be Israel understood as how things *might not be*: exile and loss, alienation and resentment, but, instead of annihilation, renewal, restoration, reconciliation, and (in theological language) redemption. So that paradigmatic experience, the one beginning in 586 and ending in ca. 450, written down in that written Torah of Moses, made its mark.

That pattern of appeal to political means and of defining Israel as a political entity, permanently inscribed in the Torah of God to Moses at Sinai, would define for all Israels over all time that matter of resentment demanding recapitulation: leaving home, coming home. What is that one systemic trait that marks all Judaisms and sets them apart from all other religious systems, viewed jointly and severally? The religious ecology of Judaisms is dictated by that perpetual asking of the question, who are we? That trait of self-consciousness, that incapacity to accept the group as a given and its data – way of life, world-view, constituting the world of an Israel, a Jewish people, in the here and now – is the one thing draws together Judaisms from beginning to end. Jews' persistent passion for self-definition characterizes all of the Judaisms they have made for themselves. What others take as the given the Jews perceive as the received, the special, the extraordinary. And that perception of the remarkable character of what to other groups is the absolute datum of all being requires explanation.

The union of politics and psychology sustained the indicative character of the initial paradigm. Since the formative pattern imposed that perpetual, self-conscious uncertainty, treating the life of the group as conditional and discontinuous, Jews have asked themselves who they are and invented Judaisms to answer that question. Accordingly, on account of the definitive paradigm – ecology in an intellectual form – affecting their group-life in various contexts, no circumstances have permitted Jews to take for granted their existence as a group. Looking back on Scripture and its message, Jews have ordinarily treated as special, subject to conditions and therefore uncertain what (in their view) other groups enjoyed as unconditional and simply given. Why the paradigm renewed itself is clear: this particular view of matters generated expectations that could not be met, hence created resentment – and then provided comfort and hope that made possible coping with that resentment.

Specifically, each Judaism retells in its own way and with its distinctive emphases the tale of the Five Books of Moses, the story of a no-people that becomes a people, that has what it gets only on condition, and that can lose it all by virtue of its own sin. That is a terrifying, unsettling story for a social group to tell of itself, because it imposes acute self-consciousness, chronic insecurity, upon what should be the level plane and firm foundation of society. That is to say, the collection of diverse materials joined into a single tale on the occasion of the original exile and restoration because of the repetition in age succeeding age also precipitates the recapitulation of the interior experience of exile and restoration – always because of sin and atonement. To conclude this picture of the paradigm common to all Judaisms at the point at which we began, let me account for the systemic power that will undergird the politics of any Judaism.

The power of religion, Judaism(s), to form an independent variable in the life of Israel(s) throughout all time and so to impose its imprint upon the politics, also, of all Judaisms that set forth a politics, flows from an ever-renewed source. It is the source of resentment and the resolution of resentment. For the power of Judaisms derives from their capacity to form and reform a permanent social paradigm and to perpetuate a single corresponding psychological attitude and experience. And how was (and is) this done? Promising what could not be delivered, then providing solace for the consequent disappointment, the system at hand – the pentateuchal one, to which all subsequent systems appealed – precipitated in age succeeding age the very conditions necessary for its own replication. Precipitating resentment and then remitting the consequent anguish, Judaisms renew themselves, and, in the context of Judaisms, religion itself forms a self-perpetuating fact of the ecology of religion.

From Judaisms in general, we come to the Judaism that is first exposed in the Mishnah, which, as I have already said, comprises the initial statement of a Judaic system. In the aftermath of a half-century of political disasters, from before 70 to after 135, that overturned structures and systems of centuries, a group of intellectuals forming what ultimately appeared another half-century later in the Mishnah set forth a grand design for an imagined reconstruction. That design encompassed in a single theory of all things the correct conduct of the life of society within the dominion of God. In providing for institutions and organizations of an enduring society, not merely for the inner life of individuals and families, the design quite naturally encompassed, also, politics. It was a politics represented as a (mere) recapitulation of how things had been, how things (as a matter of fact) really are. But, in fact, it was a politics imagined, not reconstructed, and the political imagination extending to both political structures and institutions and also to political systems and activities expressed an essentially theological vision. That is why I claimed in the Preface to provide an instance of how religion invents politics.

Political in its very basic design, speaking of a social entity and its power to exercise legitimate violence in governing its own affairs, the document presents its social vision in the form of a law code what is in fact the design for a social system. That is why I ask the Mishnah to tell us the political structure and system that it sets forth for the society its authorship imagines and I promise to explain the reason why it said what it said and imagined what it made up. For the law code at hand is not an account of how things were, but of how, out of the sherds and remnants of an indeterminate past, its authorship proposed to reconstruct the world.

The Mishnah therefore constitutes a profoundly utopian document, in the tradition of the political theory in the form of a fantasy, a kind of *Staatsroman* of ancient times, to be compared therefore to Plato's *Republic* and Aristotle's *Politics*.[10] The Mishnah provides a sustained example of systemic thinking, in a systematic and orderly way, about political questions about which, in point of fact, its authorship could do absolutely nothing in reality. Why politics in particular, and not, for example, teleology in eschatological form? Why ignore theological

---

[10]I use the word "utopian" in its ordinary sense: never-never land. But in the concluding chapters, the other sense of "utopia," which is, "no where in particular," as against the contrary word (invented by Jonathan Z. Smith), "locative," will form a principal component of my analysis.

issues about the nature of God and address social issues about the utilization of power?  These are questions of systemic analysis that require us to ask, why this, not that, this topic, not that topic, in the systemic statement?  And to answer those questions, we need to find out both how people thought and also what they meant to convey in choosing the topics they treated and in thinking about them as they did?

Conducting an analysis of the imagined politics of the document accordingly allows us entry into a mode of thought that is utterly unaffected by the variables of practical life and public policy applied to concrete problems.  Here we have an ideal example of a political structure and system flowing wholly from an imagination – but an imagination shaped by problems set by concrete reality, on the one side, and rigorous, disciplined, rational, philosophical modes of thought, on the other: political theory in its most elegant setting: the human mind, the engaged intellect.  For the Mishnah, a deeply philosophical document, manages to say one thing about many things.  The work therefore falls well within the framework of defined by the modes of philosophical thought of antiquity.

The document presents its discourses as thematic expositions, with beginnings, middles, and endings, principles and secondary developments thereof.  Throughout the Mishnah the preferred mode of layout is through themes, spelled out along the lines of the logic imbedded in those themes.  The Mishnah is divided up into six principal divisions, each expounding a single, immense topic.  The tractates of each division furthermore take up subtopics of the principal theme.  The chapters then unfold along the lines of the (to the framers) logic of the necessary dissection of the division.  Intermediate divisions of these principal divisions (we might call them chapters of tractates) are to be discerned on the basis of internal evidence, through the confluence of theme and form.  That is to say, a given intermediate division of a principal one (a chapter of a tractate) will be marked by a particular, recurrent, formal pattern in accord with which sentences are constructed, and also by a particular and distinct theme, to which these sentences are addressed.  When a new theme commences, a fresh formal pattern will be used.  Within the intermediate divisions, we are able to recognize the components, or smallest whole units of thought (hereinafter, cognitive units, defined at greater length presently), because there will be a recurrent pattern of sentence structure repeated time and again within the unit and a shifting at the commencement of the next theme.  Each point at which the recurrent pattern commences marks the beginning of a new cognitive unit.

The Mishnah's logic of cogent discourse establishes propositions that rest upon philosophical bases, e.g., through the proposal of a thesis and the composition of a list of facts that (e.g., through shared traits of a taxonomic order) prove the thesis. The Mishnah presents rules and treats stories (inclusive of history) as incidental and of merely taxonomic interest. Its logic is propositional, and its intellect does its work through a vast labor of classification, comparison and contrast generating governing rules and generalizations. The Pentateuch, by contrast, appeals to a different logic of cogent discourse from the Mishnah's. It is the cogency imparted by teleology, that is, a logic that provides an account of how things were in order to explain how things are and set forth how they should be, with the tabernacle in the wilderness the model for (and modeled after) the Temple in the Jerusalem abuilding. The Mishnah speaks in a continuing present tense, saying only how things are, indifferent to the *were* and the *will-be.* The Pentateuch focuses upon self-conscious "Israel," saying who they were and what they must become to overcome how they now are. The Mishnah understands by "Israel" as much the individual as the nation and identifies as its principal actors, the heroes of its narrative, not the family become a nation, but the priest and the householder, the woman and the slave, the adult and the child, and other castes and categories of person within an inward-looking, established, fully landed community. Given the Mishnah's authorship's interest in classifications and categories, therefore in systematic hierarchization of an orderly world, one can hardly find odd that (re)definition of the subject matter and problematic of the systemic social entity.

That purpose is accomplished, in particular, though list-making, which places on display the data of the like and the unlike and implicitly (ordinarily, not explicitly) then conveys the rule. It is this resort to list-making that accounts for the rhetorical stress on groups of examples of a common principle, three or five for instance. Once a series is established, the authorship assumes, the governing rule will be perceived. That explains why, in exposing the interior logic of its authorship's intellect, the Mishnah had to be a book of lists, with the implicit order, the nomothetic traits of a monothetic order, dictating the ordinarily unstated general and encompassing rule. And all this why? It is in order to make a single statement, endless times over, and to repeat in a mass of tangled detail precisely the same fundamental judgment. The Mishnah in its way is as blatantly repetitious in its fundamental statement as is the Pentateuch. If I had to specify a single mode of thought that for the Mishnah's authorship establishes connections between one fact and another, it is in the search for points in common and therefore also points of contrast. We seek connection between fact and fact, sentence and sentence in the subtle and balanced rhetoric of the Mishnah, by comparing and contrasting two things that are like and not alike.

At the logical level, too, the Mishnah falls into the category of familiar philosophical thought. Once we seek regularities, we propose rules. What is like another thing falls under its rule, and what is not like the other falls under the opposite rule. Accordingly, as to the species of the genus, so far as they are alike, they share the same rule. So far as they are not alike, each follows a rule contrary to that governing the other. So the work of analysis is what produces connection, and therefore the drawing of conclusions derives from comparison and contrast: the *and*, the *equal*. The proposition then that forms the conclusion concerns the essential likeness of the two offices, except where they are different, but the subterranean premise is that we can explain both likeness and difference by appeal to a principle of fundamental order and unity. To make these observations concrete, we turn to the case at hand. The important contrast comes at the outset. The high priest and king fall into a single genus, but speciation, based on traits particular to the king, then distinguishes the one from the other. All of this exercise is conducted essentially independently of Scripture; the classifications derive from the system, are viewed as autonomous constructs; traits of things define classifications and dictate what is like and what is unlike. That is how the Mishnah's authorship finds it possible to say the same thing about many things.

So the Mishnah, seen whole, turns out to repeat in many ways a single encompassing proposition. Once the question is defined, the exegetical process takes over, with its infinite capacity to make details repeat a basic premise or proposition. But the systemic statement as a whole takes as urgent and obsessively reviews a set of questions deemed ineluctable and demanding answers. And, in one way or another, those questions receive answers that are deemed self-evidently so. Accordingly, the Mishnah's system forms a closed circle. And as a matter of fact, the boundaries of the circle are political, the issues so framed that politics constitutes the principal force in the shaping of society and imagination alike; politics profoundly affects the conditions of religious belief and behavior.

As noted earlier, in the period in which the Mishnah came to closure, two political events, very well documented in a variety of writings and also in archaeology, defined the circumstances in which all Jews lived and therefore in which all Judaisms took shape. A stunning shift in the political circumstance of the Jews in the Land of Israel ("Palestine") therefore affected thought about perennial questions. The first shift was represented by the destruction of the second Temple in A.D. 70 and the second, by the complete defeat, three generations later, in 135, of the war led by Bar Kokhba to reconstruct the Temple. The one fact we know for certain is that the Mishnah's authorship did their work after Bar Kokhba's defeat. If we work our way back from the answers set forth by the Mishnah, read as answers to questions, to the question addressed by these same answers and implicit within them, we confront an obsession with order. That fact suggests a concern with chaos, such as followed the political revolution brought about by the massive defeats, over a half century, suffered by the Jews in the Land of Israel. The Temple had formed the locus for social hierarchization and organized; it lay in ruins. The city, Jerusalem, had served as the center for the life of the Jews in the country. It was no longer accessible. No wonder, then, that the sages who produced the Mishnah should have given an elaborate series of answers to the question of the right ordering and classification of all things in the worlds of society, nature, and supernature. And, in the nature of things, the answers appealed to both sound philosophy and revealed theology.

Accordingly, these events formed the question, to which the Mishnah's orderly system provided the answer. The system of the Mishnah delivers the message that through order – through the reordering of Israelite life – Israel attains that sanctification that inheres in its very being. The Mishnah is divided into six divisions, covering sixty-three tractates, 531 chapters, and encompasses six large topics. This brings us to a rapid survey of the several parts of the system, the six divisions and their sixty-two usable tractates (excluding Avot). In this survey we see in concrete and specific ways precisely what it means to speak of the Judaism of the Mishnah as a political structure and system. For throughout, what the Mishnah takes up for its topical program is the concrete expression of the power to dictate the conduct of the social entity: the rationing and rationalization of power.

**The Division of Agriculture** treats two topics, first, producing crops in accord with the Scriptural rules on the subject, second, paying the required offerings and tithes to the priests, Levites, and poor. The principal point of the Division is that the Land is holy, because God has a claim both on it and upon what it produces. God's claim must be honored by setting aside a portion of the produce for those for whom God has designated it. God's ownership must be acknowledged by observing the rules God has laid down for use of the Land. In sum, the Division is divided along these lines: (1) Rules for producing crops in a state of holiness – tractates *Kilayim, Shebiit, Orlah*; (2) Rules for disposing of crops in accord with the rules of holiness – tractates *Peah*,

*Demai, Terumot, Maaserot, Maaser Sheni, Hallah, Bikkurim, Berakhot.*

**The Division of Appointed Times** forms a system in which the advent of a holy day, like the Sabbath of creation, sanctifies the life of the Israelite village through imposing on the village rules on the model of those of the Temple. The purpose of the system, therefore, is to bring into alignment the moment of sanctification of the village and the life of the home with the moment of sanctification of the Temple on those same occasions of appointed times. The underlying and generative theory of the system is that the village is the mirror image of the Temple. If things are done in one way in the Temple, they will be done in the opposite way in the village. Together the village and the Temple on the occasion of the holy day therefore form a single continuum, a completed creation, thus awaiting sanctification.

The division is made up of two quite distinct sets of materials. First, it addresses what one does in the sacred space of the Temple on the occasion of sacred time, as distinct from what one does in that same sacred space on ordinary, undifferentiated days, which is a subject worked out in Holy Things. Second, the Division defines how for the occasion of the holy day one creates a corresponding space in one's own circumstance, and what one does, within that space, during sacred time. The issue of the Temple and cult on the special occasion of festivals is treated in tractates *Pesahim, Sheqalim, Yoma, Sukkah,* and *Hagigah.* Three further tractates, *Rosh Hashshanah, Taanit,* and *Megillah,* are necessary to complete the discussion. The matter of the rigid definition of the outlines in the village, of a sacred space, delineated by the limits within which one may move on the Sabbath and festival, and of the specification of those things which one may not do within that space in sacred time, is in *Shabbat, Erubin, Besah,* and *Moed Qatan.* While the twelve tractates of the Division appear to fall into two distinct groups, joined merely by a common theme, in fact they relate through a shared, generative metaphor. It is the comparison, in the context of sacred time, of the spatial life of the Temple to the spatial life of the village, with activities and restrictions to be specified for each, upon the common occasion of the Sabbath or festival. The Mishnah's purpose therefore is to correlate the sanctity of the Temple, as defined by the holy day, with the restrictions of space and of action which make the life of the village different and holy, as defined by the holy day.

**The Division of Women** defines the women in the social economy of Israel's supernatural and natural reality. Women acquire definition wholly in relationship to men, who impart form to the Israelite social economy. The status of women is effected through both supernatural and natural, this-worldly action. What man and woman do on earth provokes a response in heaven, and the correspondences are perfect. So women are defined and secured both in heaven and here on earth, and that position is always and invariably relative to men. The principal interest for the Mishnah is the point at which a woman becomes, and ceases to be, holy to a particular man, that is, enters and leaves the marital union. These transfers of women are the dangerous and disorderly points in the relationship of woman to man, therefore, the Mishnah states, to society as well.

The formation of the marriage comes under discussion in *Qiddushin* and *Ketubot*, as well as in *Yebamot*. The rules for the duration of the marriage are scattered throughout, but derive especially from parts of *Ketubot*, *Nedarim*, and *Nazir*, on the one side, and the paramount unit of *Sotah*, on the other. The dissolution of the marriage is dealt with in *Gittin*, as well as in *Yebamot*. We see very clearly, therefore, that important overall are issues of the transfer of property, along with women, covered in *Ketubot* and to some measure in *Qiddushin*, and the proper documentation of the transfer of women and property, treated in *Ketubot* and *Gittin*. The critical issues therefore turn upon legal documents – writs of divorce, for example – and legal recognition of changes in the ownership of property, e.g., through the collection of the settlement of a marriage contract by a widow, through the provision of a dowry, or through the disposition of the property of a woman during the period in which she is married. Within this orderly world of documentary and procedural concerns a place is made for the disorderly conception of the marriage not formed by human volition but decreed in heaven, the levirate connection. *Yebamot* states that supernature sanctifies a woman to a man (under the conditions of the levirate connection). What it says by indirection is that man sanctifies too: man, like God, can sanctify that relationship between a man and a woman, and can also effect the cessation of the sanctity of that same relationship. Five of the seven tractates of the Division of Women are devoted to the formation and dissolution of the marital bond. Of them, three treat what is done by man here on earth, that is, formation of a marital bond through betrothal and marriage contract and dissolution through divorce and its consequences: *Qiddushin*, *Ketubot*, and *Gittin*. One of them is devoted to what is done by woman here on earth: *Sotah*. And *Yebamot*, greatest of the seven in size and in formal and substantive brilliance, deals with the corresponding heavenly intervention into the formation and end of a marriage: the effect of death upon both forming the marital bond and dissolving it through death. The other two tractates, *Nedarim* and *Nazir*, draw into one the two realms of reality, heaven and earth, as they work out the effects of vows, perhaps because vows taken by women and subject to the confirmation or abrogation of the father or husband make a deep impact upon the marital life of the woman who has taken them.

**The Division of Damages** comprises two subsystems, which fit together in a logical way. One part presents rules for the normal conduct of civil society. These cover commerce, trade, real estate, and other matters of everyday intercourse, as well as mishaps, such as damages by chattels and persons, fraud, overcharge, interest, and the like, in that same context of everyday social life. The other part describes the institutions governing the normal conduct of civil society, that is, courts of administration, and the penalties at the disposal of the government for the enforcement of the law. The two subjects form a single tight and systematic dissertation on the nature of Israelite society and its economic, social, and political relationships, as the Mishnah envisages them.

The main point of the first of the two parts of the Division is expressed in the sustained unfolding of the three *Babas, Baba Qamma, Baba Mesia,* and *Baba Batra.* It is that the task of society is to maintain perfect stasis, to preserve the prevailing situation, and to secure the stability of all relationships. To this end, in the interchanges of buying and selling, giving and taking, borrowing and lending, it is important that there be an essential equality of interchange. No party in the end should have more than what he had at the outset, and none should be the victim of a sizable shift in fortune and circumstance. All parties' rights to, and in, this stable and unchanging economy of society are to be preserved. When the condition of a person is violated, so far as possible the law will secure the restoration of the antecedent status.

An appropriate appendix to the *Babas* is at *Abodah Zarah,* which deals with the orderly governance of transactions and relationships between Israelite society and the outside world, the realm of idolatry, relationships which are subject to certain special considerations. These are generated by the fact that Israelites may not derive benefit (e.g., through commercial transactions) from anything which has served in the worship of an idol. Consequently, commercial transactions suffer limitations on account of extrinsic considerations of cultic taboos. While these cover both special occasions, e.g., fairs and festivals of idolatry, and general matters, that is, what Israelites may buy and sell, the main practical illustrations of the principles of the matter pertain to wine. The Mishnah supposes that gentiles routinely make use, for a libation, of a drop of any sort of wine to which they have access. It therefore is taken for granted that wine over which gentiles have had control is forbidden for Israelite use, and also that such wine is prohibited for Israelites to buy and sell. This other matter – ordinary everyday relationships with the gentile world, with special reference to trade and commerce – concludes what the Mishnah has to say about all those matters of civil and criminal law which together define everyday relationships within the Israelite nation and between that nation and all others in the world among whom, in Palestine as abroad, they lived side by side.

The other part of the Division describes the institutions of Israelite government and politics. This is in two main aspects, first, the description of the institutions and their jurisdiction, with reference to courts, conceived as both judicial and administrative agencies, and, second, the extensive discussion of criminal penalties. The penalties are three: death, banishment, and flogging. There are four ways by which a person convicted of a capital crime may be put to death. The Mishnah organizes a vast amount of information on what sorts of capital crimes are punishable by which of the four modes of execution. That information is alleged to derive from Scripture. But the facts are many, and the relevant verses few. What the Mishnah clearly contributes to this exercise is a first-rate piece of organization and elucidation of available facts. Where the facts come from we do not know. The Mishnah tractate *Sanhedrin* further describes the way in which trials are conducted in both monetary and capital cases and pays attention to the possibilities of perjury. The matter of banishment brings the Mishnah to a rather routine restatement by flogging and application of that mode of punishment conclude the discussion. Our selection from the Mishnah derives from Mishnah-tractate Sanhedrin, because that is where the reward and punishment involved in eternal life, or life in the world to come, takes its place within the larger category of penalty for violating the law of the Torah.

The character and interests of the Division of Damages present probative evidence of the larger program of the philosophers of the Mishnah. Their intention is to create nothing less than a full-scale Israelite government, subject to the administration of sages. This government is fully supplied with a constitution and bylaws (*Sanhedrin, Makkot*). It makes provision for a court system and procedures (*Shebuot, Sanhedrin, Makkot*), as well as a full set of laws governing civil society (*Baba Qamma, Baba Mesia, Baba Batra*) and criminal justice (*Sanhedrin, Makkot*). This government, moreover, mediates between its own community and the outside ("pagan") world. Through its system of laws it expresses its judgment of the others and at the same time defines, protects, and defends its own society and social frontiers (*Abodah Zarah*). It even makes provision for procedures of remission, to expiate its own errors (Horayot).

   **The Division of Holy Things** presents a system of sacrifice and
sanctuary: Matters concerning the praxis of the altar and maintenance
of the sanctuary.    The praxis of the altar, specifically, involves
sacrifice and things set aside for sacrifice and so deemed consecrated.
The topic covers these among the eleven tractates of the present
Division:  *Zebahim* and part of *Hullin, Menahot, Temurah, Keritot,*
part of *Meilah, Tamid, and Qinnim.*  The maintenance of the sanctuary
(inclusive of the personnel) in dealt with in *Bekhorot, Arakhin,* part of
*Meilah, Middot,* and part of *Hullin.*  Viewed from a distance,
therefore, the Mishnah's tractates divide themselves up into the
following groups (in parentheses are tractates containing relevant
materials):  (1) Rules for the altar and the praxis of the cult – *Zebahim
Menahot, Hullin, Keritot, Tamid, Qinnim (Bekhorot, Meilah);* (2)
Rules for the altar and the animals set aside for the cult – *Arakhin,
Temurah, Meilah (Bekhorot);* and (3) Rules for the altar and support of
the Temple staff and buildings – *Bekhorot, Middot (Hullin, Arakhin,
Meilah, Tamid).*  In a word, this Division speaks of the sacrificial cult
and the sanctuary in which the cult is conducted.  The law pays special
attention to the matter of the status of the property of the altar and of
the sanctuary, both materials to be utilized in the actual sacrificial
rites, and property the value of which supports the cult and sanctuary
in general.  Both are deemed  to be sanctified, that is: "holy things."
The Division of Holy Things centers upon the everyday and rules
always applicable to the cult.

   **The Division of Purities** presents a very simple system of three
principal parts:   sources of uncleanness, objects and substances
susceptible to uncleanness, and modes of purification from uncleanness.
So it tells the story of what makes a given sort of object unclean and
what makes it clean.   The tractates on these several topics are as
follows:    (1) sources of uncleanness – *Ohalot, Negaim, Niddah,
Makhshirin, Zabim, Tebul Yom;* (2) objects and substances susceptible to
uncleanness – *Kelim, Tohorot, Uqsin;* and (3) modes of purification –
*Parah, Miqvaot, Yadayim.*   Viewed as a whole, the Division of
Purities treats the interplay of persons, food, and liquids.   Dry
inanimate objects or food are not susceptible to uncleanness.  What is
wet is susceptible.  So liquids activate the system.  What is unclean,
moreover, emerges from uncleanness through the operation of liquids,
specifically, through immersion in fit water of requisite volume and in
natural condition. Liquids thus deactivate the system.  Thus, water in
its natural condition is what concludes the process by removing
uncleanness.  Water in its unnatural condition, that is, deliberately
affected by human agency, is what imparts susceptibility to
uncleanness to begin with. The uncleanness of persons, furthermore, is

signified by body liquids or flux in the case of the menstruating woman (*Niddah*) and the *zab* (Zabim).  Corpse uncleanness is conceived to be a kind of effluent, a viscous gas, which flows like liquid.  Utensils for their part receive uncleanness when they form receptacles able to contain liquid.  In sum, we have a system in which the invisible flow of fluid-like substances or powers serve to put food, drink, and receptacles into the status of uncleanness and to remove those things from that status.  Whether or not we call the system "metaphysical," it certainly has no material base but is conditioned upon highly abstract notions.  Thus in material terms, the effect of liquid is upon food, drink, utensils, and man.  The consequence has to do with who may eat and drink what food and liquid, and what food and drink may be consumed in which pots and pans.  These loci are specified by tractates on utensils (Kelim) and on food and drink (Tohorot and Uqsin).

In reviewing this account of the program of the Judaism of the Mishnah, the reader must wonder what of Scripture.  For if, as we realize, all Judaisms appeal to the Hebrew Scriptures ("Old Testament," "written Torah"), then should an account of the politics of Judaism not begin in that same generative document?  And how is it legitimate to read the Mishnah as an autonomous statement and not merely a secondary expansion and revision of the generative one that is contained, for politics, in Exodus, Leviticus, and Deuteronomy?  To answer that question and show the autonomy, from Scripture, of the Judaism of the Mishnah requires a brief survey of the relationship of the Mishnah to Scripture.  On that basis, we shall see how the authorship of the Mishnah has picked and chosen, within Scripture, to find whatever suited its purposes and contributed to the formation of its system.  And once we see that picking and choosing has gone on, then the criteria for sorting out what pertains and what does not turn out to derive from the system that guides the choices, and not from that system among which choices are made.

On the surface, Scripture plays little role in the Mishnaic system.  The Mishnah's authorship rarely cites a verse of Scripture, refers to Scripture as an entity, links its own ideas to those of Scripture, or lays claim to originate in what Scripture has said, even by indirect or remote allusion to a Scriptural verse of teaching.  So, superficially, the Mishnah is totally indifferent to Scripture.  That impression, moreover, is reinforced by the traits of the language of the Mishnah.  The framers of Mishnaic discourse, amazingly, never attempt to imitate the language of Scripture, as do those of the Essene writings at Qumran.  The very redactional structure of Scripture, found to serviceable to the writer of the Temple scroll, remarkably, is of no interest whatever to the organizers of the Mishnah and its tractates, except in a very few cases (Leviticus 16, Yoma; Exodus 12; Pesahim).

Formally, redactionally, and linguistically the Mishnah stands in splendid isolation from Scripture. It is not possible to point in other Judaisms, before the one set forth in the Mishnah, to many parallels, that is, cases of anonymous books, received as holy, in which the forms and formulations (specific verses) of Scripture play so slight a role. People who wrote holy books commonly imitated the Scripture's language. They cited concrete verses. They claimed at the very least that direct revelation had come to them, as in the angelic discourses of IV Ezra and Baruch, so that what they say stands on an equal plane with Scripture. The internal evidence of the Mishnah's sixty-two usable tractates (excluding Abot), by contrast, in no way suggests that anyone pretended to talk like Moses and write like Moses, claimed to cite and correctly interpret things that Moses had said, or even alleged to have had a revelation like that of Moses and so to stand on the mountain with Moses. There is none of this. So the claim of Scriptural authority for the Mishnah's doctrines and institutions is difficult to locate within the internal evidence of the Mishnah itself. Let me now state the facts of the relationship of the Mishnah to Scripture.

First, there are tractates which simply repeat in their own words precisely what Scripture has to say, and at best serve to amplify and complete the basic ideas of Scripture. For example, all of the cultic tractates of the second division, the one on Appointed Times, which tell what one is supposed to do in the Temple on the various special days of the year, and the bulk of the cultic tractates of the fifth division, which deals with Holy Things, simply restate facts of Scripture. For another example, all of those tractates of the sixth division, on Purities, which specify sources of uncleanness, depend completely on information supplied by Scripture. I have demonstrated in detail that every important statement in Niddah, on menstrual uncleanness, and the most fundamental notions of Zabim, on the uncleanness of the person with flux referred to in Leviticus Chapter Fifteen, as well as every detail in Negaim, on the uncleanness of the person or house suffering the uncleanness described at Leviticus Chapters Thirteen and Fourteen – all of these tractates serve only to restate the basic facts of Scripture and to complement those facts with other important ones. Were the politics of the Mishnah to derive from tractates that stand in relationship to Mishnah as utter dependents, then we should turn forthwith to the politics of Scripture, and simply point to those minor details in which the framers of the document at hand revised the inherited system. But the politics of the Mishnah rarely appeals to the political structures set forth, e.g., in Exodus or

Deuteronomy or Leviticus, and the political system imagined by the framers of the Mishnah never appeals for precedent to the workings of the political system set forth, for instance, in the books of Joshua, Judges, Samuel, and Kings.

There are, second, tractates which take up facts of Scripture but work them out in a way in which those Scriptural facts cannot have led us to predict. A supposition concerning what is important about the facts, utterly remote from the supposition of Scripture, will explain why the Mishnah-tractates under discussion say the original things they say in confronting those Scripturally provided facts. For one example, Scripture takes for granted that the red cow will be burned in a state of uncleanness, because it is burned outside the camp-Temple. The priestly writers cannot have imagined that a state of cultic cleanness was to be attained outside of the cult. The absolute datum of tractate Parah, by contrast, is that cultic cleanness not only can be attained outside of the "tent of meeting." The red cow was to be burned in a state of cleanness even exceeding that cultic cleanness required in the Temple itself. The problematic which generates the intellectual agendum of Parah, therefore, is how to work out the conduct of the rite of burning the cow in relationship to the Temple: Is it to be done in exactly the same way, or in exactly the opposite way? This mode of contrastive and analogical thinking helps us to understand the generative problematic of such tractates as Erubin and Besah, to mention only two.

Third, there are, predictably, many tractates which either take up problems in no way suggested by Scripture, or begin from facts at best merely relevant to facts of Scripture. In the former category are Tohorot, on the cleanness of foods, with its companion, Uqsin; Demai, on doubtfully tithed produce; Tamid, on the conduct of the daily whole-offering; Baba Batra, on rules of real estate transactions and certain other commercial and property relationships, and so on. In the latter category are Ohalot, which spins out its strange problems within the theory that a tent and a utensil are to be compared to one another (!); Kelim, on the susceptibility to uncleanness of various sorts of utensils; Miqvaot, on the sorts of water which effect purification from uncleanness; Ketubot and Gittin, on the documents of marriage and divorce; and many others. These tractates draw on facts of Scripture. But the problem confronted in these tractates in no way responds to problems important to Scripture. What we have here is a prior program of inquiry, which will make ample provision for facts of Scripture in an inquiry to begin with generated essentially outside of the framework of Scripture. First comes the problem or topic, then – if possible – comes attention to Scripture. And as we shall see, while our authorship draws richly upon the heritage of Scripture, the political structure and system of the Mishnah in no way proves symmetrical to those of Scripture.

So there we have it. Some tractates merely repeat what we find in Scripture. Some are totally independent of Scripture. And some fall in between. Clearly, we are no closer to a definitive answer to the question of the relationship of Scripture to the Mishnah than we were when we described the state of thought on the very same questions in the third and fourth centuries. We find everything and its opposite. But to offer a final answer to the question of Scripture-Mishnah relationships, we have to take that fact seriously. The Mishnah in no way is so remote from Scripture as its formal omission of citations of verses of Scripture suggests. In no way can it be described as contingent upon, and secondary to Scripture, as many of its third century apologists claimed. But the right answer is not that it is somewhere in between. Scripture confronts the framers of the Mishnah as revelation, not merely as a source of facts. But the framers of the Mishnah had their own world with which to deal. They made statements in the framework and fellowship of their own age and generation. They were bound, therefore, to come to Scripture with a set of questions generated other than in Scripture. They brought their own ideas about what was going to be important in Scripture. And that is what justifies our asking about their structure and their system, not only about how they have reshaped the politics of ancient Israel as portrayed in scriptural stories and rules.

The philosophers of the Mishnah conceded to Scripture the highest authority. At the same time what they chose to hear, within the authoritative statements of Scripture, will in the end form a statement of its own. To state matters simply: all of Scripture is authoritative. But only some of Scripture is relevant. And what happened is that the framers and philosophers of the tradition of the Mishnah came to Scripture when they had reason to. That is to say, they brought to Scripture a program of questions and inquiries framed essentially among themselves. So they were highly selective. That is why their program itself constituted a statement *upon* the meaning of Scripture. They and their apologists of one sort hastened to add, their program consisted of a statement *of* the meaning of Scripture. But that issue hardly demands attention in this context.

So much for the topical program and its relationship to Scripture. Let us now turn to the questions of power: who dominates whom, why, and by what means? Answers to these questions to begin with will not derive from data that tells us to whom the Mishnah is addressed. For whom are the Mishnah's system's answer to critical and urgent questions self-evidently valid? The building block of Mishnaic discourse, the circumstance addressed whenever the issues of concrete society and material transactions are taken up, is the householder and his establishment, which is the basic unit of production and also the fundamental building block of society. But, as we shall see, that is not the case when the Mishnah speaks of politics. The Mishnah knows about all sorts of economic activities. But for the Mishnah the center and focus of interest lie in the village. The village is made up of households, each a unit of production in farming. The households are constructed by, and around, the householder, father of an extended family, including his sons and their wives and children, his servants, his slaves (bondsmen), the craftsmen to whom he entrusts tasks he does not choose to do. When it comes to politics, by contrast, the Mishnah's framers take no interest in village or town or city (polis); they know only Jerusalem and everywhere else, without differentiation; and they know not the householder and his establishment but other social classifications and entities entirely.

The economics of the Mishnah is profoundly locative, in line with the simple fact that the concerns of householders are in transactions in land. Their measurement of value is expressed in acreage of top, middle, and bottom grade. Through real estate critical transactions are worked out. The marriage settlement depends upon real property. Civil penalties are exacted through payment of real property. The principal transactions to be taken up are those of the householder who owns beasts which do damage or suffer it; who harvests his crops and must set aside and so by his own word and deed sanctify them for use by the castes scheduled from on high; who uses or sells his crops and feeds his family; and who, if he is fortunate, will acquire still more land. None of this has any bearing upon the politics of the document. That politics takes place no where in particular, but in the Holy Land as a whole.

This underlines the disjuncture between the Mishnah's economics and its politics, as our categorical analysis in Parts Two and Three will show us in detail. For it is to householders that the Mishnah is addressed. The householder (not necessarily head of a family, not necessarily a male, but always a landholder) forms the pivot of society and its bulwark, the units of which the village is composed, the corporate component of the society of Israel in the limits of the village and the Land. The householder, as I said, is the building block of the house of Israel, of its *economy* in the classic sense of the word. That simple fact will take center stage when we consider the politics of the house of Israel, which exhibit a stunning shift in principles of category formation.

But if there is a disjuncture between the generative metaphor of the Mishnah's economics and the one that is spun out in its politics, the systemic message is the same in both cases. The message of the document as a whole concerns order and stability. The one thing the Mishnah does not want to tell us is about change, how things come to be what they are. The Mishnah's pretense is that all of these have come to rest. They compose a world in stasis, perfect and complete, made holy because it is complete and perfect. It is an economy embedded on a social system awaiting the divine act of sanctification which, as at the creation of the world, would set the seal of holy rest upon an again-complete creation, just as in the beginning. There is no place for the actors when what is besought is no action whatsoever, but only perfection, which is unchanging. There is room only for a description of how things are: the present tense, the sequence of completed statements and static problems. All the action lies within, in how these statements are made. Once they come to full expression, with nothing left to say, there also is nothing left to do, no need for actors, whether the political entities comprising king, scribes, priests, or the economic entities comprising householders.

The Mishnah's principal message expressed through the categorical media of economics and politics alike, the message that makes the Judaism of this document and of its social components distinctive and cogent, is that man[11] is at the center of creation, the head of all creatures upon earth, corresponding to God in heaven, in whose image man is made. Who this man is – whether householder, whether priest, monarch, or sage – shifts from topic to topic, but the priority of the human (male's) will and attitude in the disposition of important questions everywhere forms the premise of discourse. The way in which the Mishnah makes this simple and fundamental statement is to impute power to man to inaugurate and initiate those corresponding processes, sanctification and uncleanness, which play so critical a role in the Mishnah's account of reality. The will of man, expressed through the deed of man, is the active power in the world. Will and deed constitute those actors of creation which work upon neutral realms, subject to either sanctification or uncleanness: the Temple and table, the field and family, the altar and hearth, woman, time, space, transactions in the material world and in the world above as well. An object, a substance, a transaction, even a phrase or a sentence is inert but may be made holy, when the interplay of the will

---

[11]Woman is subordinate and dependent. Man is the norm and the normal. That is why I can say only "man," rather than, in this context, "the human being."

and deed of man arouses or generates its potential to be sanctified. Each may be treated as ordinary or (where relevant) made unclean by the neglect of the will and inattentive act of man.

The entire system of uncleanness and holiness for instance awaits the intervention of man, which imparts the capacity to become unclean upon what was formerly inert, or which removes the capacity to impart cleanness from what was formerly in its natural and puissant condition. So too in the other ranges of reality, man is at the center on earth, just as is God in heaven. Man is counterpart and partner and creation, in that, like God he has power over the status and condition of creation, putting everything in its proper place, calling everything by its rightful name. So, stated briefly, the question taken up by the Mishnah and answered by Judaism is, What can a man do? And the answer laid down by the Mishnah is, Man, through will and deed, is master of this world, the measure of all things. Since when the Mishnah thinks of man, it means the Israelite, who is the subject and actor of its system, the statement is clear. This man is Israel, who can do what he wills. In the aftermath of the two wars, the message of the Mishnah cannot have proved more pertinent – or poignant and tragic.

It would carry us far afield to follow the fate of the Mishnah's structure and system from 200 to the present. And it would also prove beside the point, since the continuators of the Mishnah, in the literature of exegesis and application of its law, of codification and restatement of its principles, reshaped the Mishnah, seen not as a system but as a composite of authoritative details alone, into the structures and systems of their own choosing. Accordingly, the Mishnah stands as a single, whole systemic structure for only a brief moment. The politics of Judaism would over time draw forth new systemic compositions, in response to successive crises, urgent questions yielding self-evidently valid answers. What the Mishnah's authorship contributed to the later politics of Judaisms was the simple proposition that a Judaism would be, whatever else it would constitute, an essentially political statement. That is what would last out of this initial system. Now to spell out the structure of the politics of the Mishnah and the way in which that political system is imagined to have done its work. Now to describe the political structure of the Judaism of the Mishnah.

# Part Two
# THE ECONOMICS OF A JUDAISM

# 4

# Why Does Judaism Have an Economics?

Let me begin with a simple piece of evidence that the ancient sages of Judaism recognized cycles of abundance and scarcity, if they did not call them business cycles.[1]  Sages most certainly understood the principles of market economics as they affected the market mechanism and manipulated those principles to achieve their own goals, as the following story indicates:

> A pair of birds in Jerusalem went up in price to a gold denar.
>
> Said Rabban Simeon b. Gamaliel, "By this sanctuary! I shall not rest tonight until they shall be sold at silver denars."
>
> He entered the court and taught, "The woman who is subject to five confirmed miscarriages or five confirmed fluxes brings only a single offering, and she eats animal-sacrifices, and the rest of the offerings do not remain as an obligation for her."
>
> And pairs of birds stood on that very day at a quarter-denar each, [one hundredth of the former price, the demand having been drastically reduced]."
>
> (M. Keritot 1:7K-Q)

The story shows that sages recognized the effect upon prices of diminished demand and were prepared to intervene in the market. Now to the more general question at hand: what is an economics, and does Judaism have one, and, if so, why?

An economics is a theory about the rational disposition of scarce resources.  The key word is "rational," of course, since what is reasonable in one setting or culture is incomprehensible in another, and

---

[1]The Inaugural Saul Reinfeld Lecture in Judaic Studies at Connecticut College New London, Connecticut on Wednesday, April 13, 1988.

in due course I shall explain the rational of the economics of Judaism. But so far as a social entity knows how and why scarce resources are assigned to, or end up in the hands of, one person, rather than some other, or one institution or class or other social organization, rather than some other, that social entity has an economics. A religion, such as Judaism (defined presently), need not have an economics, and most religions do not have an economic theory at all. Christianity prior to the Middle Ages, for example, had no economics, even though it had by then developed a rich and complex politics. And sayings relevant to an economics, answering questions concerning the definition of wealth, property, production and the unit of production, ownership, the determination of price and value and the like, – sayings relevant to economics in general may take shape within a religion, without that religion's setting forth an economics at all. For opinions on this and that, sayings about mercy to the poor, recommendations of right action, fairness, honesty, and the like – all these components of economics do not by themselves add up to an economics.

Only a sustained and systematic, internally coherent theory that over all and in an encompassing way explains why this, not that, defines market in relationship to ownership, production in relationship to price, above all, constitutes an economics. In the case of a religion, moreover, the presence of a theory on wealth and ownership, production and consumption, requires explanation. What we want to know, in particular, is what a particular religion wishes to express through its statements within the realm of economics, and why it is through economics in particular that the religion finds it necessary to make those statements. When, therefore, I ask, why does Judaism have an economics? I mean to answer that particular question: why does Judaism make its statement, in part, by discussing in a systematic and cogent way and within an encompassing theory the matter of the rational disposition of scarce resources?

Economics from Aristotle to Quesnay and Riqueti, in the eighteenth century, dealt with not the science of wealth but rather "the management of the social household, first the city, then the state."[2] Economics disembedded from politics developed only in the eighteenth century. Prior to that time, it formed a principal part of the study of political economy. That is to say, economics formed a component of the

---

[2]Elizabeth Fox-Genovese, *The Origins of Physiocracy. Economic Revolution and Social Order in Eighteenth-Century France* (Ithaca and London: Cornell University Press, 1985), p. 9. See also Karl Polanyi, *The Livelihood of Man.* Edited by Harry W. Pearson (New York, San Francisco, and London: Academic Press, 1977), p. 7.

larger sociopolitical order and dealt with the organization and management of the household (*oikos*). The city (*polis*) was conceived as comprising a set of households. Political economy, therefore, presented the theory of the construction of society, the village, town, or city, out of households, a neat and orderly, intensely classical and, of course, utterly fictive conception. One part of that larger political economy confronted issues of the household and its definition as the principal unit of economic production, the market and its function within the larger political structure, and the nature and definition of wealth. And the reason that one important Judaism had an economics was that that Judaism proposed to tell the Jews how to build an ideal society, a holy society, and in order to make its statement, that Judaism appealed to the correct, hence, the rational distribution of scarce resources: to distributive, rather than to market, economics, as we shall see. It was only through appeal to ancient principles of distributive economics, resting on the temple, priesthood, and cult, that the Judaism at hand found it possible to say what it wished to say in politic economy.

### I. The Economics of Judaism: Which Judaism? Which Economics?

The Judaism the economics of which is under study is the one that rested on the myth of Moses' receiving the Torah at Sinai in two media, written and oral. The written one corresponded to the Hebrew Bible or Old Testament. The oral one was ultimately written down by the sages of Judaism in late antiquity, beginning with the composition of the Mishnah, the Mishnah, a utopian system expressed in the form of a law-code, closed at ca. A.D. 200. The initial statement of that Judaism is represented by the Mishnah. The Judaism of the dual Torah, bearing the adjectives normative, talmudic, rabbinic, classical, and the like, unfolded through the exegesis of the two Torahs, written and oral, Scripture and Mishnah, through the first seven centuries of the Common Era (=A.D.) and yielded as its authoritative document the Talmud of Babylonia or Bavli. But only the initial and fundamental document of that Judaism forms the object of study here. My purpose here is to describe the economics of (a) Judaism in the context of in systemic context, to offer an account of economics in the foundation-document of the canon of the Judaism of the dual Torah.

When we place the economics, or, more really, the political economics of the Mishnah into the context of Greco-Roman economic thought, we gain a clearer picture of the power of economics to serve in the expression and detailed exposition of a utopian design for society. For, as Robert Lekachman states, "We see the economics of Plato and

Aristotle somewhat differently when we realize that what they were discussing above all was the good life, the just state, and the happy man."[3] They sought a unified science of society. And that serves as a suitable definition, also, for the program of the framers of the Mishnah. The authorship of the Mishnah covered every important problem that any treatise on economics, covering not only the rules of household management covered in an *oikonomikos*, but also the law of money-making, found it necessary to discuss, and on that basis, I claim to describe in some modest detail what I conceive to have been the economics of Judaism as the Mishnah's authorship defined Judaism and as the ancient world understood the science of economics, or, in its context, political economy. But let me start from the beginning, and that means, turn to the familiar definition of our subject.

The Mishnah, the initial statement of the Judaism of the dual Torah, not only encompasses but integrates economics within its larger system. That particular Judaism, indeed, makes its statement, also, through the exquisite details of rules and regulations governing the householder, the market, and wealth. The Mishnah's remarkably successful capacity to make its systemic statement, also, through the concerns of economics, its capacity to accomplish the detailed exegesis of economics within its larger social vision and system – these lack a significant counterpart in the generality of philosophy and theology in ancient times. Only in Aristotle do we find a great system-builder who encompassed, within his systemic statement, economic theory. Plato forms no important counterpart, and, as to Christianity, down to the end of late antiquity, in the seventh century, economics as a matter of theory enjoyed no position whatsoever. In theologies of Christianity, for one example, we find slight interest in, or use of, theories on the household, markets, and wealth, in the framing of the Christian statement, which bears no judgment that we may identify as a statement upon, or of, economics. Only when we turn to Aristotle do we find a counterpart to the truly remarkable accomplishment of the authorship of the Mishnah in engaging economics in the service of its larger systemic statement. Indeed, as the Mishnah's authorship's power of the extraordinarily detailed exegesis of economics as a systemic component becomes clear to us, we shall conclude that, among the social theorists of antiquity, the framers of the Mishnah take first place in the sophistication and profundity of their thought within political economy.[4]

---

[3]Robert Lekachman, *History of Economic Ideas* (New York: Harper & Bros., 1959), p. 4.
[4]That considerable claim of mine forms the *leitmotif* of this essay.

But the fact that both Aristotle and the authorship of the Mishnah appealed to economic theory in spelling out their ideas by itself does not require us to bring into juxtaposition, for purposes of comparison and contrast, the economic thought of the two writings, Aristotle's and the Mishnaic sages'. What requires that work is the simple fact that the Mishnah came forth in the age of the Second Sophistic, and, in diverse ways, adheres to the attitudes and agenda of that movement.[5] Not only so, but when we do read Aristotle's thought on economic theory, we find clear and detailed propositions in common between him and our authorship. But there is yet a third reason. Both Aristotle and the sages of the Mishnah thought deeply and sustainedly about economic issues. The power of economics as framed by Aristotle, the only economic theorist of antiquity worthy of the name was to develop the relationship between the economy to society as a whole.[6] And the framers of the Mishnah did precisely that: they incorporated issues of economics, even at a profound theoretical level, into the system of society as a whole, as they proposed to construct society. That is why to paraphrase Polanyi's judgment of Aristotle, the authorship of the Mishnah will be seen as attacking the problem of man's livelihood within a system of sanctification of a holy people with a radicalism of which no later religious thinkers about utopias were capable. None has ever penetrated deeper into the material organization of man's life under the aspect of God's rule. In effect, they posed, in all its breadth, the question of the critical, indeed definitive place occupied by the economy in society under God's rule. That is what we shall see in the remarkable statement, within an even more subtle idiom, of the economics of Judaism as the framers of the Mishnah defined that economics.

Just as through economics, Aristotle made the larger point that animated his system as a whole, so through economics did the framers of the Mishnah. The theory of both, moreover, falls into the same classification of economic theory, namely, the theory of distributive economics, familiar in the Near and Middle East from Sumerian times down to, but not including, the age of Aristotle himself. Before proceeding, let me define market and distributive economics, since these form the two economic theories at issue in antiquity, and, among them, the far more ancient, the distributive, shaped the economic thought of the two important systems of antiquity that made their statement, also, through economics, those of Aristotle and the Mishnah. In market

---

[5]This is a topic that in future work I shall treat in its own terms, but we do have to take note of the fact even now.

[6]Polanyi, "Aristotle Discovers the Economy," p. 79.

economics merchants transfer goods from place to place in response to the working of the market mechanism, which is expressed in price. In distributive economics, by contrast, traders move goods from point to point in response to political commands. In market economics, merchants make the market work by calculations of profit and loss. In distributive economics, there is no risk of loss on a transaction.[7] In market economics, money forms an arbitrary measure of value, a unit of account. In distributive economics, money gives way to barter and bears only intrinsic value, as do the goods for which it is exchanged. It is understood as "something that people accept not for its inherent value in use but because of what it will buy."[8] The idea of money requires the transaction to be complete in the exchange not of goods but of coins. The alternative is the barter transaction, in which, in theory at least, the exchange takes place when goods change hands. Clearly, therefore, in the Mishnah's conception of the market and of wealth, distributive, not market, economics shapes details of all transactions. In distributive economics money is an instrument of direct exchange between buyers and sellers, not the basic resource in the process of production and distribution that it is in market economics.

## II. The Distributive Economics of the Judaism of the Dual Torah

That distributive mode of economics, rationalized within theology and also fully realized in the detail of law, will not have astonished the framers of social systems from ancient Sumerian times, three thousand years before the time of the Mishnah, onward. For from the beginning of recorded time, temples or governments imposed the economics of distribution, and market economics, where feasible at all, competed with the economics of politics, organization, and administration. From remote antiquity onward, a market economy coexisted with a distributive economy.[9] Distributive economic theory

---

[7]All: Davisson and Harper, *European Economic History*, p. 130.

[8]*Ibid.*, p. 131.

[9]See Morris Silver, *Economic Structures of the Ancient Near East* (London and Sydney: Croom Helm, 1985), and J. Wansbrough's review of that book in *Bulletin of the London School of Oriental and African Studies* 50 (1987): 361-2. In this and prior studies Silver has successfully refuted the thesis of Polanyi that "there were not and could not be circumstances conducive to a market economy" (Wansbrough, p. 362). But the distinction between distributive and market economics has no bearing whatsoever upon whether or not, in remote antiquity, there was no such thing as a market in an economic sense, as Polanyi maintained. My argument focuses only upon economic theory. But, as is clear, I take for granted that Silver and those he represents have established as

characteristic of ancient temples and governments, which served as the storage points for an economy conceived to be self-supporting and self-sustaining, involved something other than a simultaneous exchange of legally recognized rights in property and its use; one party gave up scarce goods, the other party did not do so, but received those goods for other than market considerations. Free disposition of property, in distributive economics, found limitations in rules of an other-than-market character, e.g., taboos with no bearing upon the rational utilization of resources and individual decisions on the disposition of assets.

If, for example, the private person who possesses property may not sell that property to anyone of his choice, or may not sell it permanently, then the possessor of the property does not exercise fully free choice in response to market conditions.[10] The reason is that he cannot gain the optimum price for the land at a given moment, set by considerations of supply and demand for land or (more really) for the produce of land of a particular character. Another, a co-owner, in addition to the householder in possession of a piece of property, has a say. The decisions of that other owner are not governed solely (or at all) by market considerations. In the case of temple communities or god-kings, land ownership and control fall into the hands of an entity other than the private person, whether we call it the temple, priesthood, the government, the gild, or even the poor (!). Then, with private property and its use placed under limitations and constraints of an other-than-market origin, market trading is not possible: "While there could be a considerable development of governmental status distribution and some marginal barter, there could not develop a price-making market."[11] Private property in land, not merely in control of production, was required for the formation of a market economics in the conditions of antiquity, when ownership of production derived from ownership of land.

A further mark of the distributive economy is that transactions take the form of commodities of real value, that is, barter, and not of

---

fact the coexistence of market and distributive economics, such as I claim to discern, also, in the system of the Mishnah.

[10]Presently we shall note the integral relationship of a theory of ownership of property, specifically, a conception of property being private, and a theory of market economics. A mark of a distributive economics will be systemic intervention into not only the rationing (distribution) of resources but also of the means of production.

[11]Davisson and Harper, p. 125.

symbolic value, that is, money.   In ancient Mesopotamia, with its
distributive economics, while silver was the medium of exchange, it
was used in ingots and required weighing at each transfer.[12]  That
conception dominates in the Mishnah.    Finally, in distributive
economics, profit is a subordinate consideration, and, in the hands of so
sophisticated a mind as Aristotle's and as the Mishnah's authorship's,
profit is treated as unnatural.   Competing with market economics in the
Mishnah is a fully developed and amply instantiated, if never
articulated, distributive economics.   The Mishnah's authorship took
over the economics of the Priestly Code, itself a restatement, in the
idiom of the Israelite priesthood, of the distributive economics of
temples and kings beginning with the Sumerians and Egyptians and
coming down to the Greeks.  Market-economics was an innovation, its
economics not fully understood, at the time of the Priestly Code, and,
for reasons of their own, the framers of the Mishnah fully adopted and
exhaustively spelled out that distributive economics, even while
setting forth a plan for the economic life of "Israel" in a market
economy.

That old and well established theory of economics, in the received
Scriptures, is accurately represented by the Priestly Code, spelled out
in the rules of the biblical books of Leviticus and Numbers, upon which
the Mishnah's authorship drew very heavily.  The economic program
of the Mishnah, as a matter of fact, derived its values and also its
details from the Priestly Code and other priestly writings within the
pentateuchal mosaic.   Indeed, at point after point, that authorship
clearly intended merely to spin out details of the rules set forth in
Scripture in general, and, in economic issues such as the rational use of
scarce resources, the Priestly Code in particular.  The Priestly Code
assigned portions of the crop to the priesthood and Levites as well as to
the caste comprising the poor; it intervened in the market processes
affecting real estate by insisting that land could not be permanently
alienated but reverted to its "original" ownership every fifty years; it
treated some produce as unmarketable even though it was entirely fit;
it exacted for the temple a share of the crop; it imposed regulations on
the labor force that were not shaped by market considerations but by
religious taboos, e.g., days on which work might not be performed, or
might be performed only in a diminished capacity.

In these and numerous other details, the Priestly Code stated in the
Israelite-priestly idiom and in matters of detail the long established
principles of distributive economics and so conformed to thousands of

---

[12]A. Leo Oppenheim, *Ancient Mesopotamia.  Portrait of a Dead Civilization*
(Chicago and London: The University of Chicago Press, 1972), p. 87.

years of that distributive economics that treated private property as stipulative and merely conditional and the market as subordinate and subject to close political supervision. Market economics, coming into being in Greece in the very period – the sixth century B.C. – in which the Priestly Code was composed. Aristotle theorized about an economics entirely beyond anyone's ken and stated as principle the values of an economics (and a social system, too) long since transcended. Market economics, moreover, had been conveyed in practice to the Middle East a century and a half or so later by Alexander. By the time of the Mishnah, seven centuries after the Pentateuch was closed, market economics was well established as the economics of the world economy in which, as a matter of fact, the land of Israel and Israel, that is, the Jews of Palestine, had been fully incorporated. Theories of fixed value, distribution of scarce resources by appeal to other than the rationality of the market – these represented anachronisms. But, as the Mishnah's sages' prohibition against profit, which they called "usury" and their odd conception of a true value inherent in a commodity shows us, the framers of the Mishnah developed a dual economics, partly market, partly distributive. That is the fact that permits us to treat as matters of economic theory a range of rules that, in market economics, can have no point of entry whatsoever.

Only when we have grasped the general terms within which those concrete rules are worked out shall we understand the mixed economics characteristic of the Judaism of the Mishnah. A distributive economics, we now realize full well, is one that substitutes for the market as the price-fixing mechanism for the distribution of goods the instrumentality of the state or some other central organization, in the case of Scripture's economics in the Priestly Code of ca. A.D. 500, the Temple. In such an economics, in the words of Davisson and Harper,

> Such an organization will involve people's giving and receiving, producing and consuming, according to their status.[13]

Substituting for the market as a rationing device, the distributive economy dealt with "the actual things that are distributed," while in markets, "purchases and sales are usually made for money, not directly for other commodities or services."[14]

The definition of market economics calls to our attention the contrary traits of distributive economics, in particular, the intervention of authority other than the market in controlling both production and distribution of scarce goods. In the case of the Mishnah, the temple

---

[13]Davisson and Harper, p. 115.
[14]*Ibid.*, p. 123.

requires the recognition of the status of certain individual participants – in addition to the householder – in the transaction of distributing the material goods of the economy, in particular, portions of the crop. Priests, Levites, and the poor have a claim on the crop independent of their role in the production of the crop, e.g., in labor, in land ownership, in investment of seed and the like. Not only so, but the market is not the sole point of transfer of value. For material goods of the economy are directed to the temple – so in the theory of the Mishnah – without any regard for the working of the market. When it comes to the claim of the temple and priesthood upon the productive economy, there is no consideration of the exchange of material value for material value, let alone of the intervention of considerations of supply and demand, the worth of the goods as against the worth of the services supplied by the temple, and the like.[15]  Davisson and Harper state of the market, "Even politically powerful interests and corporations must agree to accept the market decisions whether or not the outcome of a particular market transaction favors a person of high status."[16]  But in the Mishnah, that simply is not so. And, we shall further observe, the temple taboos imposed upon the productive economy considerations of a non-market, non-productive character, in consequence of which the maximization of productivity forms only one among several competing considerations, and not the most important one, in the planning of production.

This brings us to the fundamental and necessary trait of market economics, private property. Davisson and Harper further state,

> Private ownership of property...is an essential condition of the market, but its existence does not guarantee that a market will exist or that contractual exchanges will occur [that can reach a conclusion with a simultaneous exchange of legally recognized rights in property and its use]. To be sure, in the absence of private property in the ancient Near East and early medieval Europe, we find a distributive economic order. Is there, then, some relation of cause and effect between private property and the operation of a market? It seems that insofar as there is monolithic ownership and control of property (as in the Sumerian temple communities or with the god-king pharaoh of Egypt) there can be no development of a market. Where private property was so limited, there could be no market trading. While there could be a considerable development of governmental status distribution

---

[15]True, the ideology of the Priestly Code insisted that payment of the temple taxes insured that God would "bless" the country with ample harvests, large herds, big families, and the like. But these factors in shaping of public opinion, therefore of considerations of demand, on their own do not – and cannot – fall into the classification of economic facts.

[16]Davisson and Harper, p. 123.

and some marginal barter, there could not develop a price-making market.[17]

That statement again draws our attention to the datum of the Mishnah, which informs, by the way, its economics as well: that God owns the land and that the household holds the land in joint tenancy with God. Private ownership does not extend to the land at all.[18] That simple fact imposes upon the Mishnah's economic theory the principles of distributive economics, even while the framers of that theory address a world of market economics. It accounts for the mixed economics – market, distributive – of the Mishnah. Not only so, but as we just noted, the mortal owner-partner with God in the management of the household is not free to make decisions based solely on maximizing productivity; other considerations as to the use of land, as much as to the disposition of the crop, intervened.

Both Aristotle and the framers of the Mishnah addressed economic theory not only within the framework of distributive economics. They also acknowledged the facts of market economics, even while reaffirming (each party in its own terms and context) the higher (Aristotle: "natural," thus more natural, Mishnah authorship: "holy" and hence holier) value associated with distributive economics. For Aristotle, therefore, the criterion of correct economic action derived from a larger concern to uncover natural, as against unnatural, ways of conducting affairs, and for the sages of the Mishnah, the counterpart criterion appealed to the theology of the Priestly Code, with its conception of the magical character of the land the Jews held as their own, which they called (and still call) "the land of Israel." This land was subject to particular requirements, because God owned this land in particular and through the temple and the priesthood constituted the joint owner, along with the Israelite householder, of every acre.

### III. Why Does Judaism Have an Economics?

The Mishnah is a document of political economy, in which the two critical classifications are the village, *polis*, and the household, *oikos*. Since, however, the Mishnah's framers conceived of the world as God's possession and handiwork, theirs was the design of a university in which the God's and humanity's realms flowed together. In their

---

[17]*Ibid.*, pp. 124-125.
[18]But God does not lay claim to joint ownership of other goods and services of the economy, apart from the land and its produce, with the result that private ownership of the commercial and manufacturing economy assuredly prevailed, one of the reasons I refer to the Mishnah's economic theory as a mixed one.

statement bears comparison, therefore, to Plato's *Republic* and
Aristotle's *Politics* as a utopian program (*Staatsroman*) of a society as a
political entity, encompassing, also, its economics; but pertinent to the
comparison also is Augustine's conception of a city of God and a city of
man. In the Mishnah we find thinkers attempting, in acute detail, to
think through how God and humanity form a single *polis* and a single
*oikos*, a shared political economy, one village and one household on
earth as it is in heaven.[19]

The Mishnah's sages placed economics, both market and
distributive, in the center of their system, devoting two of their six
divisions to it (the first and the fourth, for distributive and market
economics, respectively), and succeeded in making their statement
through economics in a sustained and detailed way far beyond the
merely generalizing manner in which Aristotle did. And no one in
antiquity came near Aristotle, as I said. It was with remarkable success
that the sages of Judaism presented an economics wholly coordinated in
a systemic way with a politics. The framers of the Mishnah joined
together the premises of two distinct economic theories, market
economics. And these two distinct theories, moreover, coexisted on the
foundations of an economics of reciprocity, joining heaven to earth.[20]

---

[19]That is why I conceive the more profound inquiry to address the politics of
Judaism, as the Mishnah presents that politics: the city of God which is the city
of humanity, unlike the distinct cities conceived by Augustine. The matter is
neatly expressed in numerous specific rules. See for example Roger Brooks,
*Support for the Poor in the Mishnaic Law of Agriculture: Tractate Peah* (Chico:
Scholars Press for Brown Judaic Studies, 1983), p. 49 to Mishnah-tractate Peah
1:4-5: "...The Mishnah's framers regard the Land as the exclusive property of
God. When Israelite farmers claim it as their own and grow food on it, they
must pay for using God's earth. Householders thus must leave a portion of the
yield unharvested as *peah* and give this food over to God's chosen
representatives, the poor. The underlying theory is that householders are
tenant farmers who pay taxes to their landlord, God." In this concrete way the
interpenetration of the realms of God and humanity is expressed. That
conception of the household and the village made up of households, the *oikos*
and the *polis*, yields not only an economics, such as we treat here in Chapters
Four through Six and Seven (market, distributive economics, respectively), but
also a politics. And the politics is the foundation for the economics, as we shall
repeatedly observe.

[20]But it seems to me not productive to pursue as an issue of theoretical
economics the notion of an exchange between heaven and earth, that is,
between God and Israel. That conception leads us deep into territory beyond
the substance of economics, into intangibles that we cannot grasp, measure or
weigh. Accordingly, I leave out of this account any notion of an economics of
reciprocity and deal only with (re)distribution and market exchange. I also

The conception of God's enjoying standing and power within the domain of economic life formed not a theological but an economic fact, on the basis of which decisions on the allocation of scarce resources and on the nature of wealth and ownership were reached and carried out in law. That simple fact constitutes the single indicative trait of the Judaism of the Mishnah, its power to translate theological conviction into exquisitely detailed rules for everyday life. Let me spell out how, in economics, the sages of the Mishnah made their theological statement.

### IV. The Distributive Economics of Judaism and the Theology of Judaism

The economic data with which the Mishnah's framers made their statement came to them from the Priestly Code. On the face of matters, therefore, the authorship of the document appealed to an economic theory that derived from an ancient age (we would say it was seven hundred years old, back to ca. 500 B.C., but they would say it was fourteen hundred years old, back to Sinai, which would bear a date of ca. 1200 B.C.). The truly anachronistic character of the Mishnah's distributive economics[21] becomes clear, however, when we realize that by the fourth century B.C., the Middle East received and used the legacy of Greece, brought by Alexander, in which a type of private property, prerequisite to the development of the market and available for the free use of the holder of that property independent of the priesthood or other government intervention, had developed.[22] For the theory of the Mishnah both the market and the distributive systems form one system and represent two components of one system. So we deal

---

omit reference to "householding" as too vague; no one imagines that Israel's economy in its land was a subsistence economy, certainly not at any point, from the sixth century B.C. forward, covered by the pentateuchal law-codes or their successors. So I see no point of interest in householding, because it is irrelevant, nor can I cope with "reciprocity," because it is a category covering economic relations between units that are not this-worldly (to put it mildly).

[21]For an account of archaizing tendency of the Second Sophistic in general, that is to say, the age of philosophy in which the Mishnah's authors did their work, see E. L. Bowie, "Greeks and their Past in the Second Sophistic," in M. I. Finley, ed., *Studies in Ancient Society* (London and Boston: Routledge & Kegan Paul, 1974), pp. 166-209. Bowie shows that "the archaism of language and style known as Atticism is only part of a wider tendency, a tendency that prevails in literature not only in style but also in choice of theme and treatment, and that equally affects other areas of cultural activity." I shall address this matter more systematically in my coming study of the Mishnah in the context of the philosophy of the Second Sophistic.

[22]Davisson and Harper, p. 125.

with a single theory, holding together two distinct economics. What we shall now see is how the distributive component of the Mishnah's economic theory reshapes the three principal categories that have occupied our attention, the household, the market, and wealth. But we ask, first of all, why the system of the Mishnah appealed to economics to begin with, and the answer to that question comes to us from theology, not economics. What the Mishnah's authorship wished to say, we shall now see, they could express only by utilizing the principal categories of economics under study here.

At the center of the Mishnah's economics is the disposition of resources with unremitting regard to the status of recipients in the transaction. In no way does the economics of Judaism in its initial statement conform to the definition of market economics just now cited. Our task therefore is now to understand in detail the foundation of the principles of distribution that define the theory of economics within the larger system of the Mishnah. In this way we grasp how profoundly the economics of the system has been shaped by the larger systemic statement and message.[23] The Mishnah's distributive economics derives from the theory that the temple and its scheduled castes on earth exercise God's claim to the ownership of the holy land. It is, in fact, a theology that comes to expression in the details of material transactions. The theology derives from the conviction expressed in the Psalm, "The earth is the Lord's." That conviction is a statement of ownership in a literal sense. God owns the earth. But the particular earth that God owns is the land of Israel, and, within that land, the particular earth is land in the land of Israel that is owned by an Israelite. With that Israelite, a land-owner in the land of Israel, God is co-owner.

From that theological principle, spun out of the notion that when Israelites occupy the land that God has given to the Israelites, namely, the land of Israel, that land is transformed, and so too are the principles of ownership and distribution of the land, all else flows. The economics of the Judaism rests upon the theory of the ownership of a designated piece of real estate, ownership that is shared between

_____

[23]Whether or not other economic theories express broader systemic values or are simply disembedded from systems and structures is not at issue in this account. It seems to me clear that all expositions of Aristotle's economics find it possible to show the coherence of his economics with his larger systemic, philosophical concerns. But why Aristotelian economics, read in light of Scripture, much like the economics of the Judaism of the Mishnah, formed out of the marriage of Aristotle and Scripture, should have served Latin Christianity so long (and so well) as it did, I do not know.

God and partners of a certain genus of humanity whose occupancy of that designated piece of real estate, but no other, affects the character of the dirt in question. The theology consists in an account of what happens when ground of a certain locale is subject to the residency and ownership of persons of a certain genus of humanity. The generative conception of the theology involves a theory of the effect – the enchantment and transformation – that results from the intersection of "being Israel": land, people, individual person alike. But let us turn directly to the economics of it all.

Since God owns the land of Israel, God – represented by, or embodied through, the temple and priesthood and other scheduled castes – joins each householder who also owns land in the land of Israel as an active partner, indeed, as senior partner, in possession of the landed domain. God not only demands a share of the crop, hence comprises a householder. God also dictates rules and conditions concerning production, therefore controls the householder's utilization of the means of production. Furthermore, it goes without saying, God additionally has provided as a lasting inheritance to Israel, the people, the enduring wealth of the country, which is to remain stable and stationary and not to change hands in such wise that one grows richer, the other poorer. Every detail of the distributive economics therefore restates that single point: *the earth is the Lord's.* That explains why the householder is partner of the Lord in ownership of the land, so that the Lord takes his share of the crop at the exact moment at which the householder asserts his ownership of his portion.[24]

But the on-going partnership between God and Israel in the sanctification and possession of the land is not a narrowly secular

---

[24]It is not only at the exact moment, but, as a matter of fact, in response to the householder's own decision and intention that God takes an interest in the crop. Before the householder exercises his ownership of the land through disposing of the crop, God does not exercise his ownership, except passively, by dictating the conduct of the means of production. What this means is that, within the anthropology of the Mishnaic system, God responds to man's emotions, attitudes, and intentions, and so reveals what I believe we may call anthropopathism. The conception of God as emotionally consubstantial with man therefore is embedded, even, in the economics. In this connection, Abraham J. Heschel, *The Prophets* (Philadelphia: Jewish Publication Society of America, 1958) explores the anthropological theology of prophetic writings along the same lines. But I know no study of the emotional correspondences between God and man other than my *Incarnation of God. The Character of Divinity in Formative Judaism* (Philadelphia: Fortress Press, 1988), in which the matter plays no central role.

arrangement. Both parties share in the process of the sanctification of
the land, which accounts for, and justifies, Israel's very possession of
the land. The Israelite landowner has a particular role in effecting the
sanctification of the land, in that, land is holy and subject to the rules
of God only when the Israelite landowner owns land in the land of
Israel. Once more, land located elsewhere owned by Israelites, and
land located in the land of Israel but not owned by Israelites, has no
material relationship to the processes of sanctification, in utilization
and in the disposition of the products of the land, that are at the heart
of the distributive economics at hand. That fact is demonstrated by the
conception about the character of the land, and of God's relationship to
it, that the longer Israel has lived in the land of Israel, the holier that
part of the land. Israel's dwelling in the land makes it holy. "Areas in
which Israelites have lived for longer periods of time are holier and
are subject to more rigorous restrictions,"[25] than those in which Israel
has lived for a shorter period. The laws of the sabbatical year apply
more strictly to the territories in which Israel lived before and after
586. Areas occupied only before but not after, or vice versa, are subject to
fewer restrictions. This has an important implication for the nature of
God's ownership of the land. Newman comments, "In Leviticus the land
is sanctified by God alone, who dwells in it and who has given it to
Israel, his people. The Mishnah's framers by contrast, claim that
Israelites also play an active part in sanctifying the land."[26]
Accordingly, in the Mishnah's system, the partnership of Israel,
represented by the householder, with God in ownership of the land
affects the very character of the land itself, making it different from
other land, imparting to it the status of sanctification through the
presence of the two sources of sanctification, God and the Israelite, the
Israelite householder in particular.

That explains why, in the case of the conception of ownership of
wealth set forth by the authorship of the Mishnah, a conception
informed by the rules of Leviticus, God's joint ownership and tenancy
with the farmer imposed a dual economics, the one, a distributive
economic order, the other, a market system pure and simple. The one
partner, God, had no strong interest in the market system; the other
partner, the householder, was assumed to have only such an interest in
the rational utilization and increase of scarce resources, land and crops,
herds and chattels. God's share was to be distributed in accord with
God's rules, the farmer keeping the rest. That is what I mean by a

---

[25]Louis E. Newman, *The Sanctity of the Seventh Year: A Study of Mishnah-
Tractate Shebiit* (Chico: Scholars Press for Brown Judaic Studies, 1983), p. 19.
[26]*Ibid.*, p. 19.

mixed system, one partner framing policy in line with a system of distributive economics, the other in market economics. The authorship of the Mishnah thus effected and realized in a systematic way rules governing land use, placement of diverse types of crops, rights of ownership, alongside provision of part of the crop to those whom God had designated as recipients of his share of the produce. That explains why that authorship could not imagine a market economy at all, and why the administered market (which, as we noted, is no market at all) in which government – priests' government – supposedly distributed status and sustained economic relationships of barter took the place of the market. What falls into the system of sanctification is what grows from the land through the householder's own labor ("cultivated"), is useful to the householder for sustaining life ("food"). God owns the land, the householder is the sharecropper, and the wealth of the householder therefore is the land that God allows for the householder's share and use. Wealth consists of land and what land produces, crops and cattle, as well as a large labor force, comprising the children of a growing population.

At the end we have to listen not only to what the authorship of the Mishnah says, but also to what it does not treat. What are the scarce resources that the economics of Judaism ignores? The economics of the system expresses in tacit omissions a judgment concerning the dimensions of the economy that to begin with falls subject to the enchantment of sanctification expressed in glorious triviality by our authorship. For matching the explicit rules are the authorship's ominous silences. Its land-centeredness permits its economics to have no bearing not only upon the economy comprising Jews who were not householders, but also Jews who lived overseas. The Mishnah's distributive economics is for the "Israel" of "the land of Israel" to which the Mishnah speaks. There is no address to the economics of "Israel" outside of the land. For distributive economics governs only agricultural produce of the land of Israel, and, it follows, market economics, everything else, and everywhere else. No wonder, then, that the framers of the Talmud of Babylonia, addressing, as they did, Jews who did not live on holy or sanctified dirt, took no interest whatsoever in the Mishnah-tractates upon which we have focused here, the ones that state in rich detail the theory of a distributive economics of God as owner, scheduled caste as surrogate, temple as focus, and enlandisement as rationale, for an utterly fictive system.

Strictly speaking, the economics of the Mishnah is not an economics at all. The reason is that in the Mishnah's system, economics is embedded in an encompassing structure, to which economic considerations are subordinated, forming merely instrumental components of a statement made not in response to, but merely through, economics. And economics can emerge as an autonomous and governing theory only when disembedded from politics and society.[27] Economic institutions, such as the market, the wage system, a theory of private ownership, and the like, in no way can have served the system of the Mishnah, not because in their moral or ethical value they proved less, or more, suitable than competing institutions, such as the sacerdotal system of production and distribution, a theory of divine-human joint tenancy, and a system made up of both wages for labor and also fees for correct genealogy, that the Mishnah's framers adopted. Economics viewed in its own terms cannot have served the system of the Mishnah because the system-builders viewed nothing in its own terms, but all things in the framework of the social system they proposed to construct. I earlier observed that Christian theologians for the first seven centuries simply ignored economics, having no theory to contribute to economic thought and no sustained interest in the subject. But when we realize the character and function of economics in the system of the Mishnah, we realize that the same reason accounts for the presence of an economics as for its absence.

Not all Judaic religious systems – statements of a world-view and a way of life addressed to a well defined social entity – have made

---

[27]That interest in whether or not economics is "embedded" or "disembedded" explains, once more, why I have tried to avoid those components of Polanyi's interpretation that have come under interesting criticism. I find especially suggestive the comments of Sally Humphreys, "Thus, what disturbed the philosophers of the fourth century was not, as Polanyi thought, an increase in profit-making on price differentials, but the disembedding or structural differentiation of the economy, leading to the application of 'economic' criteria and standards of behavior in a wide range of situations recognized as economic above all by the fact that money was involved; the old civic virtues of generosity and self-sufficiency were being replaced by the market attitudes of the traders." See Sally C. Humphreys, "History, Economics, and Anthropology: The Work of Karl Polanyi," *History & Theory* 8 (1969): 211. Note also Otto Erb, *Wirtschaft und Gesellschaft im Denken der hellenischen Antike* (Berlin: 1939), cited by her. Humphreys asks an interesting question: "Would a decrease in the importance of market institutions in a society which had reached this level of differentiation produce a revival of the attitudes whose loss Aristotle and Polanyi deplored? In the Roman Empire the state increasingly had to take over the functions of the market system in order to ensure an adequate supply and distribution of food to the city population. This change was accompanied by an increase in private redistribution...The process of bureaucratization of the economy and the rise under the influence of Christianity of new attitudes to economic matters has never really been studied."

judgments upon precisely those issues that conventionally comprise economics.[28] The priestly code did. We look in vain, in the counterpart rules of a priestly community, the Essenes at Qumran, for an interest in the same questions. The authorship of the Priestly Code concerned itself with distributive economics, true value, the reversion of property to its "original" owner, and other fundamental conceptions that everything belonged in place, and that there was a given order that

---

[28]See Barry Gordon, "Biblical and Early Judeo-Christian Thought: Genesis to Augustine," in S. Todd Lowry, ed., *Pre-Classical Economic Thought. From the Greeks to the Scottish Enlightenment* (Boston, Dordrecht, Lancaster: Kluwer Academic Publishers), pp. 43-67, and the commentary by Roman A. Ohrenstein, "Some Socioeconomic Aspects of Judaic Thought," *ibid.*, pp. 68-76. Note also the following items, among many:

R. Barraclough, *Economic Structures in the Bible* (Canberra: Zadok Centre, 1980).

Roland de Vaux, *Ancient Israel* (London: Darton, Longman and Todd, 1978).

Barry Gordon, *Economic Analysis before Adam Smith: Hesiod to Lessius* (London: MacMillan, 1975).

*Ibid.*, "Lending at Interest: Some Jewish, Greek, and Christian Approaches, 800 B.C. – A.D. 100," *History of Political Economy*, 1982. 14:406-26.

Frederick C. Grant, The Economic Background of the Gospels (New York: Russell and Russell, 1973) (Repr. of 1926 ed.).

B. J. Meislin and M. L. Cohen, "Backgrounds of the Biblical Law against Usury," *Comparative Studies in Society and History 6* (1963-4).

Ben Nelson, *The Idea of Usury* (Chicago and London: University of Chicago Press, 1969).

E. Neufeld, "Socio-Economic Background of Yobel and Shemitta," *Rivista degli studi orientali 33* (1958): 53-124.

Robert North, *Sociology of the Biblical Jubilee* (Rome: Pontifical Biblical Institute, 1954).

Roman A. Ohrenstein, "Economic Thought in Talmudic Literature in the Light of Modern Economics," *American Journal of Economics and Sociology 27* (1968): 185-96.

*Idem.*, "Economic Self-Interest and Social Progress in Talmudic Literature," *American Journal of Economics and Sociology 27* (1970): 59-70.

*Idem.*, "Economic Aspects of Organized Religion in Perspective: The Early Phase," *The Nassau Review* (1970): 27-43.

*Idem.*, "Economic Analysis in Talmudic Literature: Some Ancient Studies of Value," *American Journal of Economics and Sociology* (1979): 38.

*Idem.*, "Some Studies of Value in Talmudic Literature in the Light of Modern Economics," *The Nassau Review 4* (1981): 48-70.

Morris Silver, *Prophets and Markets: The Political Economy of Ancient Israel* (Boston: Kluwer-Nijhoff, 1983).

J. Viner, "The Economic Doctrines of the Christian Fathers," *History of Political Economy 10* (1978): 9-45.

constituted the right arrangement and disposition of material wealth. So too, as we shall see, did the authorship of the Mishnah. But I find slight equivalent interest in the law-codes of the Essenes of Qumran in these same matters, and there is no counterpart to the sustained and detailed attention to them accorded by the authorship of the Mishnah. For the whole of antiquity, we recognize, Christian theologians and jurisprudents (after Constantine) managed to say practically nothing about matters of economic theory. Only with the advent of Aristotle in the life of the Christian intellect in the West do we find a counterpart interest to that of the authorship of the Mishnah. That authorship made a choice, and we can explain why this, not that, when we realize that the requirements of the system of the Mishnah encompasses, also, the task of framing an economic theory as a medium for the statement of the system's main points concerning sanctification.

What I have shown is that the Mishnah is a document of political economy, in which the two critical classifications are the village, *polis*, and the household, *oikos*. Since, however, the Mishnah's framers conceived of the world as God's possession and handiwork, theirs was the design of a universe in which the God's and humanity's realms flowed together. The result is a distributive economics, familiar from most ancient times onward, but a distributive economics that, in the same system, coexisted with a kind of market economics.[29] In their statement bears comparison, therefore, to Plato's *Republic* and Aristotle's *Politics* as a utopian program (*Staatsroman*) of a society as a political entity, encompassing, also, its economics; but pertinent to the comparison also is Augustine's conception of a city of God and a city of man. In the Mishnah we find thinkers attempting, in acute detail, to think through how God and humanity form a single *polis* and a single *oikos*, a shared political economy, one village and one household on earth as it is in heaven.[30]

---

[29]I explain this matter in my *Economics of Judaism. The Initial Statement* (in press).

[30]That is why I conceive the more profound inquiry to address the politics of Judaism, as the Mishnah presents that politics: the city of God which is the city of humanity, unlike the distinct cities conceived by Augustine. The matter is neatly expressed in numerous specific rules. See, for example, Brooks, p. 49, to Mishnah-tractate Peah 1:4-5: "...The Mishnah's framers regard the Land as the exclusive property of God. When Israelite farmers claim it as their own and grow food on it, they must pay for using God's earth. Householders thus must leave a portion of the yield unharvested as *peah* and give this food over to God's chosen representatives, the poor. The underlying theory is that householders are tenant farmers who pay taxes to their landlord, God." In this concrete way the interpenetration of the realms of God and humanity is

The Mishnah's sages placed economics, both market (for civil transactions) and distributive (for sacred transactions, e.g., with scheduled castes and the temple), in the center of their system, devoting two of their six divisions to it (the first and the fourth, for the distributive and the market economics, respectively), and succeeded in making their statement through economics in a sustained and detailed way far beyond the manner in which Aristotle did. And no one in antiquity came near Aristotle, as I said. It was with remarkable success that the sages of Judaism presented an economics wholly coordinated in a systemic way with a politics. In this proposed kind of study of religion and economics, therefore, we find ourselves on the border between sociology and economics, following how the sociology of economics – and therefore this kind of inquiry concerning religious materials places us squarely into the middle of discourse on political economy. Compared to the work of Plato and Aristotle, the Mishnah's system presents the single most successful political economy accomplished in antiquity.

### V. Jews in Economies and the Economics of Judaism:
### The Case of Salo W. Baron

The economics of Judaism, as the economics of the Jews, is hardly an unexplored field of inquiry.[31] Indeed, any study of pertinent topics, whether of the Jews' economics or of the Jews' own economy, of the Jews in economic life or of the economics of Judaism, takes its place in a long, if somewhat irregular and uneven, line of works on the subject. The most important and best known statement on the economics of Judaism purports to account, by appeal to the economics of Judaism and the economic behavior of Jews, for the origins of modern capitalism.

---

expressed. That conception of the household and the village made up of households, the oikos and the polis, yields not only an economics but also a politics. And the politics is the foundation for the economics.

[31]For an introduction to the economic study of talmudic literature, see Roman A. Ohrenstein, "Economic Thought in Talmudic Literature in the Light of Modern Economics," *The American Journal of Economics and Sociology* 27 (1968): 185-96, who cites earlier writings on the subject, cf. p. 185, n. 3. Ohrenstein's "Economic Self-Interest and Social Progress in Talmudic Literature: A Further Study of Ancient Economic Thought and its Modern Significance," *American Journal of Economics and Sociology* 29 (1970): 59-70, typifies the perfectly dreadful work in hand in that field. I do not here treat Tamari's work on Jewish ethics vis-à-vis economics, because that seems to me a methodologically still more primitive work than any under discussion here.

Werner Sombart, *The Jews and Modern Capitalism*,[32] in 1911 set the issues of the economics of Judaism within a racist framework, maintaining that Jews exhibited an aptitude for modern capitalism, and that aptitude derives in part from the Jewish religion, in part from the Jews' national characteristics. Jewish intellectuality, teleological mode of thought, energy, mobility, adaptability, Jews' affinity for liberalism and capitalism, – all of these accounted for the role of Jews in the creation of the economics of capitalism, which dominated. Sombart appealed, in particular, to the anthropology of the Jew, maintaining that the Jews comprise a distinct anthropological group. Jewish qualities persist throughout their history: "constancy in the attitude of the Jews to the peoples among whom they dwelt, hatred of the Jews, Jewish elasticity." "The economic activities of the Jew also show a remarkable constancy." Sombart even found the knowledge of economics among the rabbis of the Talmud to be remarkable. In the end Sombart appealed to the fact that the Jews constitute a "Southern people transplanted among Northern peoples." The Jews exhibited a nomadic spirit through their history. Sombart contrasted "the cold North and the warm South," and held that "Jewish characteristics are due to a peculiar environment." So he appealed to what he found to be the correlation between Jewish intellectuality and desert life, Jewish adaptability and nomad life, and wrote about "Jewish energy and their Southern origin," "'Sylvanism' and Feudalism compared with 'Saharaism' and Capitalism," and ended, of course, with the theme of the Jews and money and the Jews and the Ghetto.

The romantic and racist view of the Jews as a single continuing people with innate characteristics which scientific scholarship can identify and explain of course formed the premise for Sombart's particular interest, in the economic characteristics of the Jew and the relationship of this racial traits to the Jews' origin in the desert. While thoroughly discredited, these views have nonetheless generated a long sequence of books on Jews' economic behavior. Today people continue to conceive "Jewish economic history" as a cogent subject that follows not only synchronic and determinate, but also diachronic and indeterminate lines and dimensions. Such books have taken and now take as the generative category the Jews' constituting a distinct economy, or their formation of a social unit of internally consistent economic action and therefore thought, the possibility of describing, analyzing, and interpreting the Jews within the science of economics.

---

[32]The edition I consulted is Werner Sombart, *The Jews and Modern Capitalism*. With a new introduction by Samuel Z. Klausner. Translated by M. Epstein (New Brunswick and London: Transaction Books, 1982).

But that category and its premise themselves still await definition and demonstration, and these to this day are yet lacking. Consequently, while a considerable literature on "the Jews' economic history" takes for granted that there is a single, economically cogent group, the Jews, which has had a single ("an") economic history, and which, therefore, forms a distinctive unit of economic action and thought, the foundations for that literature remain somewhat infirm.[33]

The conception of Jews' having an economic history, part of the larger, indeed encompassing, notion of the Jews' have had a single history as a people, one people, has outlived the demise of the racist rendition of the matter by Sombart. But what happens when we take seriously the problems of conception and method that render fictive and merely imposed a diachronic history of the Jews, unitary, harmonious, and continuous, and when we realize that the secondary and derivative conception of a diachronic economics of the Jews is equally dubious? Whether or not it is racist, that unitary conception of the Jews as a single, distinctive, on-going historical entity, a social group forming also a cogent unit of economic action, is surely romantic. Whatever the salubrious ideological consequences, such an economics bypasses every fundamental question of definition and method If the Jews do not form a distinct economy, then how can we speak of the Jews in particular in an account of economic history? If, moreover, the Jews do not form a distinct component of a larger economy, then what do we learn about economics when we know that (some) Jews do this, others, that? And if Jews, in a given place and circumstance, constitute a distinct economic unit within a larger economy, then how study Jews' economic action out of the larger economic context which they help define and of which they form a component? The upshot of these question is simple: how shall we address those questions concerning rational action with regard to scarcity that do, after all, draw our attention when we contemplate, among other entities, the social entities that Jews have formed, and now form, in the world? And this brings us to the work of Salo W. Baron in social and economic history of the Jews, since in Baron's definition of the matter we are able to see precisely how this kind of study should not be done – and why.

---

[33]I hasten to state at the outset that Jews' role in diverse economies, so far as that role is distinctive, surely permits us to appeal as an independent variable to the fact that certain economic actors are Jews. But what trait or quality about those actors as Jews explains the distinctive traits of Jews as a group – if any does – requires careful analysis in a comparative framework, e.g., Jews as a distinct component of a variety of economies. None of these entirely valid and intellectually rigorous inquires is under discussion here.

Salo W. Baron[34] claims to know about economic trends among Jews in the second, third, and fourth centuries. As evidence he cites episodic statements of rabbis, as in the following:

> In those days R. Simon ben Laqish coined that portentous homily which, for generations after, was to be quoted in endless variations: "'You shall not cut yourselves,' this means you shall not divide yourselves into separate groups...." Before the battle for ethnic-religious survival, the inner class struggle receded.[35]
>
> Age-old antagonisms, to be sure, did not disappear overnight. The conflict between the scholarly class and "the people of the land" continued for several generations...
>
> Class differences as such likewise receded into the background as the extremes of wealth and poverty were leveled down by the unrelenting pressure of Roman exploitation. Rarely do we now hear descriptions of such reckless display of wealth as characterized the generation of Martha, daughter of Boethos, before the fall of Jerusalem. Even the consciously exaggerated reports of the wealth of the patriarchal house in the days of Judah I fell far short of what we know about the conspicuous consumption of the Herodian court and aristocracy....

It would be difficult to find a better example of overinterpretation of evidence to begin with irrelevant to the point than Baron's concluding sentence of the opening paragraph of this abstract. Not having shown that there was an inner class struggle or even spelled out what he means by class struggle, how he knows the category applies, let alone the evidence for social stratification on which such judgments rest, Baron leaps into his explanation for why the class struggle receded. That is not the only evidence of what can only be regarded as indifference to critical issues characteristic of writing on Jews' economies, but it is probative. The rest of the passage shows how on the basis of no sustained argument whatsoever, Baron invokes a variety of categories of economic history and analysis of his time, e.g., conspicuous consumption, class struggle ("inner" presumably different from "outer"), and on and on.

---

[34]*A Social and Religious History of the Jews* (New York: Columbia University Press, 1952) II. *Ancient Times,* Part II, pp. 241-260. Compare my "Why No Science in Judaism?" in *From Description to Conviction* (Atlanta: Scholars Press for Brown Judaic Studies, 1987), on the counterpart problems of intellect exhibited by Saul Lieberman, Baron's contemporary. I place the matter into a still broader context in Paradigms in Passage: *Paradigms in Passage: Patterns of Change in the Contemporary Study of Judaism.* (Lanham: University Press of America, 1988. Studies in Judaism Series.)
[35]Baron, p. 241.

When discussing economic policies, which draw us closer to the subject of this book, Baron presents a discussion some may deem fatuous.[36] Precisely how he frames the issues of economic theory will show why:

> Economic Policies: Here too we may observe the tremendous influence of talmudic legislation upon Jewish economy.

The premise that there was (a) Jewish economy, and that talmudic legislation affected economic action, is simply unsubstantiated. How Baron knows that people did what rabbis said they should, or that Jews formed an economy in which people could make decisions in accord with sages' instructions, he does not say. The premise of all that follows, then, is vacant. More to the point of our interest in matters of economic theory, we turn to Baron's program of discourse on what he has called "policies":

> The rabbis constantly tried to maintain interclass equilibrium. They did not denounce riches, as some early Christians did, but they emphasized the merely relative value of great fortunes....The persistent accentuation of collective economic responsibility made the Jewish system of public welfare highly effective. While there was much poverty among the Jews, the community, through its numerous charitable institutions, took more or less adequate care of the needy.

> Man's right, as well as duty, to earn a living and his freedom of disposing of property were safeguarded by rabbinic law and ethics only in so far as they did not conflict with the common weal....

> Private ownership, too, was hedged with many legal restrictions and moral injunctions in favor of over-all communal control....

> Rabbinic law also extended unusual protection to neighbors....

> Nor did the individual enjoy complete mastery over testamentary dispositions....

> Apart from favoring discriminatory treatment of apostates, who were supposed to be dead to their families, the rabbis evinced great concern for the claims of minor children to support from their fathers' estate....

> In a period of economic scarcity social interest demanded also communal control over wasteful practices even with one's own possessions....

How this mélange of this and that – something akin to economic policy, some odd observations on public priority over private interest that sounds suspiciously contemporary (to 1952), counsel about not throwing away bread crumbs – adds up to "economic policies" I cannot

---

[36]*Ibid.*, pp. 251-255.

say. But the data deserves a still closer scrutiny, since Baron represents the state of economic analysis of Judaism and so exemplifies precisely the problem I propose to solve in a different way. Here is his "man's right" paragraph, complete:

> Man's right, as well as duty, to earn a living and his freedom of disposing of property were safeguarded by rabbinic law and ethics only in so far as they did not conflict with the common weal. Extremists like R. Simon ben Yohai insisted that the biblical injunction, "This book of the law shall not depart out of thy mouth, but thou shalt meditate therein day and night," postulated wholehearted devotion to the study of Torah at the expense of all economic endeavors. But R. Ishmael effectively countered by quoting the equally scriptural blessing, "That thou mayest gather in thy corn and thy wine and thine oil." Two centuries later, the Babylonian Abbaye, who had started as a poor man and through hard labor and night work in the fields had amassed some wealth, observed tersely, "Many have followed the way of R. Ishmael and succeeded; others did as R. Simeon ben Yohai and failed." Sheer romanticism induced their compeer, R. Judah bar Ila'i, to contend that in olden times people had made the study of the law a full-time occupation, and devoted only little effort to earning a living, and hence had proved successful in both.... R. Simeon ben Yohai himself conceded, however, that day and night meditation had been possible only to a generation living on Mannah or to priestly recipients of heave-offerings.... In practice the rabbis could at best secure, as we shall see, certain economic privileges for a minority of students, relying upon the overwhelming majority of the population to supply society's needs to economically productive work.

From the right to earn a living being limited by the common weal, we jump to study of the Torah as the alternative to productive labor. That move of Baron's I cannot myself claim to interpret. I see no connection between the balance between "freedom of disposing of property" and "conflict with the common weal," on the one side, and " the issue of work as against study, on the other. The rest of the discussion concerns only that latter matter, and the paragraph falls to pieces by the end in a sequence of unconnected sayings joined by a pseudo-narrative ("two centuries later...") and an equally meretricious pretense of sustained argument "...himself conceded"), all resting on the belief that the sayings assigned to various sages really were said by them.

This reading by Baron of how "the Jews" policies and behavior in economics are to be studied should not be set aside as idiosyncratic. The obvious flaws of historical method, the clear limitations in even so simple a matter as the competent construction of a paragraph – these should not obscure the fact that Baron's construction of the Jewish economy and Jewish economic policy is representative and not at all idiosyncratic. The received conception first of all imputes to the Jews a single economic history, which can be traced diachronically. Proof lies in works in both English and Hebrew. Take for example the book entitled, *Economic History of the Jews*, assigned to Salo W. Baron, Arcadius Kahan, and others, edited by Nachum Gross.[37] Baron wrote Chapters One through Seven, Kahan, Eight through Ten, of Part One, "general survey," and the titles of these sequential chapters follow: "the first temple period, exile and restoration, the second temple period, the talmudic era, the Muslim Middle Ages, medieval Christendom, economic doctrines, the early modern period, the transition period, the modern period." That, I contend, is a program of diachronic economic history. These chapters can have been composed and presented in the sequence before us only if the author assumed that a single group, with a continuous, linear history, formed also a cogent and distinct economic entity, with its own, continuous, linear, economic history.

"Economic doctrines" as Baron expounds them are amply familiar to us: bits and pieces of this and that. The remainder of the book covers these topics: agriculture, industry, services, and each part is subdivided, e.g., under services: "banking and bankers, brokers, contractors, court Jews, department stores, Jewish autonomous finances, market days and fairs, mintmasters and moneyers, moneylending, peddling, secondhand goods, slave trade, spice trade, stock exchanges." Here again, we may be sure, data on department stores derive from one time and place, those on slave trade, from another. But laid forth sequentially, the chapter titles indicate a conception of a single unitary and continuous economic history, in which any fact concerning any Jew at any time or place connects with any fact concerning any other Jew at any other time or place, the whole forming a cogent economy. Nor should work in Hebrew be expected to exhibit a more critical definition of what is subject to discourse. The same Nachum Gross edited *Jews in Economic Life. Collected Essays In Memory of Arkadius Kahan (1920-1982).*[38] Here is the portrait of a field, as sequential essays outline that field:

The Economic Activities of the Jews

The Cardinal Elements of the Economy of Palestine during the Herodian Period

---

[37]New York: Schocken, 1975.
[38]Jerusalem: The Zalman Shazar Center for the Furtherance of the Study of Jewish History, 1985.

The Economy of Jewish Communities in the Golan in the Mishna and Talmud Period

The Itinerant Peddler in Roman Palestine

The German Econo 4%in the 13th-14th Centuries:  The Framework and Conditions for the Economic Activity of the Jews

On the Participation of Jewish Businessmen in the Production and Marketing of Salt in Sixteenth Century Poland and Lithuania

Economic Activities of Jews in the Caribbean in Colonial Times

Jewish Guilds in Turkey in the Sixteenth to Nineteenth Centuries

and on and on.  Nor do I exaggerate the utter confusion generated by the conception of "the Jews" as an economic entity, continuous from beginning to the present.  The juxtaposition of these two papers seems to me to make the point rather sharply:

Jewish Population and Occupations in Sherifian Morocco

On the Economic Activities of the Moldavian Jews in the Second Half of the 18th and the First Half of the 19th Centuries

There is no need to ask what one thing has to do with the other. We just take for granted that Jews are Jews wherever they lived, whenever they thrived, and whatever Jews' occupations were in Sherifian Morocco bears a self-evident relationship to whatever Moldavian Jews did for a living half a world and a whole civilization distant.  Having cited the juxtaposition of titles, with justified confidence I simply rest my case.

# 5

## The Mishnah's Distributive Economics: Householder, Market, Wealth

A market is a series of transactions by buyer and seller where prices measure the scarcity of a commodity on the market. A high price indicates that the quantity of a given commodity on a market is low when measured against buyer demand; lower prices indicate that the quantity is great when measured against buyer demand...It is an essential point of market trading that the political authority of the society (government, temple, guilds) gives up control of production and distribution to this impersonal mechanism. The market mechanism of exchange must determine the use of resources regardless of the status of the individual participants to the transaction, regardless of the relation of the individuals to the transaction and to each other.[1]

In market economics merchants transfer goods from place to place in response to the working of the market mechanism, which is expressed in price.[2] In distributive economics, by contrast, traders move goods from point to point in response to political commands. In market economics, merchants make the market work by calculations of profit and loss. In distributive economics, there is no risk of loss on a transaction.[3] In market economics, money forms an arbitrary measure of value, a unit of account. In distributive economics, money gives way to barter and bears only intrinsic value, as do the goods for which it is exchanged. It is understood as "something that people accept not for its

---

[1]Davisson and Harper, p. 123
[2]A few points in this paper review what was said briefly in the foregoing. I beg the reader's indulgence.
[3]All: Davisson and Harper, p. 130.

inherent value in use but because of what it will buy."[4]  The idea of
money requires the transaction to be complete in the exchange not of
goods but of coins.  The alternative is the barter transaction, in which,
in theory at least, the exchange takes place when goods change hands.
In distributive economics money is an instrument of direct exchange
between buyers and sellers, not the basic resource in the process of
production and distribution that it is in market economics.  Our task is
now to understand in detail the foundation of the principles of
distribution that define the theory of economics within the larger
system of the Mishnah, ca. A.D. 200, the initial document in the
Judaism of the dual Torah that predominated from late antiquity to our
own day.  In this way we grasp how profoundly the economics of the
system has been shaped by the larger systemic statement and message.[5]

In one sentence, the Mishnah's distributive economics derives from
the theory that the temple and its scheduled castes on earth exercise
God's claim to the ownership of the holy land,.  Since God owns the
Land of Israel, God – through the temple and priesthood and other
scheduled castes – joins each householder as an active partner, indeed,
as senior partner, in possession of the landed domain.  God not only
demands a share of the crop, hence comprises a householder.  God also
dictates rules and conditions concerning production, therefore controls
the means of production.  Furthermore, it goes without saying, God
additionally has provided as a lasting inheritance to Israel, the
people, the enduring wealth of the country, which is to remain stable
and stationary and not to change hands in such wise that one grows
richer, the other poorer.  Every detail of the distributive economics
therefore restates that single point: *the earth is the Lord's.*  That
explains why the householder is partner of the Lord in ownership of
the land, so that the Lord takes his share of the crop at the exact
moment at which the householder asserts his ownership of his
portion.[6]

---

[4]*Ibid.*, p. 131.

[5]Whether or not other economic theories express broader systemic values or
are simply disembedded from systems and structures is not at issue in this
account. It seems to me clear that all expositions of Aristotle's economics find
it possible to show the coherence of his economics with his larger systemic,
philosophical concerns.  But why Aristotelian economics, read in light of
Scripture, much like the economics of the Judaism of the Mishnah, formed out
of the marriage of Aristotle and Scripture, should have served Latin
Christianity so long (and so well) as it did, I do not know.

[6]As we shall see, it is not only at the exact moment, but, as a matter of fact, in
response to the householder's own decision and intention that God takes an
interest in the crop.  Before the householder exercises his ownership of the

But the on-going partnership between God and Israel in the sanctification and possession of the land is not a narrowly secular arrangement. Both parties share in the process of the sanctification of the land, which accounts for, and justifies, Israel's very possession of the land. For a further conception about the character of the land, and of God's relationship to it, is that the longer Israel has lived in the land of Israel, the holier that part of the land. Israel's dwelling in the land makes it holy. "Areas in which Israelites have lived for longer periods of time are holier and are subject to more rigorous restrictions,"[7] than those in which Israel has lived for a shorter period. The laws of the sabbatical year apply more strictly to the territories in which Israel lived before and after 586. Areas occupied only before but not after, or vice versa, are subject to fewer restrictions. This has an important implication for the nature of God's ownership of the land. Newman comments, "In Leviticus the land is sanctified by God alone, who dwells in it and who has given it to Israel, his people. The Mishnah's framers by contrast, claim that Israelites also play an active part in sanctifying the land."[8] Accordingly, in the Mishnah's system, the partnership of Israel, represented by the householder, with God in ownership of the land affects the very character of the land itself, making it different from other land, imparting to it the status of sanctification through the presence of the two sources of sanctification, God and the Israelite, the Israelite householder in particular, as we shall presently see.

To understand the full impact of that one conception, we must recall that the Mishnah's utopian vision is realized in the exquisite detail of rules. Hence before proceeding to the secondary exposition of the implications for the distributive theory of economics of God's ownership of the land, we turn to a particular statement of the rules to

---

land through disposing of the crop, God does not exercise his ownership, except passively, by dictating the conduct of the means of production. What this means is that, within the anthropology of the Mishnaic system, God responds to man's emotions, attitudes, and intentions, and so reveals what I believe we may call anthropopathism. The conception of God as emotionally consubstantial with man therefore is embedded, even, in the economics, as we shall presently see. In this connection, Heschel (*The Prophets*), 1963 explores the anthropological theology of prophetic writings along the same lines. But I know no study of the emotional correspondences between God and man other than my *Incarnation of God. The Character of Divinity in Formative Judaism* (Philadelphia: Fortress Press, 1988), in which the matter plays no central role.
[7]Newman, p. 19.
[8]*Ibid.*, p. 19.

see what it means, in rich exegesis, to conceive that God and the householder have formed a partnership in joint tenancy of the land that the householder owns. The tractate on tithing, Maaserot, gives expression to the definition of the householder's relationship to his partner and joint tenant in possession of the land, God, meaning, the priesthood.[9] The basic point is that produce may be tithed as soon as it ripens, for, as Jaffee says, "at this point the crop becomes valuable as property." But one is required to pay the tithes only when the householder "actually claims his harvested produce as personal property."[10] That moment arrives when the householder brings untithed produce from the field to the house, or when he prepares untithed produce for sale in the market.[11] The reason is that that is the point at which the householder claims the produce for his own benefit and gain, at which point the partner, God, is to receive the portions that belong to him. The authorship of the tractate, for its part, develops a quite subordinate issue, as Jaffee defines it:

> The framers of the tractate, however, are troubled by their own notion that produce need be tithed only after it has been claimed as property. What disturbs them is that now there normally will be a lengthy period of time – beginning with the ripening of the crop and extending until well after the harvest – during which the produce will remain untithed. It is precisely during this indeterminate period prior to tithing, however, that some of the produce is likely to be eaten by those who harvest it or who are otherwise involved in its processing or transport. This is what concerns Tractate Maaserot, for untithed produce presents a taxonomical problem. On the one hand, such produce is not sacred food, restricted for the use of priests, for the dues have not yet been designated within the produce and set aside from it for their meals. On the other hand, the produce cannot be used as profane or common food, for it is capable of yielding offerings which stand under the claim of God. Untithed produce, it follows, is subject to a special set of rules which take account of its ambiguous character...produce which is neither sacred nor profane, neither wholly God's nor wholly man's.[12]

The upshot is that that produce may not be eaten in meals, but it may be used for a snack or in some other informal way. Again Jaffee: "The point is that the anomalous character of untithed food prevent it

---

[9]Martin S. Jaffee, *Mishnah's Theology of Tithing: A Study of Tractate Maaserot* (Chico: Scholars Press for Brown Judaic Studies, 1981), p. 1. In Chapter Eight, below, I review in detail Jaffee's ideas in his own words, as I have put them together to make the points important for this study.
[10]*Ibid.*, p. 1.
[11]*Ibid.*, p. 1.
[12]*Ibid.*, p. 2.

from serving the normal purpose of food which is sanctified to priests or of tithed food which is available for the use of commoners." A variety or rules then govern the use of untithed produce from the time of its ripening in the field, through the harvest field, until the point at which it is taken into the courtyard of the householder or sold in the market, at which the produce must be tithed. At that moment before the householder exercises his property rights, he must give the partner's share to Him. Jaffee formulates this matter as follows:

> God's claim to the tithes of the produce...is made only when the produce itself becomes of value to the farmer. Only after produce has ripened may we expect the farmer to use it in his own meals or sell it to others for use in theirs. Thus God's claim to it is first provoked and must therefore be protected from that point onward...the produce is permitted as food only if the farmer acknowledges God's prior claim, e.g., by refraining from eating it as he would his own produce....Once God's claim against the produce is satisfied by the removal of the tithes, the produce is released for use in all daily meals. It is now common food.[13]

The process is precipitated by the householder's evaluation of the state of the crop. Priests have a claim, as God's surrogates, not whenever they wish, but only when the householder determines that the crop is of value to him, so Jaffee: "God's claims against the Land's produce...are only reflexes of those very claims on the part of Israelite farmers. God's interest in his share of the harvest is first provoked by the desire of the farmer for the ripened fruit of his labor...God acts and wills in response to human intentions."[14] The centrality of the householder to the entire system of the Mishnah cannot be stated with greater force than this.

That distributive mode of economics, rationalized within theology and also fully realized in the detail of law, will not have astonished the framers of social systems from ancient Sumerian times, three thousand years before the time of the Mishnah, onward. For from the beginning of recorded time, temples or governments imposed the economics of distribution, and market economics, where feasible at all, competed with the economics of politics, organization, and administration. From remote antiquity onward, a market economy coexisted with a distributive economy.[15] Distributive economic theory

---

[13]*Ibid.*, p. 4.

[14]*Ibid.*, p. 5.

[15]See Silver, *Economic Structures of the Ancient Near East,* and J. Wansbrough's review of that book in *Bulletin of the London School of Oriental and African Studies* 50 (1987): 361-2. In this and prior studies Silver has successfully refuted the thesis of Polanyi that "there were not and could not be

characteristic of ancient temples and governments, which served as the storage points for an economy conceived to be self-supporting and self-sustaining, involved something other than a simultaneous exchange of legally recognized rights in property and its use; one party gave up scarce goods, the other party did not do so, but received those goods for other than market considerations. Free disposition of property, in distributive economics, found limitations in rules of an other-than-market character, e.g., taboos with no bearing upon the rational utilization of resources and individual decisions on the disposition of assets.

If, for example, the private person who possesses property may not sell that property to anyone of his choice, or may not sell it permanently, then the possessor of the property does not exercise fully free choice in response to market conditions. The reason is that he cannot gain the optimum price for the land at a given moment, set by considerations of supply and demand for land or (more really) for the produce of land of a particular character. Another owner, besides the human possessor of a piece of property, has a say. The decisions of that other owner are not governed solely (or at all) by market considerations. In the case of temple communities or god-kings, land ownership and control fall into the hands of an entity other than the private person, whether we call it the temple, priesthood, the government, the gild, or even the poor (!). Then, with private property and its use placed under limitations and constraints of an other-than-market origin, market trading is not possible: "While there could be a considerable development of governmental status distribution and some marginal barter, there could not develop a price-making market."[16] Private property in land, not merely in control of production, was required for the formation of a market economics in the conditions of antiquity, when ownership of production derived from ownership of land.

---

circumstances conducive to a market economy" (Wansbrough, p. 362). But the distinction between distributive and market economics has no bearing whatsoever upon whether or not, in remote antiquity, there was no such thing as a market in an economic sense, as Polanyi maintained. My argument focuses only upon economic theory. But, as is clear, I take for granted that Silver and those he represents have established as fact the coexistence of market and distributive economics, such as I claim to discern, also, in the system of the Mishnah.

[16]Davisson and Harper, p. 125.

A further mark of the distributive economy is that transactions take the form of commodities of real value, that is, barter, and not of symbolic value, that is, money. In ancient Mesopotamia, with its distributive economics, while silver was the medium of exchange, it was used in ingots and required weighing at each transfer.[17] We already have noticed in our survey of the working of the market that that conception dominates in the Mishnah. Finally, we recognize that, in distributive economics, profit is a subordinate consideration, and, in the hands of so sophisticated a mind as Aristotle's and as the Mishnah's authorship's, profit is treated as unnatural. We need hardly review the positions already established to claim that, competing with market economics in the Mishnah is a fully developed and amply instantiated, if never articulated, distributive economics. The Mishnah's authorship took over the economics of the Priestly Code, itself a restatement, in the idiom of the Israelite priesthood, of the distributive economics of temples and kings beginning with the Sumerians and Egyptians and coming down to the Greeks. Market economics was an innovation, its economics not fully understood, at the time of the Priestly Code, and, for reasons of their own, the framers of the Mishnah fully adopted and exhaustively spelled out that distributive economics, even while setting forth a plan for the economic life of "Israel" in a market economy.

That old and well established theory of economics, in the received Scriptures, is accurately represented by the Priestly Code, spelled out in the rules of the biblical books of Leviticus and Numbers, upon which the Mishnah's authorship drew very heavily. The economic program of the Mishnah, as a matter of fact, derived its values and also its details from the Priestly Code and other priestly writings within the pentateuchal mosaic. Indeed, at point after point, that authorship clearly intended merely to spin out details of the rules set forth in Scripture in general, and, in economic issues such as the rational use of scarce resources, the Priestly Code in particular. The Priestly Code assigned portions of the crop to the priesthood and Levites as well as to the caste comprising the poor; it intervened in the market-processes affecting real estate by insisting that land could not be permanently alienated but reverted to its "original" ownership every fifty years; it treated some produce as unmarketable even though it was entirely fit; it exacted for the temple a share of the crop; it imposed regulations on the labor force that were not shaped by market considerations but by

---

[17]Oppenheim, p. 87.

religious taboos, e.g., days on which work might not be performed, or might be performed only in a diminished capacity.[18]

In these and numerous other details, the Priestly Code stated in the Israelite-priestly idiom and in matters of detail the long established principles of distributive economics and so conformed to thousands of years of that distributive economics that treated private property as stipulative and merely conditional and the market as subordinate and subject to close political supervision. Market economics, coming into being in Greece in the very period – the sixth century B.C. – in which the Priestly Code was composed. Aristotle, as we have seen, theorized about an economics entirely beyond anyone's ken and stated as principle the values of an economics (and a social system, too) long since transcended. Market economics, moreover, had been conveyed in practice to the Middle East a century and a half or so later by Alexander. By the time of the Mishnah, seven centuries after the Pentateuch was closed, market economics was well established as the economics of the world economy in which, as a matter of fact, the land of Israel and Israel, that is, the Jews of Palestine, had been fully incorporated. Theories of fixed value, distribution of scarce resources by appeal to other than the rationality of the market – these represented anachronisms. But, as our encounter with the prohibition against profit called "usury" has already shown us, the framers of the Mishnah developed a dual economics, partly market, partly distributive. That is the fact that permits us to treat as matters of economic theory a range of rules that, in market economics, can have no point of entry whatsoever.

Only when we have grasped the general terms within which those concrete rules are worked out shall we understand the mixed economics characteristic of the Judaism of the Mishnah. A distributive economics, we now realize full well, is one that substitutes for the market as the price-fixing mechanism for the distribution of goods the instrumentality of the state or some other central organization, in the case of Scripture's economics in the Priestly Code of ca. A.D. 500, the Temple. In such an economics, in the words of Davisson and Harper,

> Such an organization will involve people's giving and receiving, producing and consuming, according to their status.[19]

Substituting for the market as a rationing device, the distributive economy dealt with "the actual things that are distributed," while in

---

[18]In due course we shall review pertinent verses of Scripture in our detailed examination of the distributive economics of the Mishnah.
[19]Davisson and Harper, p. 115.

markets, "purchases and sales are usually made for money, not directly for other commodities or services."[20]

The definition of market economics cited above calls to our attention the contrary traits of distributive economics, in particular, the intervention of authority other than the market in controlling both production and distribution of scarce goods. In the case of the Mishnah, the temple requires the recognition of the status of certain individual participants – in addition to the householder – in the transaction of distributing the material goods of the economy, in particular, portions of the crop. Priests, Levites, and the poor have a claim on the crop independent of their role in the production of the crop, e.g., in labor, in land ownership, in investment of seed and the like. Not only so, but the market is not the sole point of transfer of value. For material goods of the economy are directed to the temple – so in the theory of the Mishnah – without any regard for the working of the market. When it comes to the claim of the temple and priesthood upon the productive economy, there is no consideration of the exchange of material value for material value, let alone of the intervention of considerations of supply and demand, the worth of the goods as against the worth of the services supplied by the temple, and the like.[21] Davisson and Harper state of the market, "Even politically powerful interests and corporations must agree to accept the market decisions whether or not the outcome of a particular market transaction favors a person of high status."[22] But in the Mishnah, that simply is not so. And, we shall further observe, the temple taboos imposed upon the productive economy considerations of a non-market, non-productive character, in consequence of which the maximization of productivity forms only one among several competing considerations, and not the most important one, in the planning of production.

This brings us to the fundamental and necessary trait of market economics, private property. Davisson and Harper further state,

> Private ownership of property...is an essential condition of the market, but its existence does not guarantee that a market will exist or that contractual exchanges will occur [that can reach a conclusion with a simultaneous exchange of legally recognized rights in property and its

---

[20]*Ibid.*, p. 123.

[21]True, the ideology of the Priestly Code insisted that payment of the temple taxes insured that God would "bless" the country with ample harvests, large herds, big families, and the like. But these factors in shaping of public opinion, therefore of considerations of demand, on their own do not – and cannot – fall into the classification of economic facts.

[22]Davisson and Harper, p. 123.

use]. To be sure, in the absence of private property in the ancient
Near East and early medieval Europe, we find a distributive economic
order. Is there, then, some relation of cause and effect between
private property and the operation of a market? It seems that insofar
as there is monolithic ownership and control of property (as in the
Sumerian temple communities or with the god-king pharaoh of Egypt)
there can be no development of a market. Where private property
was so limited, there could be no market trading. While there could
be a considerable development of governmental status distribution
and some marginal barter, there could not develop a price-making
market.[23]

That statement again draws our attention to the datum of the
Mishnah, which informs, by the way, its economics as well: that God
owns the land and that the household holds the land in joint tenancy
with God. Private ownership does not extend to the land at all.[24] That
simple fact imposes upon the Mishnah's economic theory the principles
of distributive economics, even while the framers of that theory
address a world of market economics. It accounts for the mixed
economics – market, distributive – of the Mishnah. Not only so, but as
we just noted, the mortal owner-partner with God in the management of
the household is not free to make decisions based solely on maximizing
productivity; other considerations as to the use of land, as much as to
the disposition of the crop, intervened.

In the conception of the authorship of the Mishnah, therefore, all
land was held in joint tenancy, with the householder as one partner,
God as the other. That mixed ownership then placed side by side two
economic systems, one distributive, resting on control of property by the
temple acting in behalf of the owner of the land, who was god, the
other the market system in which private persons owned property and
with legal sanction could use it and transfer title without intervention
from any other power. As Davisson and Harper state, "For an economic
system to be a market system, exchanges of private property must be
accompanied by simultaneous exchanges of legally recognizes rights in
property and its use."[25] To the degree that the private person, the
householder in our system's instance, shared those rights with another
and functioned within limits imposed by that other, the consequent

---

[23]*Ibid.*, pp. 124-125.
[24]But as we shall observe in due course, God does not lay claim to joint
ownership of other goods and services of the economy, apart from the land and
its produce, with the result that private ownership of the commercial and
manufacturing economy assuredly prevailed, one of the reasons I refer to the
Mishnah's economic theory as a mixed one.
[25]Davisson and Harper, p. 124.

economy was not wholly a market economy at all. That is the case, particularly, when other-than-market considerations affected the use of land or other good and when the other defined limits bearing no congruence to the policies and plans of the (secular) partner, the householder.

Before proceeding, let me catalogue what is at stake in the claim that God makes against the householder's crops and herds. The disposition of God's designated share of the crop is laid out, all together, as follows:

> [The Mishnah] requires the separation of four gifts from all edible and cultivated agriculture produce before that produce may be eaten. [1] Heave-offering is the first gift to be separated. It is given to the priest, who eats it in conditions of cleanness. No fixed amount is set for this gift, but one-fiftieth is deemed an average quantity...[2] First tithe, one-tenth, is given to the Levite, who separates from it [3] a further tenth [i.e., one hundredth of the whole] as heave-offering of the tithe and gives it to the priest...[4a] Second tithe, one tenth, then is separated from the remainder of the produce [for consumption in Jerusalem]. [4b] During the third and sixth years of the sabbatical cycle poor man's tithe is separated instead of second tithe. In the case of bread [5] a further dough-offering is separated after the other tithe. This consists of one twenty-fourth part of the whole...and is given to the priest. Produce from which all tithes have been separated is called..."set right" or "fully tithed," "unconsecrated." The faithful separation of all of the Mishnah's tithes means that slightly less than 22% (or, in the case of bread made by an individual, slightly less than 26%) of one's produce is set aside...This is a considerable amount of produce which the owner cedes (over and above the amount paid in taxes to the Roman authorities from 64 B.C.E. onwards).[26]

The priests have a claim upon parts of the animal slaughtered for the cult, and also the one slaughtered for secular purposes. Specifically, the shoulder and two cheeks and maw of a beast slaughtered for secular purposes are to be given to the priest. The priests have a claim on the first of the fleece (Dt. 18:4, M. Hul. 11:1ff.). The firstborn male offspring of cattle must be given to the priest. The firstborn of man and of an ass must be redeemed, and the money goes to the priest. The firstborn of clean cattle must be slaughtered in the temple. If it was blemished, the priest gets it and may do with it as he likes. Clearly, we deal with a formidable claim. Let me now spell out its rationale.

In the case of the conception of ownership of wealth set forth by the authorship of the Mishnah, a conception informed by the rules of

---

[26]Richard S. Sarason, *A History of the Mishnaic Law of Agriculture. Section Three. A Study of Tractate Demai* (Leiden: E. J. Brill, 1979), p. 9.

Leviticus, God's joint ownership and tenancy with the farmer imposed a dual economics, the one, a distributive economic order, the other, a market system pure and simple. The one partner, God, had no strong interest in the market system; the other partner, the householder, was assumed to have only such an interest in the rational utilization and increase of scarce resources, land and crops, herds and chattels. God's share was to be distributed in accord with God's rules, the farmer keeping the rest. That is what I mean by a mixed system, one partner framing policy in line with a system of distributive economics, the other in market economics. The authorship of the Mishnah thus effected and realized in a systematic way rules governing land use, placement of diverse types of crops, rights of ownership, alongside provision of part of the crop to those whom God had designated as recipients of his share of the produce. That explains why that authorship could not imagine a market economy at all, and why the administered market (which, as we noted, is no market at all) in which government – priests' government – supposedly distributed status and sustained economic relationships of barter took the place of the market.

The true anachronism of the Mishnah's economics therefore becomes clear, when we realize that by the fourth century B.C., the Middle East received and used the legacy of Greece, brought by Alexander, in which a type of private property, prerequisite to the development of the market and available for the free use of the holder of that property independent of the priesthood or other government intervention, had developed.[27] For the theory of the Mishnah both the market and the distributive systems form one system and represent two components of one system. So we deal with a single theory, holding together two distinct economics. What we shall now see is how the distributive component of the Mishnah's economic theory reshapes the three principal categories that have occupied our attention, the household, the market, and wealth.

The householder is represented by the Mishnah's authorship as a tenant-farmer, a sharecropper on land owned by God. Brooks spells this out as follows:

> As a tenant-farmer [the householder] works God's Land and enjoys its yield, with the result that a portion of all that he produces belongs to God. In order to pay this obligation Israelites render to the priests grain as heave-offering, tithes, and other priestly rations. Similarly, a specific portion of the Land's yield is set aside, by chance alone, for the poor. So underlying the designation of both priestly rations and poor-offerings is a single theory: God owns the entire Land of Israel

---

[27]Davisson and Harper, p. 125.

and, because of this ownership, a portion of each crop must be paid to him as a sort of sacred tax. According to the Mishnah's framers, God claims that which is owed him and then gives it to those under his special care, the poor and the priests.[28]

The task of the householder, therefore, is to give over to God, through the representatives designated by him in his discourses with Moses, God's share of the crop.

We have now to ask, precisely how does God assert his claim to his portion of the crop? The way in which we know God's portion of the crop is through some sort of accident that separates grain from the normal crop. This is taken to represent God's intervention in matters, in line with the casting of lots, e.g., with the Urim and Thummim, or in the story of Esther, constitutes the way of finding out God's preference. Designating God's portion by the workings of chance is illustrated by the category of the forgotten sheaf, an offering separated when the farmer has completed reaping the field and binds the grain into sheaves. A sheaf forgotten by all involved in the processing then becomes the forgotten sheaf that is the property of the poor (M. Pe. 5:7). Single grapes that fall due to no identifiable cause during the harvest fall into the category of the separated grape. Clusters that grow without shoulders or pendants are defective and go to the poor (M. Pe. 7:4). When the farmer thins the vineyard, the law of the defective cluster begins to apply; that is the point at which the householder asserts his right of ownership (M. Pe. 7:5).

Produce that is designated without any intention of the householder and not by identifiable cause has been chosen by God. That portion of the crop is what goes to the poor, or, under other circumstances, to the priest (hence: offering that is raised up for priestly rations). As Brooks explains, "Whether it is the grain that happens to grow in the rear corner of the field (and that the farmer himself will later designate as *peah*) or the stalks that by chance fall aside from the edge of the farmer's sickle (gleanings), all this food apportioned seemingly by accident must be left for the poor. So the framers of the Mishnah believe that God alone determines what produce falls into the category of poor-offerings."[29] The same consideration affects the designation of produce for the priests' rations. The procedure for designating those rations at the threshing floor is for the priest to declare that the priestly ration ("heave-offering") is isolated in one part of the pile of grain. Whatever the householder then grabs from the pile falls into the status of sanctified grain, and

---

[28]Brooks, p. 18.
[29]*Ibid.*, p. 18.

there can be no measuring nor designing specific grain.  Again Brooks: "It is through chance alone that God determines which particular grain in which quantity will fall into the category of priestly rations."  The householder's partner can be relied upon, therefore, to make his selection of the shared crop.

When God does so forms yet another detail in which the system as a whole restates its prevailing and single principle of joint ownership.  The point at which the joint holder of the land, God, demands asserts his rights of ownership and so also demands his share of the crop is when the householder asserts his ownership of the crop.  When the field is reaped, the laws for providing for the caste of the poor come into effect (M. Pe. 4:6-7).  When the grain pile at the threshing floor is smoothed over, then produce becomes subject to the separation of tithes (M. Pe. 4:8).  There are two such points in the process of reaping the grain, first, when the householder harvests the grain, claiming it for himself.  Then a bit of food left at random goes for the poor.  Then, when the farmer collects the grain at the threshing floor, God asserts ownership of his share, and that is what goes to the priests.[30]  The sole difference in procedure is that while the poor persons' share is designated by the accident of leaving a corner of the field unharvested, dropping a few stalks accidentally, forgetting sheaves, and the like, the householder is the one who designates what is to serve as the priestly ration.  Here he takes an active role, since he is the one to set aside produce for the priests.  In this latter act the householder serves as God's partner, in sharing the crop, but also as God's agent, in designating and delivering the share of God to the priest.  But the householder in no way may intervene in the process.  "Householders must not in any way interfere as God apportions the grain."[31]

Since the Mishnah's framers regard the land as God's property; when Israelite farmers claim it as their own, and grow food on it, they must pay for using God's earth.  The householder therefore must leave a portion of the field unharvested as *peah* and give this food over to God's chosen representatives, the poor.  The underlying theory is that householders are tenant farmers who pay taxes to their landlord, God.[32]  The point at which the divine taxes become valid is "the critical moment when he takes possession of the food. Before smoothing over the grain pile he may dispose of the food freely; he has not yet claimed full ownership of it and so need not separate tithes (cf. M. Maaserot 1:1).  Once the farmer has processed the grain, he has

[30]*Ibid.*, pp. 18-19.
[31]*Ibid.*, p. 20.
[32]*Ibid.*, p. 49.

claimed ownership. This arouses the intense interest of God, the farmer's agricultural partner. The householder must pay to God a part of the profits.[33]

The cattle are to be tithed three times a year (M. Bekh. 9:1-8), with the priests given the tithed beasts for use in the temple. Tithing cattle derives from Lev. 27:32-33: "And all the tithe of herds and flocks, every tenth animal of all that pass under the herdsman's staff, shall be holy to the Lord (and given to the temple)." The beast is brought to Jerusalem, the blood and fat are offered up, and the owner gets the meat, to eat in the city.

Disposition of the crop also involves presenting to the temple priesthood the first fruits of the crops. But only householders are liable to present first fruits of their produce. Others are exempt. This negative rule bears in its way the same message as the positive one. Those who do not own the land are not liable to bring first fruits, even though they own them as sharecroppers. Those who own land but are proselytes, or who do not fully own the land, may not make the recitation. Only full ownership of the land permits one to carry out the rite. God's claim is limited to what God has made and distributed, the land. This is a mark that the householder occupies a distinctive place in the scheme of things.[34] First fruits are thereby distinguished from other agricultural gifts, obligation to provide which apply to all. The relationship between ownership of land and the obligation to bring first fruits and make the recitation that accompanies their offering constitutes the critical issue of much of the tractate, Bikkurim, on the subject of first fruits.

The effect of distributive economics upon the station of the householder should not be missed. The system at hand, after all, distributed more than scarce material resources; it also parcelled out equally valued, it non-material, goods such as status and standing. Owning land conferred a place in Israel's history that owning mere money did not. For what is interesting here is that the owner arrogates to himself a first-person narrative that, in fact, in its original scriptural context refers to all Israelites. But when the text, Dt. 26:1-11, that the householder must recite refers to "Behold, now I bring the first fruit of the ground which you, O Lord, have given me," the authorship of the Mishnah understands that reference is made, in particular, to the householder, who alone can say, "which *you* have

---

[33]*Ibid.*, p 51.
[34]See Margaret Wenig Rubenstein, "A Commentary on Mishnah-Tosefta Bikkurim, Chapters One and Two," in W. S. Green, ed. *Approaches to Ancient Judaism* (Chico: Scholars Press for Brown Judaic Studies, 1981) 3:47-87.

given *me*." That fundamental theory of what it means to be a householder may be expressed in a single sentence: the householder is normative Israel. All others take up positions, within Israel, in relationship to him. For, in his monopoly of the right to make the required recitation, the householder *is* Israel, when the sacred history of Israel is recited with the presentation of the first fruits. The householder's own personal history then conforms to the statements made in the text, but then that personal history becomes Israel in the here and now. The picture of landownership in Deuteronomy (Dt. 26:1-11) emphasizes that God has kept his promise to give the people the land of Israel. The interest of the priestly code reads the offerings of first fruits, now identified with the sheaf of grain known as the *omer* (Lev. 23:9-21), sets the presentation of the sheaf of the first fruits of the harvest into the sabbatical system, now the concluding Sabbath of the feast of unleavened bread; this is then waved for seven full weeks, counting fifty days to the morrow after the seventh Sabbath. This forms one of the many significations of the relationship between the Sabbath, the land, and the Lord, who owns the land and sanctifies the Sabbath.[35]

Let us take as an example of the Mishnah's authorship's indifference to the commercial economy and its participants a simple fact. It is that the Sabbatical year does not cancel payments which would prevent Israelite merchants from conducting their business. The *prozbul* a legal fiction, allows for normal transactions. Commercial credit, fines, assessments for damages, and the like, are not released by the Sabbatical year. Secured loans remain collectable. Newman explains, "This is because the Mishnah's authorities regard the collateral as a temporary repayment of the loan until the borrower actually repays the money he owes. Since these loans are deemed not to be outstanding, they cannot be cancelled by the Sabbatical year. Loans turned over to a court for collection are not cancelled."[36] The net effect of this remission of the full effects of the law is to exclude from the sabbatical system the entire commercial economy.

No wonder then that the householder stands alone in sharing with God ownership of the land, and, it follows, it is the householder alone, among all Israelites, who can effect an act of intention and designation that transforms the status of produce from secular or neutral to sacred. That power of consecration matches the control over Israel's history that is assigned, through the law of firstfruits, to the householder. How so? The householder's produce becomes consecrated as heave-

---

[35]*Ibid.*, 49-50.
[36]Newman, p. 199.

offering only through the intention or thought and the deed of the Israelite householder. The householder is the one – the only one – who has the power to cause produce to be deemed holy. This he does by (in Avery-Peck's words) "formulating the intention to consecrate produce as the priestly gift. Then he pronounces a formula by which he orally designates a portion of his produce to be heave-offering. Finally, he effects his intention by physically separating that portion from the rest of the batch. Through these thoughts and actions the householder determines what produce, and how much of it, is to be deemed holy."[37] While human intention in general plays a central role, because of the arena defined by the law, namely, the disposition of the crop by its mortal owner, it is the intention of the householder in particular that is determinative. That intention is what changes the substance at hand from secular to holy, for holiness does not inhere but only is imputed by the householder.[38] Avery-Peck makes this matter clear in his summary of the main interests of the tractate, Terumot:

> The topics of the tractate reveal the point which its framers wish to make...first, the role of the Israelite in the designation and separation of heave-offering; second, his responsibility to protect the priestly due for the priest; and, third, the part he plays in the ultimate disposition of the offering. The tractate as a whole thus speaks about common Israelites. It proposes to delineate their responsibility as regards all aspects of the designation and disposition of the priestly gift. Its particular rules, moreover, make clear the centrality of the Israelite's own intentions and perceptions. At each point these determine the status of sanctification of produce which the Israelite sets aside as the priest's share. Through the Israelite's powers of intention, produce first comes to be deemed holy. Later, the holiness of the priest's gift may be encroached upon only through actions which the Israelite performs purposely. Finally, the offering no longer is considered holy when the Israelite himself does not deem it to be edible.[39]

When we take into account that the particular Israelite with the power to designate produce as heave-offering is only the householder, and it is the produce of the farm that is at stake, we understand how central, indeed, unique and crucial, a role is reserved for the householder in the processes of sanctification, that is, in this context, the disposition of scarce resources outside of normal market transactions and relationships.

---

[37]Alan J. [Avery-]Peck, *The Priestly Gift in Mishnah. A Study of Tractate Terumot* (Chico: Scholars Press for Brown Judaic Studies, 1981), p. 3.
[38]*Ibid.*, p. 3.
[39]*Ibid.*, p. 21.

The householder, for the system of the Mishnah, therefore occupies an exalted position as God's partner. Consequently, the opinions, attitudes, plans, and intentions of the householder form the centerpiece of the system. Indeed, the will and intention of the householder, in matters of the disposition of scarce resources in particular, are what make the system work. For one example among many, at M. Kil. 7:6, we find that the action and attitude of the householder set aside the violation of the taboo which, had the householder deliberately done the deed, would have rendered forfeit the entire vineyard. If a usurper who sow a vineyard with mixed seeds and the vineyard left his possession, the rightful owner must cut down the sown crop immediately. If he does so, however, there is no consequence to the prior presence of what should have been prohibited. The decision and action of the landowner make all the difference, e.g., if a wind hurled vines on top of grain, the householder cuts the vines at once and there is no further penalty, since the householder bears no responsibility for the violation.

In respect to the taboos against mixed species, not only the householder, but any other person, is subject to the law. We can see the consequence, in that the owner of a garment made of mixed fibers, wool and linen, bears responsibility for the law-violation. Here the owner of the garment is the responsible party, e.g., "Clothes dealers and tailors may carry garments of diverse kinds in the course of their work, provided that they do not intend to use them as garments" (M. Kil. 9:5-6). This proves that the owner of the garment is the one who bears responsibility for violating the law and underlines the fact that, as to mixed seeds, it is the householder who is wholly in charge. That proves that the premise of the premise of all rules of mixed seeds and mixed species, Kilayim, is that the householder's judgment is what is decisive. For the householder is the archetypal owner, master of a domain; the craftsman or manufacturer, tradesmen or merchant, is in his model.

Intervention of God – that is to say, the considerations of cult and taboo, not solely those of market and trade and value – into land ownership is total and complete. No householder can sell his land permanently, if he received it by inheritance. Lev. 25:10 has land revert after fifty years, in the Jubilee, to the original owner. What does not revert? The portion of the firstborn, inheritance of one who inherits his wife's estate, inheritance of the one who enters into Levirate massage (M. Bekh 8:10). Consequently, the householder cannot alienate his property and invest his capital in some other medium. The cultic rule imposes a valuation on the real estate that otherwise it cannot have enjoyed, and, at the same time, freezes in land the equity of the householder. An other-than-market consideration overrides the market's valuation of the land. This consideration affects not only the householder's land, but also his residence. Specifically, a house in a walled city cannot be permanently sold but reverts to the original owner, so Lev. 25:25-34. Tractate Arakhin in Chapters Seven and Eight goes over this rule. When someone dedicates a field, and another person then buys it (redeems it) from the temple, he may not do so permanently. The field or the house reverts at the jubilee. At issue is only the field of possession, which is one that is received by inheritance, so Lev. 27:16-25/Mishnah-tractate Arakhin 7:1-8:3. The field received as an inheritance and the dwelling house in a walled city, which are to revert to the "original" owner, are treated at Lev. 25:25-34/Mishnah-tractate Arakhin 9:1-8. The sale here is assumed to be brought about because of need, "If your brother becomes poor and sells part of his property..." (Lev. 25:25). The intervention of the law into the disposition of the capital of the household that is in the form of the herds and the flocks derives from Ex. 13:2, Num. 18:15-18. Invalidated holy things are sold in the marketplace, but the blemished firstling may not be sold in the marketplace (M. Bekh. 5:1). Here too the Mishnah's framers invent nothing but integrate into their larger statement rules of Scripture deemed systemically urgent.

The Mishnah's economics of the householder confirms to the theory of the market. As we now realize, the Mishnah's economics knows the market, but it is not a market economics. Distributive economics, that is, the distribution of scarce goods and services not through the market mechanism, involves designation of recipients who do not form normal participants or undifferentiated constituents of the market. These scheduled castes[40] lay an enormous claim, therefore, upon the resources of the economy, that is, the harvest of the household, for reasons other than their providing a quid pro quo.

One such designated group is the poor, who do not own a share of the Land. They are comparable to the priests and Levites, likewise not given a share of the Land (Dt. 18:1-5), and, like the sacerdotal castes,

---

[40]Since at stake here is hierarchization, I am justified in invoking the notion of caste, in line with Louis Dumont, *Homo Hierarchicus* (Chicago: University of Chicago Press, 1982). I refer to "scheduled" ones in particular, because there are other castes – groups of persons bearing the same indicative traits, e.g., women, slaves, minors – that are hierarchized in the Mishnah's vast hierarchization of all social reality, but that are not accorded a special share in, or claim upon, the distribution of scarce resources, as are the priests, Levites, and poor. The ones on the schedule within the larger hierarchical structure then fall into the classification I have invoked here.

the poor therefore receive a share of the crop.[41]   The rationale always
is the same: God is the partner, in ownership of the land, with the
householder.  Consequently, God's share of the crop is apportioned to
the castes or classes who form the surrogate for God in the division of
the crops among the rightful owners.  The rules governing the poor's
share occur in tractate Peah, that is, "the corner-offering for the poor,"
which asserts that the poor have a claim on the produce of the land.[42]
In point of fact there are several such portions of the crop reserved for
the caste of the poor.  The first is the rear corner of the field, peah,
Lev. 19:9, 23:22; then come gleanings, Lev. 19:9, 23:22; the forgotten
sheaf Dt. 24:19; the separated grape, Lev. 19:10; the defective cluster
Lev. 19:10, Dt. 24:21, and poor man's tithe, Dt. 26:12, a tenth of the crop
separated in the third and sixth years of the sabbatical cycle and
handed over to the poor.  Some of these offerings therefore involve
leftovers or rejected portions of the crop, others quite marketable
produce.

To understand the true character of this support for the poor, we
must take account of the simple fact that it is not support accorded out
of sympathy or social concern.  The system of the Mishnah knows a
quite distinct source of eleemosynary support for the poor, in addition to
the provision of God's share of the crop to them.  It was a system of soup
kitchens.  Through them transient poor are supported (M. Pe. 8:7), and
the community maintains a soup kitchen as well.  We should not
therefore confuse the holy, Godly rights of the scheduled castes, on the
one side, with the social benefits of supporting the poor, on the other.
The former constitute a chapter in distributive economics, the latter do
not.  The difference is in the rights of ownership.  In the case of the
scheduled castes, the poor stand in for the "other Householder," who is
God, and the disposition of the crop follows rules of distribution
decreed by God, that is to say, by the priesthood that forms the
authorship of parts of the Pentateuch, and the editorship of the whole
of the Pentateuch, as the framers of the Mishnah among all Israel
possessed the document.

The rationale for poor relief, in its several forms, differs in
Scripture.  The priestly authorship of Leviticus identifies God as the
cause: "You shall leave them for the poor and for the sojourner: I am the
Lord your God" (Lev. 19:9-10), 23:22).  The Deuteronomist promises that

---

[41]The poor do not have to separate from food they receive as a scheduled caste
the share that the priesthood would otherwise claim (M. Pe. 8:2-4). Since God
cannot lay claim on the same share twice, produce designated as *peah* is
exempt from separation of tithes (M. Pe. 1:6).
[42]Brooks, p. 1.

God will reward those who do the same, but does not invoke God's name and ownership. Rather, he gives an essentially eleemosynary reason: "When you reap your harvest in your field and have forgotten a sheaf in the field, you shall not go back to get it. It shall be for the sojourner, the fatherless and the widow, that the Lord your God may bless you in all the work of your hands...You shall remember that you were a slave in the land of Egypt, therefore I command you to do this" (Dt. 24:19-22). The reason then has nothing to do with God's ownership of the whole land. It is, rather, that the Israelites too were once members of the scheduled caste of slaves, and that is why they must now act generously. Here too we discern two distinct forms of poor-relief, the one an expression of the land-theology of the priestly writings, the other of the social concern of the deuteronomic code.

Distributive economics accords an ample share in the scarce resources of the economy not only to the scheduled castes, but also to a particular location, namely, Jerusalem. Indeed, assigning a share of the crop to Jerusalem, without a corresponding outlay by participants in the Jerusalem market, corresponds explicitly to assigning a share of the crop to the scheduled castes. This is accomplished by treating as comparable the tithe of the crop given to the poor and the tithe of the crop delivered for consumption in Jerusalem. Specifically, in the first, second, fourth, and fifth years of the Sabbatical cycle,[43] the tithe that the householder separates from his crop is devoted not to the needs of the poor but to the maintenance of Jerusalem. This is accomplished by requiring the householder to bring to Jerusalem and consume there a tenth of his crop or the monetary equivalent thereof (Dt. 14:22-26). The result is to provide for Jerusalem an artificially inflated supply of food, and so to keep under control the cost of food in the Jerusalem market on the occasion of pilgrim festivals.when large numbers of tourists will have come to the city. Compensating for the inflated demand, the sizable supply will have lowered food costs in Jerusalem, but only at the expense of removing from the supply available in the rest of the country approximately 10% of the crop. The farmer, that is, the householder, is responsible for designating the portion of the crop and transporting it.[44]

The impact of the produce's having been in Jerusalem upon the status of the produce is considerable. Food that has been designated as second tithe, that is, consecrated, must be used only in the way in which produce of its type is normally used. Before the produce has been in

---

[43]In the third and sixth years, the tithe goes to the poor.
[44]Peter J. Haas, *A History of the Mishnaic Law of Agriculture. Tractate Maaser Sheni* (Chico: Scholars Press for Brown Judaic Studies, 1980), p. 1.

Jerusalem, it is sold at local market prices, it may be sold at the lowest prevailing price, and so on (M. M. S. 3:5-4:8). Then the money received is brought to Jerusalem. But once the produce itself has entered Jerusalem, it enters a different status altogether. At that point, the produce is holy and may no longer be sold. Then, in Jerusalem itself, it must be eaten by the householder or those to whom he gives the food.

We have now to identify that component of the goods and services of the market that is subjected to distributive, rather than market, economics, within the mixed economics at hand. It is, in particular, food that is subjected to the distributive system at hand – food and, in point of fact, nothing else, certainly not capital, or even money. Manufactured goods and services, that is, shoes on the last, medical and educational services, the services of clerks and scribes, goods in trade, commercial ventures of all kinds – none of these is subjected to the tithes and other sacerdotal offerings. The possibility of the mixed economics, market and distributive alike, rests upon the upshot of the claim that God owns the holy land. It is the land that God owns, and not the factory or shop, stall and store, ship and wagon, and other instruments and means of production. Indeed, the sole unit of production for which the Mishnah legislates in rich and profound exegetical detail is the agricultural one. The distributive component of the economy, therefore, is the one responsible for the production of food, inclusive of the raising of sheep, goats, and cattle.

The agricultural produce of which God owns a share is explicitly what is marketable: it is that which is edible, tended, grown in the Land of Israel, harvested as a crop, and can be stored (M. Pe. 1:4-5). These traits, of course, characterize the produce that a householder will cultivate. Edibility guarantees use; tending defines an indicative trait of the household and further guarantees that the produce is valued by the householder, indicating by his cultivating it; the land of Israel is God's land; harvesting involves the taking of possession; and storage, like edibility, is a mark of valuing the crop. But produce that is not owned, e.g., what grows wild, what is used for feed for beasts, and seed, all are exempt; God's claim extends only to what the householder will use for his own needs and his family's and dependents'. There is no divine share in what is not owned to begin with, and that accounts also for the suspension of the designation of God's share of crops in the seventh year in the Sabbatical cycle, when the householder, for his part, exercises no rights of cultivation or ownership of in the land.

The distributive economics of the Mishnah affects not only the distribution, but also the production and utilization for the market, of agricultural goods. The supply of produce on the market, therefore, responds not only to market considerations, but also to extrinsic ones imposed by the temple and its taboos. The intervention of rules of proper slaughter into the disposition of the capital represented by beasts prepared for meat certainly imposes extra-market considerations. Tractate Hullin declares invalid for Israelite use beasts that are improperly slaughtered, or that produce certain marks of invalidity of another sort, and that vastly lowered the return on the beast. The market for meat fit for Israelite consumption was prepared to pay a premium for such meat. Among the prohibitions affecting the suitability of animals is the removal of the sinew of the hip, or sciatic nerve. Gentiles of course may purchase such meat (e.g., M. Hullin 7:2). The same is so for rules as to whether or not Israelites may slaughter a beast in behalf of a gentile (M. Hul. 2:7). Here the concern is the intention for which the beast is slaughtered. Gentiles are assumed to slaughter the beast in honor of an idol (M. Hul. 2:7E), and that would render the meat unacceptable to the Israelite market, just as is the case with wine in the whole of tractate Abodah Zarah, on idolatry. It follows that non-market considerations as to the disposition of scarce resources intervene here as well, to the detriment not only of the gentile, who loses the Israelite market for his meat, but also the Jews. For the supply of meat in their market is diminished by the consideration at hand, even though, in all other respects, the meat may be suitable for Israelite consumption and, of course, also nourishing. Both supply and demand therefore are affected by extra-market considerations. One fundamental rule for non-market economics introduces the consideration of Israel's not worshipping idols, and this affects the disposition of a variety of goods that, in all other respects, are entirely valid for sale and use in the Jews' market.

The intervention of cultic considerations in the market affects the supply of meat in a positive way. Farmers or butchers are required to slaughter beasts even against their will on the eve of the last festival day of the Festival of Sukkot, on the eve of the first festival day of Passover, on the eve of Pentecost, and on the eve of the New Year (M. Hullin 5:3). However slight the demand, butchers are forced to slaughter beasts to supply meat for the market for the festival celebration. It is taken for granted that on that occasion people will eat meat, and, in consequence, the Mishnah's framers wish to assure a large supply to meet the demand, intervening in the normal working of the market, which should set the price in such a way that supply will routinely meet demand. This is stated explicitly: "Even if the beast was worth a thousand denars, and the purchaser has only one denar, they force the butcher to slaughter the beast" (M. Hullin 5:4).[45] It follows that the supply of goods to the market is affected both negatively and positively by non-market considerations imposed in the system of distribution at hand.

Taboos affecting production of produce were not inconsiderable. Let us take, for example, the application to production of scriptural taboos as to commingling different categories of plants, animals, or fibres (Lv. 19:19, Dt. 22:9-11). That taboo certainly represents an intervention into the free conduct of the means of production for the market. In that aspect, also, the temple intervened into the economy and introduced considerations not pertinent to the market. The Mishnah-tractate devoted to these taboos, Kilayim, established criteria for distinguishing among different classes; defined what constitutes the commingling of such classes; and determined how to keep each category separate and distinct from others. Mandelbaum defines the interest of the tractate as follows: "Although the Mishnah's regulations clearly depend upon their scriptural antecedents, the conception of the law which they express is distinctive to the Mishnah...It is man, using his powers of observation, who determines what is orderly and what lies in confusion. Unlike Scripture, which takes for granted the existence of an established and immutable order, the Mishnah calls upon man to create order based upon his own perception of the world around him."[46] Man defines what constitutes a class and determines how to keep the different classes distinct from one another; man thus imposes upon an otherwise disorderly world limits and boundaries which accord with human perception of order and regularity.[47] The priestly conception of this matter, in Leviticus, is set forth by Mandelbaum as follows:

> In the view of the priestly circles which stand behind P, order is a precondition of holiness. This notion is clearly reflected in P's account

---

[45]It should be clear that some cultic requirements have no bearing upon the market, e.g., the requirement to cover up the blood of a slaughtered beast (M. Hul.. 6:1) has no bearing upon the suitability of the beast. Not cooking the beast in its mother's milk (M. Hul. 8:1) would have no bearing upon the suitability of the meat for sale in the Jews' market. So too not mixing dairy with meat produces (M. Hul. 8:2) on the face of it does not intervene in the market, but only in the practice of the home. Another instance of a cultic rule with no bearing upon the market is the requirement to let the dam go from the nest (Dt. 22:6-7/M. Hul. 12:1-2), which seems to me to have a negligible effect upon the supply of fowl in the market.

[46]Irving Mandelbaum, *A History of the Mishnaic Law of Agriculture: Kilayim. Translation and Exegesis* (Chico: Scholars Press for Brown Judaic Studies, 1982), p. ix.

[47]*Ibid.*, p. 1.

of the creation...P describes the making of a well-ordered, hierarchical world. Each type of creation is brought forth in order of ascending importance...All living things furthermore were created each according to its kind...Creation is thus an act of ordering, the purpose of which is to make the world perfect and thus prepare it to be made holy. The actual act of the sanctification of the world then takes place on the Sabbath. The point of P's laws in Leviticus...is to prevent the confusion of those classes and categories which were established at the creation. P thus commands man to restore the world from its present condition of chaos to its original orderly state and so to make the world ready once again for sanctification....The Mishnah claims that it is man, and not a set of already established rules, who decides what is orderly and what is confused.[48]

The "man" whose judgment is decisive in these matters of course is the farmer, that is to say, the householder.

An important dimension of distributive economics encompasses production, not solely distribution, of goods and services. In this matter, rules not dictated by the need to achieve maximum productivity on the farm yet governing the conduct of the household farm take first place. Among those rules dictating means and conditions of production, without regard to maximum utility of the farm, the single most important is the one that prohibits all agricultural activity in the seventh year of a seven year cycle. We may now recognize that that rule that requires fields to lie fallow in fact fructifies the soil by renewing nutrients in it. But the reason for that prohibition derives solely from theological myth, and the system at hand imposes the law solely to realize that myth: "The land shall observe a Sabbath of the Lord. Six years you may sow your field, and six years you may prune your vineyard and gather in the yield. But in the seventh year the land shall have a Sabbath of complete rest, a Sabbath of the Lord; you shall not sow your field or prune your vineyard. You shall not reap the aftergrowth of your harvest or gather the grapes of your untrimmed vines; it shall be a year of complete rest for the land. But you may eat whatever the land during its Sabbath will produce, you, your male and female slaves, the hired and bound laborers who live with you, and your cattle and the beasts in your land may eat all its yield" (Lev. 25:1-7).

Now the notion of the land's observing the Sabbath carries not a trace of recognition that the land gains from lying fallow. The priestly conception is not made explicit, except in the opening phrase, "...the land that I give you, the land shall observe a Sabbath of the Lord." Here again the priestly authorship underlines God's ownership of the

---

[48]*Ibid.*, p. 2-3.

land, God's giving to Israel[ite householders in particular] their share
of what is God's. That is why, as a matter of fact, God may also dictate
the conditions under which the land is used, when and how it will be
productive. The point here is that just as God rested from the work of
creation on the seventh day and sanctified it as a day of rest (Gen. 2:3),
so God has given the seventh year to the land as its Sabbath. The land
of Israel "is enchanted, for it enjoys a unique relationship to God and to
the people of Israel...God sanctified this land by giving it to his chosen
people as an exclusive possession. Israelites, in turn, are obligated to
work the land and to handle its produce in accordance with God's
wishes."[49] In the seventh year, therefore the householder cannot do
those things that in other years constitute their mode of asserting and
exercising ownership over the land. That is how the householders
acknowledged that God is the owner of the land alone, and they enjoy
the usufruct as a gift from God.[50]

God intervenes into the market in yet another way, namely, by
requiring the remission of debts every seventh year, an extraordinary
intervention in the normal working of the market, by which money
becomes wealth that can be accumulated. Here, we see, wealth in the
form of money cannot be accumulated but must be relinquished: " Every
seventh year you shall practice remission of debts. This shall be the
nature of the remission. Every creditor shall remit the due that he
claims from his neighbor. He shall not dun his neighbor or kinsman, for
the remission proclaimed is of the Lord. You may dun the foreigner, but
you must remit whatever is due you from your kinsmen" (Dt. 15:1-3).
The upshot is the poor do not grow poorer through accumulated debts.
But, as a matter of fact, it also means that the rich cannot become
richer. "Israelites restore equilibrium to their commercial
transactions."[51]

Mishnah-tractate Shebiit develops the prohibition against
working the land during the seventh year. The authorship of the
tractate extends the prohibition against sowing and reaping grain and
grapes to all agricultural activities, including fertilizing and
irrigating. Produce that grows of itself in the seventh year may not be
sold or otherwise used for benefit. God owns that produce, and it is
treated as having no other owner, hence, as ownerless property that
may not be sold or exchanged for personal gain. The one point
introduced by the authorship to the repertoire of facts of Scripture,
similar to the shift in regard to mixed seeds, is that the householder

[49]Newman, p. 15.
[50]*Ibid.*, pp. 115-16.
[51]*Ibid.*, p. 16.

through his actions and perceptions plays a role in determining how the agricultural restrictions of the sabbatical year apply. So Newman: "Israelite...householders have the power within specified limits to decide when, how, and where the laws of the Sabbatical year take effect. This is realized in a fundamental rule that the householder may not do anything that appears to others to transgress the law, even though the action does not actually benefit the land. Removing stones from the field for use in construction may also appear to constitute clearing the land for planting. Stockpiling manure in the field looks like fertilizing the field. Accordingly, the householder may not so act as to appear to violate the law (M. Sheb. 3:1-4:10).[52] The observance of the Sabbatical year serves to sanctify the land and express its sanctification, and that depends upon the actions and will of the people, Israel. But among the people, the ones who count are the householders.

Ceasing all productive labor on the farms in the seventh year of the sabbatical cycle dictated the conditions for supply, cutting the crop to what grew on its own without human intervention, and, further, governed what might or might not be sold in the market. For example, in the Sabbatical year a craftsman may not sell a plow and its accessories, but he may sell a sickle (M. Sheb. 5:6). The general rule is as follows: As regards any tool the use of which during the Sabbatical year is limited exclusive to the performance of an act which is a transgression, it is forbidden to sell such a tool during the Sabbatical year. But as for any tool which may be used both for work which is forbidden and for work which is permitted according to the laws of the Sabbatical year, it is permissible to sell such a tool during the Sabbatical year (M. Sheb. 5:6).[53] Along these same lines the potter may sell to an individual only so many pots as one usually needs to store produce gathered in accordance with the law (M. Sheb. 5:7).

Essentially the markets are supposed to close, in that the prevailing assumption is that everything is free. That seems to me a considerable intervention. In the eighth year, that is, the year following the Sabbatical year, people may assume that vegetables in the market no longer derive from the crop of the seventh year (M. Sheb. 6:4). All rights of ownership of crops are suspended by the advent of the Sabbatical year. Produce in that year is held to be ownerless property. That food belongs equally to all Israelites, so it is not a common commodity, like produce grown in other years. People may not use it for their own financial gain, and if they sell it or process it, it

---

[52]*Ibid.*, p. 18.
[53]*Ibid.*, p. 117.

must be done in an unusual manner. They may not hoard it but must remove it from the house if it has been stored there, at exactly the same time at which the produce is no longer found in the fields. He places the produce outside his house and makes it accessible to all.[54] Accordingly, what people have to do with their crops is remove from their house and declare ownerless whatever has grown in the Sabbatical year. When a given crop disappears from the fields, it also may not longer be stored in the household. Whatever is fit for human or animal consumption or use and is an annual is subject to the requirement of removal, meaning, declaration of being ownerless (M. Sheb. 7:1-2).

The sanctified produce of the Sabbatical year, for its part, is also subject to important restrictions. First, of course, it may not be sold in the usual manner, e.g., by volume, weight, or in fixed quantity. Second, what is ordinarily used as food may only be used for food. Nothing may be wasted. The produce is always deemed consecrated. People must use it for the correct purposes (M. Sheb. 8:1-9:1). What grows wild may be bought from anyone during the Sabbatical year, in the assumption that that has not been cultivated. The main point is that people may not stockpile edible produce and deprive others of access to that same (ownerless) produce. That is the purpose of removing stockpiled produce from the household.[55]

Other taboos governing the supply of produce to the market were hardly of so drastic a character as those concerning the production and disposition of crops in the sabbatical year. Mishnah-tractate Orlah works out the rule governing fourth year fruit, in line with Lev. 19:23, "When you come to the land and plant any kind of tree for food, you shall treat it as forbidden. For three years it shall be forbidden, it will not be eaten." In the fourth year, the fruit is placed into the status of Second Tithe, which is to say, it is to be brought to Jerusalem and consumed there.[56] That rule, like the one governing produce designated as second tithe, removes from the market a share of the produce that would ordinarily be available for sale, consequently raising the price for other produce, not subject to the same restrictions.

Disposition of a small portion – approximately 2% – of the crop to the priests intervened in the normal working of the market in two

---

[54]*Ibid.*, pp. 139-140.

[55]*Ibid.*, pp. 28-29.

[56]Howard Scott Essner, "The Mishnah Tracate *Orlah*: Translation and Commentary," in W. S. Green, ed. *Approaches to Ancient Judaism* (Chico: Scholars Press for Brown Judaic Studies, 1981) 3:105.

ways.[57]  First, the supply of produce for the market was correspondingly diminished, with the result that prices will have been affected.  This seems to me not a negligible consideration.  Second, a part of the population, namely, priests, their families and dependents, received support without corresponding investment in production of goods and services.  That is a considerable matter.  Produce in the status of heave-offering, or priestly rations, commanded a much lower price, there being a limited demand.  Produce available for "secular" use, that is to say, produce not subject to taboos limiting its market and utilization, commanded a substantially higher price.  Heave-offering derived only from the householder, constituting a portion of the yield of the vineyards and fields, and could be given only by the householder or his agent, not by any third party.  Accordingly, only the householder participated in the process.[58]  The householder designated a portion of his produce to be heave-offering and bore responsibility to protect it from common use until it was handed over to the priest.  The theory of the matter is expressed at Num. 18:8-13.  Heave-offering was to support the priest and formed part of the provision for maintaining the sacerdotal caste.  The produce was eaten in a state of cultic cleanness, only by the priest and his household.

The rules of tithing impose upon market transactions certain considerations of a non-market character, e.g., whether or not one must tithe produce that one purchases (M. Maaserot 2:5-6).  One who purchases five figs for a coin may not eat them without tithing, since they are regarded as distinct and random, so Meir.  Judah maintains that one may eat them one by one without tithing, but if he takes the purchase together as a batch, he must tithe them.  Now the net effect on the price of the figs cannot be reckoned, since one may avoid tithing the purchased figs by conducting himself in one way, rather than in another.  But to use the figs for one's family, one surely will have to gather the purchase together as a batch and taken it home.  Accordingly, untithed produce will command a correspondingly lower price at the market than tithed produce, again a consideration in the setting of the price for food in the marketplace.  The affect upon price therefore is going to be more than negligible, since ten per cent of the volume of what one purchases may, in fact, go for some other purpose than the purchaser's needs.

Distributive economics not only dictated supply (and, it follows, also, demand) but also governed who may, and may not, participate in the market at all.  Penalties for violating the law include exclusion

---

[57][Avery-]Peck, pp. 1ff.
[58]*Ibid.*, pp. 1ff.

from trading, for example: "He who is suspected of breaking the law of firstlings – they do not purchase from him meat of gazelles or untanned hides, bleached wool or dirty wool, but they do purchase from him spun wool or wool made into garments. If he is suspected of violating the restrictions of the seventh year, they do not purchase flax from him" (M. Bekh. 4:7-8). So too the following:

> "He who is suspected of selling food in the status of heave-offering as if it were unconsecrated food – they do not purchase from him even water or salt," the words of R. Judah.

> R. Simeon says, "Whatever is subject to the rules of heave-offerings and tithes they do not purchase from him."

> (M. Bekh. 4:9).

These rules intervene into the market available to such a person and affect the normal demand for food, restricting it, just as much as the rules that are reenforced here limit the supply of food as well.

A further intrusion of the market, one that causes no surprise, is the system's clear policy of favoring the temple as against the market and to assign all advantage to the temple. For example:

> All invalidated Holy Things once redeemed may be sold in the marketplace and slaughtered in the marketplace and weighed by exact volume, except for the blemished firstling and tithe of cattle. For the advantage of selling them in the market where demand is higher would fall to the owner. Invalidated Holy Things are so disposed of that the advantage falls to the sanctuary.

> (M. Bekh. 5:1A-F)

The laws against idolatry represent an enormous intrusion into the working of the market. For example, for three days before gentile festivals one may not do business with gentiles in the market (M. A.Z. 1:1ff.). There are things one may not sell to gentiles, for example, small cattle, which are used for sacrifices to idols; bears, lions, or anything which is a public danger (M. A.Z. 1:50-7). One may not sell gentiles ornaments for an idol, produce not yet harvested, land in the Holy Land (M. A.Z. 1:8-9). Trade in wine is subject to special prohibitions. Wine on which gentiles have worked is assumed to have been devoted to idolatry, and Israelites therefore may derive no benefit whatsoever from the remaining wine in the same bottle (M. A.Z. 2:3). These rules are concrete and have nothing to do with the general prohibition against idolatry (M. A. Z. 3:1-4:7). The principal consideration is the prohibition against libation-wine, which is fully worked out at M. A. Z. 4:8-12, 5:1-7. One may not lend to gentiles or borrow from them, borrow money or repay a loan, prior to a festival (M. A.Z. 1:1A-D). The marketplace in which there is an idol is subjected to prohibitions, e.g.,

"A town in which there is an idol, and in which there were shops that were adorned and shops that were not – this was a case in Beth Shean, and sages rules, 'Those which are adorned are prohibited, but those which are not adorned are permitted'" (M. A.Z. 1:4).

One may sell to a gentile nothing that may be used for idolatrous purposes (M. A.Z. 1:5). Israelite craftsmen may not make ornaments for an idol, nor may farmers sell produce as yet unplucked. One may not rent to gentiles houses or fields in the land of Israel, but may do so abroad (M. A.Z. 1:8G-M). These rules and stipulations have concrete bearing upon the market, in a way in which other laws do not, e.g., "They accept from gentiles healing for property but not for a person," (M. A. Z. 2:2), "They do not leave cattle in gentiles' inns because they are suspect in regard to bestiality" (M. A. Z. 2:1). The prohibition as to libation wine greatly intruded into relationships of all sorts, but the point at which economic action and policy were affected had to do with the production of, and trade in, wine. Gentile workers could not be employed unless constantly watched, and if a jar of wine was opened by a gentile, it was assumed to have been used for a libation, and the rest of the wine thereby to have been spoiled. This led to various complications, e.g., "Israelite craftsmen to whom a gentile sent a jar of libation-wine as their salary are permitted to say to him, 'Give us its value'" (M. A.Z. 5:7).

The definition of wealth forms a component of the rationale for the system as a whole. As we now recognize full well, the object of concern, in connection with tithing, is land and its produce. That conception is expressed in the following statement:

A general principle they stated concerning tithes:

Anything that is food, cultivated, and which grows from the earth, is subject to the law of tithes.

And yet another general principle:

Anything which at its first stage of development is food and which at its ultimate stage of development is food, even though the farmer maintains its growth in order to increase the food it will yield, is subject to the law of tithes, whether it is small or large, that is, at all points in its development.

But anything which at its first stage of development is not food, yet which at its ultimate stage of development is food, is not subject to the laws of tithes until it becomes edible.

M. Maaserot 1:1[59]

---

[59]Jaffee, p. 28

The point is that all plants cultivated by man as food are subject to the law of tithes. When the householder harvests the crop, he must designate a fixed percentage of it as heave-offering or tithes; these are sanctified and set aside from the rest of the harvested crop and handed over to the priests and other scheduled castes. Only then is the rest of the produce available to the owner. What therefore falls into the system of sanctification is what grows from the land through the householder's own labor ("cultivated"), is useful to the householder for sustaining life ("food"). God owns the land, the householder is the sharecropper, and the wealth of the householder therefore is the land that God allows for the householder's share and use.

Wealth consists of land and what land produces, crops and cattle, as well as a large labor force, comprising the children of a growing population. The link of fertility to tithing occurs at Dt. 14:22-29, in connection with the separation of the tithe and the delivery of the tithe to Jerusalem, where it is to be eaten by the householder: "that the Lord your God may bless you in all the work of your hands that you do." "Proper disposition of the tithe...will result in God's blessing of the soil and its increased productivity."[60] The conception that wealth is solely land, is expressed not only in rules for the householder but also in silence: tithe derives only from herds and agriculture produce. The artisan and craftsman, the personnel of the service economy, merchants and traders and other commercial persons – none of these has nothing to tithe While they may have possessed wealth in the form of goods and even money, the distributive economics of the Mishnah had no rules governing the disposition of that wealth, which was left without recognition. And yet, as we have seen, the market economics of the Mishnah made ample provision for the governance of wealth in other forms than real estate. On that basis – the awry theory of wealth – I maintain the Mishnah presents, side by side, two distinct theories of economics, the one a market economics, the other, a more familiar distributive economics.

Matching that rule is the authorship's ominous silences. Its land-centeredness permits its economics to have no bearing not only upon the economy comprising Jews who were not householders, but also Jews who lived overseas. The Mishnah's distributive economics is for the "Israel" of "the land of Israel" to which the Mishnah speaks. There is no address to the economics of "Israel" outside of the land. For distributive economics governs only agricultural produce of the land of Israel, and, it follows, market economics, everything else, and everywhere else. No wonder, then, that the framers of the Talmud of

---

[60]Sarason, p. 4.

Babylonia, addressing, as they did, Jews who did not live on sanctified dirt, took no interest whatsoever in the Mishnah-tractates upon which we have focused here, the ones that state in rich detail the theory of a distributive economics of God as owner, scheduled caste as surrogate, temple as focus, and enlandisement as rationale, for an utterly fictive system.

# Part Three
# THE POLITICS OF A JUDAISM

# 6

# Defining a Politics and the Politics of a Religion

> Surely, politics is made with the head, but it is certainly not made with the head alone.
>
> Max Weber[1]

Judaism falls into the classification of a political religion, because its foundation-document, the Mishnah, sets forth a view of power and the disposition of power in society that is fundamentally political. The initial system of Judaism defines within the framework of the faith a political structure and system that are integral to its religious plan for the social order. In its initial systemic statement beyond Scripture itself, this Judaism secured for the institutions of the social order the power to exercise legitimate violence for the social entity. The institutions of this particular Judaism permanently ration and rationalize the uses of that power. Why should that have been the case? Not all prior Judaisms appealed to political categories, and after the Pentateuch few of them set forth a politics at all. In the case of Judaisms, from the writing down of the highly political fantasies of the Pentateuchal compilers in ca. 450 B.C. to the formation of the

---

[1]"Politics as a Vocation," in. H. H. Gerth and C. Wright Mills, *From Max Weber: Essays in Sociology* (New York: Oxford University Press, 1958), pp. 77-128. All page references to the end of the chapter refer to this article. Quotation: p. 128. On Weber's politics, I found of special interest Jeffrey C. Alexander, *Theoretical Logic in Sociology. III. The Classical Attempt at Theoretical Synthesis: Max Weber* (Berkeley and Los Angeles: University of California Press, 1983). Note also his *Twenty Lectures. Sociological Theory Since World War II* (New York: Columbia University Press, 1987); and his *Action and its Environments. Toward a New Synthesis* (New York: Columbia University Press, 1988), both of which I read with much admiration.

Judaism that began with the Mishnah in ca. A.D. 200, moreover, no Judaism in the Land of Israel systematically incorporated politics within its system or framed part of its statement in political categories at all. But this one did, and in consequence, we classify it as a political religion and undertake to study the genus, political religion, through the species of a particular and appropriate Judaism.

What kind of politics, exactly, do we now describe? It is not a practical politics, one that describes how things actually happened, but only a utopian politics, a structure and system of a fictive and a fabricated kind: intellectuals' conception of a politics. In making up a politics, religious intellectuals' pictures of how things are supposed to be appeal to archaic systems. Politics then emerges as invention, e.g., by Heaven or in the model of Heaven, not a secular revision and reform of an existing system. To see religion – exemplified here by a Judaism in particular – in this way is to take religion seriously as a way of realizing, in classic documents, a large conception of the world. That is why we appropriately turn to a Judaism as an example of a religion that composes for itself a cogent account of the social order.

If all we analyze is a politics of utopia, a structure built nowhere in particular but only in mind and a system people made up but in point of fact in the processes of ratiocination never actually realized in social governance, then why bother? Surely reality presents sufficient cases for political inquiry. We need not be detained by someone's fantasies too. To understand what is at stake in the question taken up here, finding out in some detail just how the framers of the theory of a social system invent a politics, we may undertake an experiment in imagination. What if, selected from the debris of a ruined earth to make the voyage to build a new heaven on Jupiter, in our minds we had to invent a politics for the new planet? Consider then the challenge of reconstructing the theory of a political system afresh, using whatever we might wish from available institutions and conceptions and inventing what we needed to set forth a whole new, and valid politics. What sort of politics should we invent for our brave new world? The question, of course is one of discovering the categorical imperatives, the strategy as to policy, for the formation of a world made up de novo. We wonder, for instance, what out of the past we should take with us, and how within the utopian imagination we are to organize the political system to govern the nascent state. Cases of fabricated politics provide data about the possibilities of invention – and also, after all, the consequences.

To endure, the aborning society, like the dying one, will require the legitimate exercise of power, even of violence, to hold together and sustain itself. Some will exercise authority and so tell others what to do. So they will appeal to a theory or story of legitimation for that power, that is, a political myth. The right to exercise power will be vested in offices and institutions and also transmitted to persons qualified to staff those agencies. So there will be a theory of the structure of political institutions and an account of the way to qualify for the bureaucracy. And, too, the travelers into the unknown of social organization will also take with them a theoretical picture of how the politics will actually function, that is to say, the sources of passion, the outer limits of the arena of public and political responsibility, and the workings of public policy in proportion and proper balance.[2] All of this forms the map that in intellect and sensibility will guide the travellers as they venture into the uncharted spaces to build a new society, therefore a new politics.

In theory, just as the second century philosophers can have defined their politics in other categories entirely, so too our refugees from planet Earth will think about other political issues, besides the ones that seem to me fundamental. But before proceeding, let me specify systemic issues theoretically bearing upon any politics – surely the politics of the new earth to be built in a distant heaven – with which in this context I do not deal at all and let me explain why I do not address them. The answer will clarify the entire enterprise. The most important omitted topic is this: what exactly did the politics of Judaism conceive the Jews to be? Were they a nation? state? region? ethnos in the Greco-Roman sense? What choices were before the theorists, and what selection did they make among them? Our space-travellers would assuredly answer that question, but here we shall not. That question is dealt with systematically elsewhere, and, while political, plays no important part in the exposition of the politics of the "Israel" invented by the philosophers of the Mishnah.[3]

But there are other political questions that do make a difference, and, while a theoretical politics for a new world would surely attend to them, these political concerns are not dealt with here. They cover the definition in abstract terms of the body politic, e.g., the nature of sovereignty, how it is acquired, how it should be exercised, the characteristics of good and bad government, and in general, the relations between the ruler and the ruled. The Mishnah's philosophers think in concrete ways about abstract questions; the issues of the body

---

[2] I presently explain the origins of these categories, which are by no means introduced at random.

[3] I provide a full account of the available theories for the formative age of Judaism in my *Israel in the History of Jewish Thought* (Cambridge: Cambridge University Press, 1988).

politics concerning sovereignty prove only abstract (at least, for them), with the result that I cannot identify the epiphenomena, in concrete facts, of the applied reason that lead us back to the theory of the matter.

There is still a third range of questions of a political character, not dealt with here. Understanding why these are bypassed will illuminate the character of the analysis I propose to undertake. To be specific, I do not treat the Judaic political culture, e.g., "good breeding, courtesy, and urbanity...civility, etiquette, and correct behavior in both social and political contexts."[4] The Mishnah's picture of the training of the civil servant, that is, the sage, richly describes the traits of the political culture, since the sage forms the political instrument of power; he is the one who tells people what to do and invokes sanctions upon those who fail to keep the law. Accordingly, the reason for neglecting these weighty matters of the politics is not that these questions bear little consequence, for that is not so. It is that they are systemically inert issues. They contain information; they do not define systemic structure and composition; they provide interesting instruction, they do not address the generative problematic, which is to say, the acute and urgent questions and they do not contain elements of the self-evidently valid answers to those questions. The reason for excluding any category of political issues is not that the Mishnah fails to provide opinions on them. It is that the opinions do not lead us into the dynamics of the politics under study or clarify the character of the system that speaks, also, through this politics.

What an analysis of the politics of a religious system therefore yields is insight into not politics but the nature of that religious system: how it delivers its message through the topics it selects for detailed analysis, and what that message is, and why it chooses (in this case) politics as the appropriate medium for stating that message. But political culture in the politics of Judaism, prominent in position, is essentially peripheral to the systemic problematic. That is why, in this context, the questions at hand fall entirely outside the frame of reference of the politics we shall examine. So much for the nature of our inquiry: analysis of a theory about theoretical politics, an account of what "we" should and would do, if in terms of power we could do anything at all.

Why focus upon the politics of Judaism in particular? The politics of Judaism proves peculiarly congruent with the requirements of such a mental experiment. For this politics, as we shall see, speaks of a

---

[4]See Bernard Lewis, *The Political Language of Islam* (Chicago and London: University of Chicago Press, 1988), pp. 25ff.

structure that never was, and a system that never, in fact, came into being.  If we want to know what it is like to weave a politics out of the gossamer threads of hopeful fantasy, we can do no better than to turn for thread to the skein of the Mishnah's politics.  Here we deal with intellectuals in their pure thought, knowing only with how people imagined that things should be.  The whole political structure and system of Judaism, as portrayed in the Mishnah, were fabricated by the authorship of the document.  At the time the Mishnah's sages made up their laws, the politics to which they appealed bore no correspondence whatsoever to the politics which they knew in the concrete exercise of power.  The mental experiment, speaking of travellers into distant spaces, therefore draws our attention back to the imagination of philosophers who voyaged into unknown realms of imagination.  "Brick served them as stone, and mud served them as portar" (Gen. 11:3): they had nothing better with which to work, no facts, no experience, no problems that fell within their power for solution and resolution.

The facts of history show us why, in the politics of the Judaism of the Mishnah, we deal with an account congruent to our experiment's requirements: a made-up politics for a utopian society, just now to be sure nowhere in particular.  While in the middle second-century Rome incorporated their country, which they called the Land of Israel and the Romans called Palestine, into its imperial system, denying Jews access to their capital, Jerusalem, permanently closing their cult-center, its Temple, the authorship of the Mishnah described a government of a king and a high priest and an administration fully empowered to carry out the law through legitimate violence.  So on the surface, we shall see how religious intellectuals, philosophers rather than theologians to be sure, made up a politics.  It follows that if we want to know what a politics made up whole cloth looks like, we do well to describe, analyze, and interpret in theoretical context the politics of the Judaism at hand.

That theoretical task of inventing a state and defining the institutions and their function that bear responsibility for the social entity and therefore have the power to tell people what to do and through legitimate violence impose sanctions to enforce policy defines the agenda of any politics.  What, precisely, will any politics anywhere – that is, any theory of the legitimation of violence and its uses – need to dictate for its structure and system?[5]  We should need a

---

[5]I owe this approach to matters to Professor Francis K. Goldscheider, my colleague and dear friend, who told me that, in sociology, people have a full program of questions that require answers for the building of settlements on distant planets. My sense is that this is much as the Jesuits (among others) had

list of questions that require attention, a program of thought and planning to guide the constitution of a new politics in a new setting. Whether in the form of a constitution and bylaws, a description of institutions and their jurisdiction, a law-code, the new politics would have to set forth how power in the new age would be worked out: political institutions and their power, political classes and their responsibility, political system and its myth. Designing the structure of political institutions, dictating the course of public policy and its concrete realization in the everyday manipulation of power – these form programs of imaginative thought that we do not ordinarily associate with religious intellectuals.

Once we ask for the topics that any politics any time, anywhere – or nowhere in particular, and at no determinate time – must take up, we move from an experiment in imagination to the identification of a political theory serviceable in our inquiry. I find one such theory in the thought of Max Weber,[6] and that explains why, to identify the rubrics for my voyagers' politics, I appeal to a writing of his. There I find the six descriptive categories for political analysis utilized in my description of the politics of Judaism. These categories, formed by Weber in his "Politics as a Vocation," set forth in a realm of pure thought, are as follows: myth, institutions, administration, passion, responsibility, proportion. These seem to me to define the constituents of any political structure and system anywhere, because they define, respectively: what the politics is and how it works. They serve to identify topics that any politics, in any circumstance, is likely to address. I hardly need to add that I do not claim to contribute in any way to political theory, let alone to the study of the particular political theories to which I compare the one I analyze in detail.[7] My

---

answers in the sixteenth and seventeenth centuries for the questions of society-building in the Spanish and Portuguese New World, and the Puritans in New England. Nothing started de novo, because, to begin with, people had thought through precisely what they would need to know. The Mayflower Compact, after all, was signed aboard ship, before a single structure had been built on shore.

[6]I of course cannot argue that Weber's is the best, or the only suitable, political theory for the present purpose. Not being a political scientist, I do not know that as fact. I amplify this qualification in the next footnote.

[7] I turn to Weber not only because of my own engagement with his thought, but also because the several political scientists whom I consulted pointed me in the direction of his writings, and I found in "Politics as a Vocation" as clearly a theoretical program as I could locate. But I am not a political scientist, any more than I am a philosopher or historian of philosophy in classical antiquity.

sole claim is that Weber's catalogue of political structures provides correct categories for the politics also of Judaism. In the issues set forth by these categories I propose to describe the political structure and system proposed by the authorship of the Mishnah for the public life and politics of the Jewish people.[8]

A detailed account of Weber's definition of a politics in the abstract is now called for. Weber defines politics to encompass "any kind of independent leadership in action." By politics Weber understands, for purposes of defining politics as a vocation, "only the leadership, or the influencing of the leadership, of a political association, hence, today, of a state." And a state is defined as a political association with access to the use of physical force:

> a human community that (successfully) claims the monopoly of the legitimate use of physical force within a given territory...Hence "politics" for us means striving to share power or striving to influence the distribution of power, either among states or among groups within a state.[9]

A political question, then, means "that interests in the distribution, maintenance, or transfer of power are decisive for answering the questions and determining the decision." "He who is active in politics strives for power either as a means in serving other aims...or as 'power for power's sake,' that is, in order to enjoy the prestige-feeling that power gives."[10]

That observation frames for us the initial issue of a politics, one that must come to resolution before a political structure can be set forth, and a political system described in its functioning. It is framed by Weber in these words:

> If the state is to exist, the dominated must obey the authority claimed by the powers that be. When and why do men obey? Upon what inner justifications and upon what external means does this domination rest?[11]

Religion forms a principal mode of legitimation of domination, with its appeal to the charisma of the prophet or general. And that simple observation defines the second question that a politics must answer: the calling of the political figure, who is to exercise

---

[8]I anticipate that in a later study, I shall compare the theoretical politics of the Mishnah's Judaism with the applied politics of the Talmuds' representation of power in Israel's everyday affairs. In further studies I expect to compare the theory with the practice, and, of course, to explain the difference.

[9]Pp. 77, 78.

[10]P. 78.

[11]Pp. 77-8.

domination. A politics has to tell us who not only why people obey, but who rules and through what media, e.g., of administration, dominion is sustained.

Weber states matters in the following way:

> Organized domination, which calls for continuous administration, requires that human conduct be conditioned to obedience towards those masters who claim to be bearers of legitimate power...by virtue of this obedience, organized domination requires the control of those materials goods which...in a given case are necessary for the use of physical violence. Thus, organized domination requires control of the personal executive staff and the material implements of administration. The administrative staff, which externally represents the organization of political domination, is, of course, like any other organization, bound by obedience to the power-holder.[12]

And this leads us to the issue of personnel and management: who manages and maintains the institutions of politics and secures long-term and broad obedience to the political structure. Again Weber:

> In all political associations which are somehow extensive, that is, associations going beyond the sphere and range of the tasks of small rural districts..., political organization is necessarily managed by men interested in the management of politics

At stake in this matter is the answer to the following question: What sort of classes of persons are recruited for the administration, how are they selected and trained for the work, and what sort of positions are envisioned for them? When we can outline the program for staffing the institutions, we find a clear account of the political structure, seen from within and from the perspective of its deepest foundations and its lowest layers of permanence. Then we find out who has a stake in the management of politics.[13] We can identify not only the institutions but, more important, the political classes envisioned by a system: those who sustain an on-going and continuous engagement with the politics in its institutions.

And, it goes without saying, we further grasp a system whole only when we can explain how the political classes sustain themselves: make the living that is required to permit them to exercise the power that they seek. An account of the structure of a politics will then tell us the answers to these three questions: what are the components of power, encompassing the myth of legitimacy, to which all acts of the utilization of power to coerce appeal? How do the institutions of power, that is, the political structures, take shape? Who make up the

---

[12]P. 80.
[13]Cf. pp. 100-102.

political classes, how are they supported, and by what means do persons gain entry into the political classes of administration and bureaucracy, of leadership and domination? The answers to these three questions seem to me to form the principal components of an account of a political structure. And, as we shall see, in its somewhat odd way, the Mishnah will tell us the forms of power that it recognizes, how these forms of power to coerce are realized, and who exercises the power of coercion – telling whom what to do and why.

So much for defining what we mean by Judaism's political structures, which we treat in Part Two. How about the political system of Judaism, addressed in Part Three? Weber supplies us with the classifications of not only political institutions, but also dynamics: how a structure works, what comprise the components of a system as it functions. I find these in his discussion of the qualities that are decisive for the politician, because I find in these qualities also the traits that make possible the functioning of a political system. For the politician realizes the system, just as the system preserves the occasion for the politician to do his work. Weber finds the necessary qualities to be passion, a feeling of responsibility, and a sense of proportion, and these I translate, in systemic categories of the workings envisioned by a politics, into these matters: passion stands for why the politics works; responsibility: for what the politics accomplishes; and proportion for how the politics is imagined to function.

Weber defines the virtues of the politician in language that we may translate into the functioning of a system:

> Passion...in the sense of matter-of-factness, of passionate devotion to a cause, to the god or demon who is its overlord...the politician inwardly has to overcome a quite trivial and all-too-human enemy: a quite vulgar vanity, the deadly enemy of all matter-of-fact devotion to a cause, and of all distance, in this case, of distance towards oneself.
>
> [The politician] works with the striving for power as an unavoidable means. Therefore, "power instinct," belongs indeed to his normal qualities. The sin against the lofty spirit of his vocation...begins where this striving for power ceases to be objective and becomes purely personal self-intoxication, instead of exclusively entering the service of the cause. For ultimately there are only two kinds of deadly sins in the field of politics: lack of objectivity and irresponsibility. ...irresponsibility...suggests that he enjoy power merely for power's sake without a substantive purpose....[14]

---

[14]Pp. 115-116.

The Politics of a Judaism

The matter of proportion is left by Weber without clear exposition. My sense, however, is that his observations on the ethics of politics point toward a definition of the matter:

> The decisive means for politics is violence....Whoever contracts with violent means for whatever ends – and every politician does – is exposed to its specific consequences.[15]

That is to say, the correct proportion in the political system will weigh in the balance the costs as against the benefits of the exercise of power: violence vs. persuasion, threat vs. promise.

These have to be held in the balance, and an account of how a political system is supposed to work will instruct us on how, in fact, we are supposed to hold the whole together and so persuade people to do what they want that the exercise of naked power plays no active part in the system at all. Weber's judgment guides our inquiry: "Politics is a strong and slow boring of hard boards." It also accounts for the categories of the political system that serve this study. We ask about three matters: passion, why the politics works, responsibility, meaning, what the politics of Judaism is meant to accomplish, and proportion:, that is to say, how the politics functions, utilizing such power as it chooses to use in one way rather than in some other so to accomplish one set of goals, not another.

Out of Weber, therefore, I have drawn what seems to me a program of inquiry that yields a picture congruent to descriptive inquiries into political structures and systems under any circumstances and conditions. These categories do not derive from the data before us, for the Mishnah organizes its discourse and sets forth its system in classifications quite particular to itself. Any analysis that proposes to illuminate issues of general intelligibility will have to proceed along lines not particular to a given system, and that is why I have turned to Weber for the analytical program I bring to the Mishnah. Justification for that program will derive from the simple fact that the Mishnah's system responds in important ways to each of the questions that Weber teaches me to ask.

Clearly, I mean also to contribute to the discussion inaugurated by Max Weber's "Religious Rejections of the World and their Directions," and, in particular, his "the political sphere."[16] Weber finds tension between the brotherly ethic of salvation religions and the political

---

[15]Pp. 121, 124.
[16]H. H. Gerth and C. Wright Mills, *From Max Weber: Essays in Sociology* (New York: Oxford University Press, 1958), pp. 333ff.

orders of the world. This tension, he maintains, comes about by the rise of universalist religions, which post God ruling the whole world:

> The gods of locality, tribe, and polity were only concerned with the interests of their respective associations. They had to fight other gods like themselves, just as their communities fought, and they had to prove their divine powers in this very struggle. The problem only arose when these barriers of locality, tribe, and polity were shattered by universalist religions...The problem of tensions with the political order emerged for redemption religions out of the basic demand for brotherliness. And in politics, as in economics, the more rational the political order became, the sharper the problems of these tensions became....
>
> The state's absolute end is to safeguard (or to change) the external and internal distribution of power; ultimately this end must seem meaningless to any universalist religion of salvation. This fact has held...even more so, for foreign policy. It is absolutely essential for every political association to appeal to the naked violence of coercive means in the face of outsiders as well as in the fact of internal enemies. It is only this very appeal to violence that constitutes a political association in our terminology. The state is an association that claims the monopoly of the legitimate use of violence and cannot be defined in any other manner.[17]

But by the second century, all Judaisms addressed the world at large and proposed a universalist account of how the one God ruled all humanity in justice and in love. And yet, as we shall see, the example of a universalist religion before us not only recognized no tension between religion and the rationalities of politics and economics.

The framers of the system resorted to a deeply political reading of existence in order to convey their vision of Israel and the world as they wished to reconstruct them both. As a matter of fact, the framers of the Mishnah set forth a politics that addressed issues quite different from those Weber maintains define matters. The tensions he discerns between state power and religious vision in no way form the dynamic of the system at hand. We deal with a realm composed within, and yet, a vision of the world that encompasses the active and interventionist utilization of power, political power, including the legitimate use of violence, that, in Weber's theory, should not find a place. I hardly need to underline that, while drawing for my topical program upon Weber's "Politics as a Vocation," I claim to make no contribution whatsoever either to political science or to the study of Max Weber's intellectual heritage. The interpretation of Weber and the study of the problems on which he worked fall entirely outside of my program.

---

[17]P. 334.

Still, I do think that Weber scholarship will find in these pages occasion to ask whether, like the Confucian Chinese, the sages whose system is before us also "lacked rational matter-of-factness, impersonal rationalism, and the nature of an abstract, impersonal purpose association," such that out of their system too capitalism cannot have come, just as, in Jeffrey C. Alexander's words, "Because this normative model of instrumental rationality was lacking, the motivation for such behavior did not exist...Confucian organizations could never assume the impersonal form that allowed the instrumentally efficient responsiveness to conditions that inspired Western economic life."[18]

But what sort of data, within the Mishnah, contribute to the description of the politics of Judaism as Weber defines any politics? To identify those data of the Mishnah that contribute to a picture of the politics of the document, we have, of course, to step outside the boundary of the document altogether, which explains the resort to Weber's clear picture of what we might mean by a politics, an account that, in quite abstract terms, tells us how the disposition and rationalization of the uses of power – who can tell whom what to do and why – gain concrete and particular definition.

Identifying the correct data, within the Mishnah, proves difficult because the Mishnah speaks very concretely about cases, rarely abstractly about principles. Take the matter of the political myth, for one example. If because of the philosophical and literary traits of the systemic document we do not know the stories people told of why to obey the authority claimed by the powers that be, we do know a great deal concerning precisely the actualities of the power exercised by those authorities. We therefore move from the concrete expressions of the legitimate use of violence to the identification of those permitted to utilize violence, thence to the (likely) explanation for the right of those who do so to coerce others, thus from sanctions to institutions to myth. That will not only define the main components of the mythic foundations of the politics of Judaism. It will also identify the institutional elements of that same politics.[19]

And the case of finding myth within sanctions provides the rule. At each point, we seek in the Mishnah for evidences of the concrete

---

[18]Jeffrey C. Alexander, *Theoretical Logic in Sociology.* III. *The Classical Attempt at Theoretical Synthesis: Max Weber* (Berkeley & Los Angeles: University of California Press, 1983), p. 39.

[19]That then sets the stage for Chapter Four, and, consequently, Chapter Five as well. We shall see in Part Two that the same procedure, beginning with the concrete application of power through sanctions, guides us in identifying appropriate data to determine how the politics was supposed to function.

working of power, in particular cases. When we know how power is legitimately exercised, we may work our way back from cases involving sanctions, the naked edge of power, to the theoretical system that sorts out the issues of politics. What we do, therefore, in the case of myth, for instance, is to seek guidance in the conception of how power works as we uncover the conception of what validates power's working as it does. That is to say, to identify relevant evidence of the working of a myth is to return to our simple definition of politics. When we have surveyed what a given type of authority may legitimately do to secure conformity to the system and its rules, we may ask why authority may act in such a way, even using physical force to enforce the law and sustain the system. From the end product, the sanctions that are legitimately invoked, we may describe the myth of the politics of Judaism. And that is the rule throughout: from power in the form of sanctions to a description of the political structure and system that accounts for those sanctions and organizes power for the purposes of the social order.

But the study of politics also requires the comparison of one politics with some other. For if we know only one thing, we understand nothing. That is why, once we have identified the case for description, we face the task of defining the categorical basis for description, analysis, and interpretation. There can be no analysis without comparison and contrast, and no interpretation out of context. But with what politics shall I compare and contrast the politics of Judaism, and how shall I define the context for interpretation? If Weber provides the guidelines for the description of a political structure and system, we gain the perspective required for the analysis and interpretation of that same structure and system in the politics of Aristotle.[20]  The choice is far from random, but pointed and particular. Two reasons require it.

First of all, it is because, for Aristotle as for the philosophers of the Mishnah, politics formed a medium of choice for the making of an important part of a coherent systemic statement. The Mishnah's sages stand well within the philosophical mode of political thought that begins with Aristotle, who sees politics as a fundamental component of his system when he says, "political science...legislates as to what we are to do and what we are to abstain from;" and, as to the institutionalization of power, I cannot imagine a more ample definition

---

[20]I need hardly add that I claim no expert knowledge of Greek political theory and take my observations for purposes of comparison and contrast only by naked eye, and then only of the most obvious and accessible sightings: moon, sun, but not distant or faded stars.

of politics than that.[21] Furthermore, the two politics – the Mishnah's, Aristotle's – share in common their origins in intellectuals' theoretical and imaginative life and form an instance, within that life, of the concrete realization of a larger theory of matters. But that may be said of most political theories, which are rarely the formation of practitioners of statecraft. Not only so, but the Mishnah's world view and way of life came to expression in a world in which, as I have shown in my *Economics of Judaism*, the ideas of Aristotle, in particular, were conventional and expressed commonplace truths among intellectuals.

But there is a second, and much more compelling consideration, one that is is fundamental to the entire plan of this book. In my view political analysis comes only after economic analysis and depends upon the results of that prior inquiry into a social system's disposition of scarce resources and theory of control of means of production (to name two critical questions of the social analysis of a system's economics). When we know who commands the means of production, we then, and only then, turn to inquire about who tells whom what to do and why: who legitimately coerces others even through violence. Aristotle and the Mishnah's philosophers give the same answer about what "person" (in our century we prefer "class" or "caste" or other more abstract and impersonal categories) forms the commanding presence in control of the means of production. That is the householder (whom we shall meet again in Chapter Two and Chapter Ten). For Aristotle and for the Mishnah's sages, the fundamental unit of economic thought and the generative social metaphor of their respective systems was the householder. The givens of the thought-world of the Mishnah's framers' theory of economics, embedded in a larger systemic plan, in fact correspond point by point with the economic program of Aristotle.[22] Because the two systems – Aristotle's and the Mishnah's –

---

[21]Cited by R. G. Mulgan, *Aristotle's Political Theory* (Oxford: Clarendon Press, 1977), p. 3.

[22]The embeddedness of economics within a larger theory of social and political economy, characteristic of Aristotle's system, does not characterize the relationships between economics and politics in Judaism. My guess is that the possibility of a disembedded economics came about only with the collapse of Christian belief (via Aquinas to Aristotle) for the eighteenth century philosophers. That opened the way to modes of inquiry formerly closed by the profoundly embedded, therefore distributive, economics of the Christianity of the tradition of Aristotle. But, of course, economics followed and explained the economy, and the formation of market-economics as the regnant medium of material relationships in Western Europe came about long after the rise of capitalism. In this regard, as in so many others, I walk down a path pioneered by Weber.

appeal to precisely the same social metaphor, formed of the householder and his establishment, the fundamental unit of production, they seem to me to sustain comparison and contrast. Let me spell out this point in some detail, since it is basic to the plan of the book as a whole.

Why is it that when I seek appropriate systems for comparison and contrast, I turn, in particular, to the material relationships within society? It is because in these relationships power is realized in concrete ways; it ceases to be a hopeless abstraction and becomes a concrete case of someone's telling someone else what to do and why. Politics is about legitimate violence, power in its most naked form, and in my judgment, when we ask about power, we deal with questions of not merely control of custom or conscience but command of the means of production. I find fundamental, therefore, how, as power works itself out, the social order sorts out the position and authority, as to legitimate violence, of the one who commands the means of production, and how control of the irreducible minima of the means of production defines the social order. And that is why at that point of analytical inquiry requires me to turn to Aristotle.

Accordingly, when thinking about questions of economics, both systems – Aristotle's and the Mishnah's – begin at the same fundamental point, namely, with the one who commands the basic unit and means of production. That is the householder, and that is the fact of both systems that justifies comparing their other definitive characteristics and explaining both likenesses and differences. The point of comparison – traits in common – is not the only one of interest. It is also the point of contrast. While the economics of Aristotle and the economics of Judaism commence with the consideration of the place and power of the person ("class," "caste," economic interest) in control of the means of production, the social metaphors that animate the politics of the two systems part company. Aristotle in his *Politics* is consistent in starting with that same person ("class") when he considers issues of power. But the Mishnah's philosophers build their politics on with an altogether different set of building blocks; the householder, fundamental to their economics, does not form a subject of political discourse at all and in no way constitutes a political class or caste. In this sense, the economics of the Mishnah is disembedded from its politics, in a way in which the economics and politics of Aristotle's system are embedded within a larger and nurturing, cogent theory of political economy.

That is to say, for Aristotle, both economics and politics originate in the agglomeration of households into villages and of villages into the city or polis, which was the social metaphor of his thought on political questions. But, as we shall see, the politics of the philosophers of the Mishnah does not follow suit. Their politics begins with a quite different identification of the basic building block of thought and discourse. The politics of Judaism appeals to a fundamental building block selected out of the political entities, persons or classes, of the social order, who in no way correspond to the householder of the economics of Judaism. The economics of Judaism, as I shall explain at some length in Part Three, is disembedded from its politics.

To this point, I have treated the issue of a religion's politics as though the political religion were everywhere conceded to be a routine phenomenon. But how can we speak of the politics of – made up by – a religion at all? In answer to that question, we turn, finally, to the question of a religious politics. While in some religious traditions, Islam everywhere, Roman Catholic Christianity in Latin America, Spain, and Portugal, Judaism in the State of Israel, everyone knows that religions have politics, in others, Protestant Christianity in the West, Reform and Conservative Judaism in the USA, for instance, people do not concede that religions legitimately have, or ought to have, a politics at all. So far as in these settings we speak of religions' politics, we mean who gets to be bishop of this diocese, or to whom that synagogue pulpit is assigned. But, as is clear, what we mean by the politics of a religion is the political system that a religion, if it could, would frame for a state – any state. Not only so, but religion in its inward and mystical modes, commonly finds itself not saddled with, but contrasted against, politics, so that a mystical religion is supposed not to engage in political life at all. "Render unto Caesar..." is understood to define Christianity as not a political religion, and, indeed, for long centuries no Christianity was a political religion, which is to say, none delivered its systemic message also through a sustained and systematic theory of a politics as part of its larger systemic statement. Calling Christ "King" did not bear political implications about the legitimate use of coercion, including force, such as a politics requires (and, even in Christianity, in due course exhibited).

But, as history shows, so today we see that intellectuals, responding to other-worldly concerns, more often than not do appeal to this-worldly power of legitimate violence and therefore frame (in theory at least, but often in practice as well) a concrete and this-worldly politics. Not only so, but the religious system appears to define the independent variable, which accounts for the structure and system of the politics put forth by that religious system. My sustained argument, in Part Three, that the politics of Judaism forms part of a larger systemic statement and can be understood only in terms of the ineluctable question and self-evidently valid answer that frame the systemic statement – and that are not of a political character at all! – aims at the same conclusion. It is that religion forms the independent variable in the systemic analysis of religious systems of the social order.

Religious intellectuals, however focused in mind and imagination upon heavenly considerations, engage with the public interest and undertake to construct a politics encompassing on-going institutions to acquire and sustain worldly power. Mystics in one religious world after another prove remarkably practical in their assessment of the media of power for realizing their vision. Their vision practically and concretely shapes public affairs of women and men doing things together. And that fact characterizes all kinds of religious intellectuals. Specifically, the formation of a politics of a religion comes forth from not only mystics, such as Bernard of Clairvaux, but also prophets, such as Muhammed, and, as we shall see, also philosophers, such as the authorship of the Mishnah, the document that, with Scripture, founded Judaism.

But if some religions make up (and even realize) politics, that does not tell us what makes the politics of a religion interesting. What do we learn in the analysis of the politics of a religion, and how high are the stakes in this study? If we want to know why politics sets forth high stakes for the study of the politics of a Judaism, for example, I see two points of fundamental importance. First comes the simple and practical fact that religious imaginations – whether prophetic, mystical, or philosophical in paramount traits – have set forth political systems in structure that in the passage of time have often turned out to impart shape to the everyday realities of the social order. Today, we know, religions, the political structures and systems of which were made up long ago and wholly in intellect, now actively intervene in the formation, or reformation, of nation-states. Accordingly, our case on the surface is of more than merely antiquarian interest.[23] It follows that what begins in the theory, for instance, in

---

[23]But that is not to suggest that the contemporary politics of the State of Israel, or of the organized Jewish communities elsewhere in the world (to the degree that these form political entities at all) are understood, best or at all, by appeal to the politics defined by the Judaism studied here. I do not deal with that question at all. For one thing, no one has yet demonstrated that there is anything remotely resembling a political tradition of an on-going, linear kind, that characterizes Judaic religious systems or that accounts for Jews' political

theology and religious intellect, emerges in the concrete realm of politics and the social system.

Accordingly, a case-study of the kind of politics religious intellectuals made up for themselves within their larger design for the social world they proposed to bring into being claims acutely contemporary interest. And, as I shall show in Chapters Three through Eight, the Mishnah does set out a clear account of a political structure and system, answering fundamental questions of politics in a systematic and orderly way. It is the kind of writing that sages can have taken along to any distant, unsettled land, for reference on how to build the holy society that they will have had in mind. So the politics of a religion attracts our interest simply because, in the world as we know it, religion forms a fundamental constituent of political reality.

But there is a second point of acute interest, one that raises the stakes still higher. If through studying the politics of a religion, we learn about politics, in that same inquiry we learn still more about religion. Indeed, I should claim that if we do not study the politics of a religion that falls into the classification of a political religion, we do not understand much about that religion. For when a religion sets forth a politics, the politics will form the focus of that religion's intellectual energies and in the practical life as well will furthermore attract considerable and sustained attention. Specifically, in a political religion such as Judaism, we see how religion enjoys and (in at least the instance at hand) exercises the power to speak not only through theology or myth but also through politics.[24]

Why then do I insist that *if* a religion has a politics, then that politics demands analysis as a principal heuristic exercise? The reason is that what characterizes a well-crafted systemic statement of the social order is that every detail makes the system's main point. Through politics as much as through theology, what the system wishes to say overall, it also says in detail. For a system finds cogency in addressing a self-evidently valid response to a single urgent question, and, it must follow, the details will bear the burden of the whole. But why through politics in particular? Answers to these questions help us grasp the character of religion in its diverse manifestations: why did this system (in our case, this Judaism) bother to make up a politics at all? What type of religion will speak, also, through politics, and what type will not? And that fundamental question yields these

---

behavior. True, some assume just that. But rigorous analysis lies over the horizon of the future.

[24]As, in the case of this same Judaism, through economics!

principal parts: what statement, part of the larger theory of the social order and system, did the politics serve to make, and why was politics the uniquely appropriate medium to convey that message? These are the questions concerning the institutionalization and utilization of state power in the foundation-document of Judaism that, in my view, draw our interest and make the inquiry important.

It follows that at stake is our understanding of not only politics in the religious setting, but religion in its own right. For asking how religions would invent, and have invented, politics and political systems, states and governments for example, we frame a question that religions do answer in their own terms.[25] If I frame the question in a systemic way, wanting to know the place, within the social order planned by a religion, of politics, the message the political component of the system sets forth, and the reason that that message requires formulation in political terms, it therefore is for a simple reason. That way of inquiry – seeing things whole, as a coherent system and account of the social order – entirely accords with the way in which religions answer the question of power.

---

[25]My framing of the entire inquiry derives, of course, from the theory of the study of religion worked out by Jonathan Z. Smith in various papers, most recently, Jonathan Z. Smith, *Imagining Religion: From Babylon to Jonestown* (Chicago: The University of Chicago Press, 1982).

# 7

## The Political Myth of Judaism

> If the state is to exist, the dominated must obey the authority claimed
> by the powers that be. When and why do men obey? Upon what
> inner justifications and upon what external means does this
> domination rest?[1]

The political myth expresses that element of the world view of a
social entity that instructs people on why they should do what they
are supposed to do. It is the narrative equivalent of legitimate
violence, because it means to coerce conformity with the social order
and its norms. The political institutions envisaged by a politics convey
details of the way of life of the same entity that, in theory at least,
exercises the coercive power to secure compliance with the rules. The
management of politics, finally, forms the definition for how the
institutions secure suitable and capable staff to carry out their public
tasks. Politics, defines the concrete and material component of the
conception of a social system, and the theory of politics, defining both
how things should be and also how they should be done, forms the
critical element in a religious system.

The political myth of Judaism makes power specific and particular
to cases, above all indicating what agency or person has the power to
precipitate the working of politics as legitimate violence at all.
When, therefore, we understand the differentiating force of myth that
imparts to politics its activity and dynamism, we shall grasp what in
point of fact nowhere comes to concrete expression, while everywhere
animating the structures of the politics and propelling the system.
Accordingly, appealing to a myth of taxonomy, the system
accomplishes its tasks by explaining why this, not that, telling as its
foundation story a myth of classification of power. The myth appeals

---

[1]Max Weber, *Politics as a Vocation.*

in the end to the critical bases for the taxonomy, among institutions, of a generalized power to coerce. That is why we can move in easy stages from myth to the institutional modes of making that myth concrete and specific to cases. Specifically we analyze the mythic foundations of sanctions. When we move from sanctions to the myth expressed in the application and legitimation of those sanctions, we see a complex but cogent politics sustained by a simple myth. Let me begin this somewhat protracted survey of sanctions and their implications with a clear statement of what we shall now uncover. The encompassing framework of rules and institutions and sanctions is explained and validated by the myth of God's shared rule. That dominion, exercised by God and surrogates on earth, is focused partly in the royal palace, partly in the Temple, and partly in the court. But which part falls where and why? The political myth of Judaism serves a particular purpose, which is to answer that particular question, and, consequently, the Judaic political myth comes to expression in its details of differentiation, which permit us to answer the generative question of politics, who imposes which sanction and why?

So we begin with cases and end with cases, only in the mid-stages of analysis uncovering the narrative premises of our diverse cases that, seen altogether, form the myth of politics in the initial structure of Judaism. Through the examination of sanctions, we identify the foci of power. At that point we ask how power is differentiated. And the answer to that question, never made explicit, forms the foundation-myth of Judaism's politics. But in spelling out what must now represent an enigmatic, indeed impenetrable statement of the whole, I have skipped many stages in the argument and the examination of the evidence. So let us begin from the very beginning. How, exactly, do I propose to identify the political myth of Judaism?

While in the case of the politics of Judaism in its initial formulation, the Mishnah's ample information informs us on the institutions of politics, the mythic framework within which persuasion and inner compliance are supposed to bring about submission to legitimate power scarcely emerges. Yet institutions of political persuasion and coercion dominate not only through external coercion but also through inner obedience and appeal to good will, not only intimidation. Accordingly, we must take as a given *that* a political myth animated the structure of politics. But the authorship of the Mishnah has chosen other media for thought and expression than the narrative and teleological ones; it is a philosophical, not a historical (fictive) account that they propose to convey through their masses of detailed rules about small things. If we were to bring to the authorship of the Mishnah such questions as who tells whom what to do? they would point to the politics' imaginary king and its equally fictive high priest, with associated authorities. Here, they would tell us, in personal rather than abstract form to be sure, are the institutions of politics. But if we were to say to them, "And tell me the story (in our language: the myth) that explains on what basis you persuade people to conform," they would find considerable difficulty in bringing to the fore explicit mythic statements made by their writing.

The document contains no sustained or well-articulated account of the reasons why people should willingly conform and obey, submit to the power that the system imputes to its political principals. Yet, we shall presently see, we can delineate the main lines of the political myth of Judaism. There is a political myth, of some richness and density, and the problem only is how to locate it and draw it to the surface for systemic description. For we do find generalized appeals, as we shall see in a moment, to a prevailing myth for explaining who tells whom what to do and why. More to the point, we find in rich detail the evidences of a profound mythic composition, one that operates in enormous specificity to account for the concrete application of power: who tells whom what to do and why.

And this returns us to our basic question of method. How then are we to identify, on the basis of what the Mishnah *does* tell us, the political myth of a politics the principal statement of which does *not* to begin with record the generative myths to which the system is supposed to appeal? A myth, we recall, explains the exercise of legitimate power. Power comes to brutal expression when the state kills or maims someone or deprives a person of property. This it does through the imposition of legal sanctions for crime or sin.[2] In the absence of a myth of power, we therefore begin with power itself. That is to say, we shall work our way back from the forms of power to the intimations, within the record of legitimately violent sanctions, the intellectual and even mythic sources of legitimation for the exercise and use of that legitimate violence. For it is at the point of imposing sanctions, e.g., killing, bodily injury, denial of property, exclusion from society, that power in its naked form takes place. Then how these legitimate exercises of violence are validated will set before us such concrete evidence of the myth as we shall discover to explain,

---

[2] I do not distinguish crime from sin, since I do not think the system does. At the same time our own world does make such a distinction, and it would be confusing not to preserve it. That accounts for the usage throughout.

interprets and validate power. And, so far as there is such, that is the political myth of Judaism.[3]

Since the coming analysis of sources will prove somewhat abstruse, let me signal in advance the outcome of this inquiry. Analyzing myth from the perspective of explanations of sanctions, we shall identify four types of sanctions, deriving from four distinct institutions of political power, each bearing its own mythic explanation. The first is what God and the Heavenly court can do to people. The second is what the earthly court can do to people, and that type of sanction embodies the legitimate violence of which political theory ordinarily speaks. The third is the sanction imposed by the cult's requirements, which can deprive people of their property as legitimately as can a court. The fourth is the sanction that is self-imposed: conformity to consensus. Then the issue becomes, whose consensus, and defined by whom? Four types of coercion, including violence of various kinds, psychological and social as much as physical, are in play. The types of sanction within the system that are exercised by other than judicial-political agencies surely prove violent and legitimately coercive, even though the violence and coercion are not the same as those carried out by courts.

On that basis we can indeed differentiate among types of sanctions – and hence trace evidences of the differentiations within the mythic structure that altogether is meant to explain why various types of sanctions are put into effect. As we shall see, the exercise of power, invariably and undifferentiatedly in the name and by the authority of God in Heaven to be sure, is kept distinct. Concrete application of legitimate violence by [1] Heaven covers different matters from parts of the political and social world governed by the policy and coercion of [2] the this-worldly political classes. And both sorts of violence have to be kept distinct from the sanction effected by [3] the community, not through institutional force and expression, but through the weight of attitude and public opinion. Here, again, we find a distinct set of penalties applied to a particular range of actions. When we have seen the several separate kinds of sanction and where they apply, we shall have a full account of the workings of politics as the application of power, and from that concrete picture, we may, I think, identify the range of power and the mythic framework that has to have accommodated and legitimated diverse kinds of power.

---

[3]It goes without saying that appeal to Scripture at this point is irrelevant. People used Scripture in building their system; they did not begin their system-building by perusing Scripture. But when our analysis of the application of power invites attention to Scripture, we surely are justified in seeing what we find there.

The upshot may be stated very simply.   If because of the philosophical and literary traits of the systemic document we do not know the stories people told of why to obey the authority claimed by the powers that be, we do know a great deal concerning precisely the actualities of the power exercised by those authorities.  We therefore move from the concrete expressions of the legitimate use of violence to the identification of those permitted to utilize violence, thence to the (likely) explanation for the right of those who do so to coerce others, thus from sanctions to institutions to myth.  That will not only define the main components of the mythic foundations of the politics of Judaism.  It will also identify the institutional elements of that same politics.  What we do, therefore, seek guidance in the conception of how power works as we uncover the conception of what validates power's working as it does.  For the way to identify relevant evidence of the working of a myth is to return to our simple definition of politics.  When we have surveyed what a given type of authority may legitimately do to secure conformity to the system and its rules, we may ask why authority may act in such a way, even using physical force to enforce the law and sustain the system.  From the end product, the sanctions that are legitimately invoked, we may describe the myth of the politics of Judaism.

Our task is to figure out on the basis of the distinct realms of sanctions, which are, Heaven, earth, and the mediating range of the Temple and sacrifice, which party imposes sanctions for what crimes or sins (the distinction is ours, not the system's).   Where Heaven intervenes, do other authorities participate, and if so, what tells me which party takes charge and imposes its sanction?  Is the system differentiated, so that where earth is in charge, there is no pretense of appeal to Heaven?   Or do we find cooperation in coextensive jurisdiction, so one party penalizes an act under one circumstance, the other the same act under a different circumstance?  A survey of the sanctions forms the point at which we can differentiate the components of the power structure before us.  So we wonder whether these three estates that enjoy power and inflict sanctions of one kind or another – Heaven, earth, Temple in between – govern each its own affairs, without the intervention of the other, or whether, working together, each takes charge in collaboration with the other, so that power is parcelled out and institutions both differentiate themselves from one another but also intersect.  The survey of sanctions that follows will allow us to answer these questions and so identify the myth of politics and the exercise of power that in its initial statement Judaism put forth.

### Mishnah-tractate Sanhedrin 7:2-3

A   The religious requirement of burning [is carried out as follows]:

B.   They would bury him in manure up to his armpits, and put a towel of hard material inside one of soft material, and wrap it around his neck.

C   This [witness] pulls it to him from one side, and that witness pulls it to him at the other side, until he opens up his mouth.

D.   And one kindles a wick and throws it into his mouth, and it goes down into his bowels and burns his intestines

E   R. Judah says, "Also as to this one, if he died at their hands [through strangulation], they will not have carried out the religious requirement of burning [in the proper manner].

F.   "But they open his mouth with tongs, against his will, kindle a wick, and throw it into his mouth, and it goes down into his bowels and burns his intestines."

G.   Said R. Eleazar b. Sadoq, "The daughter of a priest committed adultery.

H.   "And they put bundles of twigs around her and burned her."

I.   They said to him, "It was because the court of that time was not expert [in the law]."

M. 7:2

A   The religious requirement of decapitation [is carried out as follows]:

B.   They would cut off his head with a sword,

C   just as the government does.

D.   R. Judah says, "This is disgusting.

E   "But they put the head on a block and chop it off with an ax."

F.   They said to him, "There is no form of death more disgusting than this one."

G.   The religious requirement of strangulation [is carried out as follows:]

H.   They would bury him in manure up to his armpits, and put a towel of hard material inside one of soft material, and wrap it around his neck.

I.   This [witness] pulls it to him from one side, and that witness pulls it to him at the other side, until he perishes.

M. 7:3

### Mishnah-tractate Sanhedrin 7:4

A   These are [the felons] who are put to death by stoning:

B.   He who has sexual relations with (1) his mother, (2) with the wife of his father, (3) with his daughter-in-law, (4) with a male, and (5) with a

C   (6) and the woman who brings an ox on top of herself;

D.   and (1) he who blasphemes, (2) he who performs an act of worship for an idol, (3) he who gives of his seed to Molech, (4) he who has a familiar spirit, and (5) he who is a soothsayer;

E   he who profanes the Sabbath,

F.  he who curses his father or his mother,

G.  he who has sexual relations with a betrothed maiden,

H.  he who beguiles [a whole town to idolatry],

I.  a sorcerer,

J.  and a stubborn and incorrigible son.

I  K.  He who has sexual relations with his mother is liable on her account because of her being his mother and because of her being his father's wife [Lev. 18:6-7, 20:11].

L.  R. Judah says, "He is liable only on account of her being his mother alone."

II  M.  He who has sexual relations with his father's wife is liable on her account because of her being his father's wife and because of her being a married woman,

N.  whether this is in the lifetime of his father or after the death of his father,

O.  whether she is only betrothed or already married [to the father].

III  P.  He who has sexual relations with his daughter-in-law is liable on her account because of her being his daughter-in-law and because of her being another man's wife

Q.  whether this is in the lifetime of his son or after the death of his son [Lev. 20:12],

R.  whether she is only betrothed or already married [to the son].

S.  He who has sexual relations with a male [Lev. 20:13, 15-16], or a cow, and the woman who brings an ox on top of herself –

T.  if the human being has committed a sin, what sin has the beast committed?

U.  But because a human being has offended through it, therefore the Scripture has said, *Let it be stoned.*

V.  Another matter:  So that the beast should not amble through the market place and people say, "This is the one on account of which Mr. So-and-so got himself stoned.

M. 7:4

There are seventeen entries, in three parts.  But they do not fall into clear-cut groups after B-C, a set of sexual crimes, six in all, and the five "religious" sins, D.  By contrast, E-J, six more items, do not appear to me to form a group which has been deliberately arranged..  The exposition of the list commences with B1-3, at the triplet, K-R, as marked. Judah's position is not repeated, but in principle he has no reason to concur with M-R.  The systematic character of the exposition is clear. The homiletical counterpart, S-V, which addresses itself to B4-5, C, in no way matches its predecessor.  It takes for granted that we have cited the relevant Scripture, requiring the ox to be stoned, and it explains that matter, U, V, with V essentially redundant of U.

Let us now go on to the expansion of the crimes for which the state imposes the death penalty here on earth.  We shall see that the politics of Judaism perceives no line of demarcation between state and church, secular and religious, even while carefully distinguishing the exercise of power by Heaven from the exercise of power by the earthly court sustaining the state.

### Mishnah-tractate Sanhedrin 7:5-11

A   *He who blasphemes* [M. 7:4D1] [Lev. 24:10] is liable only when he will have fully pronounced the divine Name.

B.   Said R. Joshua b. Qorha, "On every day of a trial they examine the witnesses with a substituted name, [such as], 'May Yosé smite Yosé.'

C   "[Once] the trial is over, they would not put him to death [on the basis of evidence given] with the euphemism, but they put out everyone and ask the most important of the witnesses, saying to him, 'Say, what exactly did you hear [in detail]?'

D.   "And he says what he heard.

E   "And the judges stand on their feet and tear their clothing, and never sew them back up.

F.   "And the second witness says, 'Also I [heard] what he heard.'

G.   "And the third witness says, 'Also I [heard] what he heard.'"

M. 7:5

A   *He who performs an act of worship for an idol* [M. 7:4D2] –

B.   all the same are the one who (1) performs an act of service, who (2) actually sacrifices, who (3) offers up incense, who (4) pours out a libation offering, who (5) bows down,

C   and the one who (6) accepts it upon himself as a god, saying to it, "You are my god."

D.   But the one who (1) hugs it, (2) kisses it, (3) polishes it, (4) sweeps it, and (5) washes it,

E   (1) anoints it, (2) puts clothing on it, and (3) puts shoes on it, [merely] transgresses a negative commandment [Ex. 20:5].

F.   He who takes a vow in its name, and he who carries out a vow made in its name transgress a negative commandment [Ex. 23:13].

G.   He who uncovers himself to Baal Peor – [he is stoned, for] this is how one performs an act of service to it.

H.   He who tosses a pebble at Merkolis [Hermes] [is stoned, for] this is how one performs an act of service to it.

M. 7:6

The primary exposition is in the distinction of B-C and D-E. The act of cultic worship is culpable by stoning. Acts of reverence, D-E, are not. F is included because it makes a corollary point. G-H bear their own exegesis and augment B-C.

A   *He who gives of his seed to Molech* [M. 7:4D3] [Lev. 20:2] is liable only when he will both have given him to Molech and have passed him through fire.

B. [If] he gave him to Molech but did not pass him through fire,

C. passed him through fire but did not give him to Molech,

D. he is not liable –

E. until he will both have given him to Molech and have passed him through fire.

F. *He who has a familiar spirit* [M. 7:D4] [Lev. 20:27] – this is one who has a Python which speaks from his armpits;

G. *and he who is a soothsayer* [M. 7:4D5] – this is one whose [spirit] speaks through his mouth –

H. lo, these are put to death by stoning.

I. And the one who makes inquiry of them is subject to a warning [Lev. 19:31, Deut. 18:10-11].

M. 7:7

The gloss takes up and applies Scripture's specifications; A-E. The rest is clear as given. F speaks of a ventriloquist, G does not. The warning carries no penalty.

A. *He who profanes the Sabbath* [M. 7:4E] – in regard to a matter, on account of the deliberate doing of which they are liable to extirpation, and on account of the inadvertent doing of which they are liable to a sin-offering.

B. *He who curses his father and his mother* [M. 7:4F] is liable only when he will have cursed them by the divine Name.

C. [If] he cursed them with a euphemism,

D. R. Meir declares him liable.

E. And sages declare him exempt.

M. 7:8

A. *He who has sexual relations with a betrothed maiden* [M. 7:4G] [Deut. 22:23-4] is liable only if she is a virgin maiden, betrothed, while she is yet in her father's house.

B. [If] two different men had sexual relations with her, the first one is put to death by stoning, and the second by strangulation.

M. 7:9

The second party, B, has not had intercourse with a virgin (M. 11:1). The maiden is between twelve and one day and twelve years six months and one day old.

A. *He who beguiles others to idolatry* [M. 7:4H] – this [refers to] an ordinary fellow who beguiles some other ordinary fellow.

B. [If] he said to him, "There is a god in such a place, who eats thus, drinks thus, does good in one way, and harm in another" –

C. against all those who are liable to the death penalty in the Torah they do not hide witnesses [for the purposes of entrapment] except for this one.

D. [If] he spoke [in such a way] to two, and they serve as witnesses against him,

E. they bring him to court and stone him.

F. [If] he spoke [in such a way] to [only] one person, [the latter then] says to him, "I have some friends who will want the same thing."

G. If he was clever and not prepared to speak in [the friend's] presence,

H. they hide witnesses on the other side of the partition,

I. and he says to him, "Tell me what you were saying to me now that we are by ourselves."

J. And the other party says to him [what he had said], and then this party says, "Now how are we going to abandon our God who is in Heaven and go and worship sticks and stones?"

K. If he repents, well and good.

L. But if he said, "This is what we are obligated to do, and this is what is good for us to do,"

M. those who stand on the other side of the partition bring him to court and stone him.

N. [*He who beguiles others is*] He who says, "I am going to worship," "I shall go and worship," "Let's go and worship," "I shall make an offering," "I shall offer incense," "I shall go and offer incense," "Let's go and offer incense," "I shall make a libation," "I shall go and make a libation," "Let's go and make a libation," "I shall bow down," "I shall go and bow down," "Let's go and bow down."

O. *He who leads [a whole town astray]* [M. 10:4H] is one who says, "Let's go and perform an act of service to an idol."

M. 7:10

The exposition of A is extensive, covering B-M. N then reverts to A, in order to establish its contrast with O. M.'s narrative, introduced by B and flowing onward through M, is clear as given.

A. *The sorcerer* [M. 7:4I] – he who does a deed is liable,

B. but not the one who merely creates an illusion.

C. R. Aqiba says in the name of R. Joshua, "Two may gather cucumbers. One gatherer may be exempt, and one gatherer may

D. "[Likewise:] He who does a deed is liable, but he who merely creates an illusion is exempt."

M. 7:11

D attributes to Joshua the distinction made at A-B. It is generally understood that C refers to one who merely creates the illusion that he is gathering cucumbers, and another who by sorcery actually does gather cucumbers. But it seems to me C may simply point out that there are conditions in which two people may do the same thing, one incurring no liability, the other incurring liability, e.g., one who gathers cucumbers in the Seventh Year after they have generally stopped being harvested will be liable for violating the laws of the Seventh Year, while one who gathers them in any other year is exempt. On that basis I introduce *likewise* at D.

### Mishnah-tractate Sanhedrin 9:1

A. And these are those who are put to death through burning:

B. (1) he who has sexual relations with both a woman and her daughter [Lev. 18:17, 20:14], and (2) a priest's daughter who committed adultery [Lev. 21:9].

C. In the same category as a woman and her daughter are []the following]: (1) his daughter, (2) his daughter's daughter, (3) his son's daughter, (4) his wife's daughter, (5) the daughter of her daughter, (6) the daughter of her son, (7) his mother-in-law, (8) the mother of his mother-in-law, and (9) the mother of his father-in-law.

D. And these are those who are put to death through decapitation:

E. (1) the murderer, and (2) the townsfolk of an apostate town [M.

F. A murderer who hit his neighbor with a stone or a piece of iron [Ex. 21:18],

G. or who pushed him under the water or into the fire, and [the other party] cannot get out of there and so perished –

H. he is liable.

I. [If] he pushed him into the water or into the fire, and he can get out of there but [nonetheless] he died, he is exempt.

J. [If] he sicked a dog on him, or sicked a snake on him, he is exempt.

K. [If] he made a snake bite him,

L. R. Judah declares him liable.

M. And sages declare him exempt.

N. He who hits his fellow, whether with a stone or with his fist,

O. and they diagnosed him as likely to die,

P. but then he got better than he was,

Q. and afterward he got worse and he died –

R. he is liable.

S. R. Nehemiah says, "He is exempt,

T. "for there is a basis to the matter [of thinking that he did not die from the original injury]."

M. 9:1

The exposition of the four modes of execution advances at M. 9:1A-C and M. 9:1D. The former is a simple list, B, which is then augmented by nine items. He who has sexual relations with any woman in the listed relationships is punished by burning. D is expanded in two parts. The remainder of this chapter deals with the murderer, E1, and after a brief interpolation at M. 10:1-3, M. 10:4 takes up the other matter, the apostate town. M. 11:1 then completes the exposition of the materials of M. 7:1-3. The point of F-H vs. I is made by the contrast. In the former instances the man obviously causes the death. In the latter, he does not. The dispute at J + K-M, and the next, at N-T, is on the application of the same principle. So far as sages are concerned, K-M, liability is not incurred. N-R takes the view that the ultimate cause of death is the blow. This brings us to the catalogue of those executed by strangling, which is as follows:

### Mishnah-tractate Sanhedrin 11:1-6

A. These are the ones who are to be strangled:

B. (1) he who hits his father and his mother [Ex. 21:15, (2) he who steals an Israelite [Ex. 21:16, Deut. 24:7, (3) an elder who defies the decision of a court, (4) a false prophet, (5) a prophet who prophesies in the name of an idol;

C. (1) he who has sexual relations with a married woman, (2) those who bear false witness against a priest's daughter and (3) against one who has sexual relations with her.

D. *He who hits his father and his mother* [B.1] is liable only if he will make a lasting bruise on them.

E. This rule is more strict in the case of the one who curses than the one who hits them.

F. For the one who curses them after they have died is liable.

G. But the one who hits them after they have died is exempt.

H. *He who steals an Israelite* [B.2] is liable only when he will have brought him into his own domain.

I. R. Judah says, "Only if he will have brought him into his own domain and will have made use of him,

J. "as it is said, *And if he deal with him as a slave or sell him* (Deut. 24:7)."

K. He who steals his son –

L. R. Ishmael, son of R. Yohanan b. Beroqah, declares him liable.

M. And sages declare him exempt.

N. [If] he stole someone who was half slave and half free –

O. R. Judah declares him liable.

P. And sages declare him exempt.

M. 11:1

A. *An elder who defies the decision of a court* [M. 11:1B3] –

B. as it is said, *If there arise a matter too hard for you in judgment, between blood and blood, between plea and plea* (Deut. 17:8) –

C. there were three courts there.

D. One was in session at the door gate of the Temple mount, one was in session at the gate of the courtyard, and one was in session in the hewn-stone chamber.

E. They come to the one which is at the gate of the Temple mount and say, "Thus I have explained the matter, and thus my colleagues have explained the matter.

F. "Thus I have ruled in the matter, and thus my colleagues have
G. If they had heard a ruling, they told it to them, and if not, they come along to that court which was at the gate of the courtyard.
H. And he says, "Thus I have explained the matter, and thus my colleagues have explained the matter.
I. "Thus I have ruled in the matter, and thus my colleagues have
J. If they had heard a ruling, they told it to them, and if not, these and those come along to the high court which was in the hewn-stone chamber,
K. from which Torah goes forth to all Israel,
L. as it is said, *From that place which the Lord shall choose* (Deut.
M. [If] he went back to his town and again ruled just as he had ruled before, he is exempt.
N. But if he instructed others to do it in that way, he is liable,
O. as it is said, *And the man who does presumptuously* (Deut.17:12).
P. He is liable only if he will give instructions to people actually to carry out the deed [in accord with the now-rejected view].
Q. A disciple of a sage who gave instruction to carry out the deed [wrongly] is exempt.
R. It turns out that the strict ruling concerning him [that he cannot give decision] is a lenient ruling concerning him [that he is not punished if he does give decisions].

M. 11:2

A. A more strict rule applies to the teachings of scribes than to the teachings of Torah.
B. He who rules, "There is no requirement to wear phylacteries," in order to transgress the teachings of the Torah, is exempt.
C. [But if he said,] "There are five partitions [in the phylactery, instead of four]," in order to add to what the scribes have taught, he is liable.

M. 11:3

The exposition of M. 11:1B3 takes up this unit, which reverts to a narrative, M. 11:2C-O + P. Q-R and M. 11:3 provide two supplements.

A. "They put him to death not in the court in his own town or in the court which is in Yabneh, but they bring him up to the high court in Jerusalem.
B. "And they keep him until the festival, and they put him to death on the festival,
C. "as it is said, *'And all the people shall hear and fear and no more do presumptuously'* (Deut. 17:13)," the words of R. Aqiba.
D. R. Judah says, "They do not delay the judgment of this one, but they put him to death at once.
E. "And they write messages and send them with messengers to every place:

F. "Mr. So-and-so, son of Mr. So-and-so, has been declared liable to the death penalty by the court."

M. 11:4

A. *A false prophet* [M. 11:1B4],
B. one who prophesies concerning something which he has not actually heard or concerning something which was not actually said
C. is put to death by man.
D. But he who holds back his prophesy, he who disregards the words of another prophet, or the prophet who transgresses his own words –
E. is put to death by Heaven,
F. as it is said, *I will require it of him* (Deut. 18:19).

M. 11:5

A. *He who prophesies in the name of an idol* [M. 11:1B5], and says, "Thus did such-and-such an idol say to me,"
B. even though he got the law right, declaring unclean that which in fact is unclean, and declaring clean that which in fact is clean.
C. *He who has sexual relations with a married woman* [M. 11:1C1] –
D. as soon as she has entered the domain of the husband in marriage, even though she has not had sexual relations with him –
E. he who has sexual relations with her – lo, this one is put to death by strangling.
F. *And those who bear false witness against the priest's daughter and against one who has sexual relations with her* [M. 11:1C2, 3] –
G. for all those who bear false witness first suffer that same mode of execution,
H. except for those who bear false witness against the priest's daughter and her lover.

M. 11:6

Two further penalties at the disposal of the earthly court are banishment and flogging, imposed in the following crimes:

**Mishnah-tractate Makkot 2:1-3**

A. These are the ones who go into exile:
B. he who kills someone accidentally.
C. (1) [If] he was rolling [the roof] with a roller, and it fell down on someone and killed him,
D. (2) [if] he was letting down a jar [from the roof], and it fell on [a man] and killed him,
E. (3) [if] one was climbing down a ladder and fell down on someone and killed him –
F. lo, this person goes into exile.
G. But: (1) if he was pulling up a roller, and it fell on [a man] and killed him,

H. (2) [if] he was drawing up a jar, and the rope broke, and [the jar] fell on a man and killed him,

I. (3) [if] he was climbing up a ladder and fell on a man and killed him,

J. lo, this one does not go into exile.

K. This is the governing principle: Whatever happens en route downward – the person goes into exile.

L. [And whatever happens] not en route downward – the person does not go into exile.

M. [If] the iron flew from the heft and killed someone,

N. Rabbi says "He does not go into exile."

O. And sages say, "He goes into exile.

P. [If] it flew from the wood which is being split,

Q. Rabbi says, "He goes into exile."

R. And sages say, "He does not go into exile."

M. 2:1

The pericope is in two distinct parts, A-L, and N-R. The former consists of two balanced triplets, as marked, followed by a "governing principle." The first three are deemed truly accidental, the second not. Num. 35:22-23 speak of dropping or hurling something and so causing death; if this is unintentional ("and without seeing him, he cast it upon him, so that he died, though he was not his enemy and did not seek his harm"), the man is exempt and goes into exile. The distinction important at M. 2:1K-L would appear to restate that conception. But this clearly is not the end of the matter, as the paired dispute indicates. Rabbi, M-O, holds the man liable because he did not examine the condition of his tool. Sages do not. Rabbi further holds the man guiltless in the case of a chip's flying from the log which is being split, P-R, and sages hold him liable. Rabbi quite reasonably invokes Deut. 19:5, "As when a man goes into the wood with his neighbor to cut down trees, and his hand strikes with the axe to cut down the tree and the iron slips from the tree...". clearly, Rabbi reads the verse to exempt the man at M and so to impose liability at P. Sages see things in the reverse. So it would seem that the entire pericope proposes to deal with the exegesis of the relevant verses, even though these have not been cited.

A. He who throws a stone into the public domain and committed homicide – lo, this one goes into exile.

B. R. Eliezer b. Jacobs says, "If after the stone left the man's hand, the other party stuck out his head and took [the stone on the head], lo, this one exempt."

C. [If] he threw the stone into his own courtyard and killed him,

D. if the victim had very right to go into there, [the other party] goes into exile.

E.  And if not, he does not go into exile,

F.  as it is said, *As when a man goes into the forest with his neighbor* (Deut. 19:5) –

G.  just as the forest is a domain in which both the victim and the one who inflected injury have every right to enter,

H.  so the courtyard belonging to the householder is excluded [from reference], since the victim had no right to go there.

I.  Abba Saul says, "Just as cutting wood is optional, so are excluded [from punishment those who do their duty, e.g.:] the father who hits his son, the master who strikes his disciple, and the court-official [who committed homicide in the doing of their duty]."

M. 2:2

I   A  The father goes into exile because of the son,

    B.  And the son goes into exile because of the father.

II  C  All go into exile because of an Israelite.

    D.  And an Israelite goes into exile on their account,

    E  except on account of a resident alien.

III F.  A resident alien goes into exile only an account of another resident alien.

    G.  "A blind person does not go into exile," the words of R. Judah.

    H.  R. Meir says, "He goes into exile."

    I.  One who bears enmity [for his victim] does not go into exile.

    J.  R. Yosé b. R. Judah says, "One who bears enmity [for his victim] is put to death,

    K.  "for he is in the status of one who is an attested danger."

    L  R. Simeon says, "There is one who bears enmity [for the victim] who goes into exile, and there is one who bears enmity who does not go into exile.

    M.  "This is the governing principle: In any case in which one has the power to say, 'He killed knowingly,' he does not go into exile.

    N.  "And if he has the power to say, 'He did not kill knowingly,' lo, this one goes into exile."

M. 2:3

M. 2:2A-B and C-H form two distinct units. Their relevance to one another is clear. Eliezer's notion is that when the man threw the stone, he could not have known that the other party would be in its path. He is exempt. The point of C-E is carefully explained at F-H. I has Abba Saul's separate and distinct reading of the same verse, accounting for the inclusion of his irrelevant saying, and the tacking on of the triplet which follows, M. 2:3A-F. The dispute at M. 2:3G-H provides yet another exegesis, now of, *and without seeing him* (Num. 35:23), which Judah takes to mean that a blind person is exempt from the law entirely. I-K refer to Num. 35:23, *though he was not his enemy and did not seek his harm.* I quite reasonably read this to mean that the law excludes such a party, even in the case of accidental death. Yosé b. R. Judah surely concurs, for the reason explained at K. Simeon takes the position that the one who bears enmity also is subject to the law of exile, as is spelled out at M-N, a fine conclusion for what is an essentially exegetical exercise.

The final sanction an earthly court imposes is flogging, and that covers a variety of crimes and sins.

### Mishnah-tractate Makkot 3:1-6

A. These are the ones who are flogged:

B. He who has sexual relations with (1) his sister, (2) the sister of his father, (3) the sister of his mother, (4) the sister of his wife, (5) the wife of his brother, (6) the wife of the brother of his father,

C. (7) with a menstruating woman,

D. (8) a widow in the case of a high priest, (9) a divorcee or a woman who has performed the rite of removing the shoe with an ordinary priest, (10) a *mamzer*-girl and (11) a *Netin*-girl with an Israelite, (12) an Israelite girl with a *Netin* or with a *mamzer*.

E. As to a widow and a divorcee, [priests] are liable in her case on two counts.

F. In the case of a divorcee and a woman who has performed the rite of removing the shoe, [a priest] is liable in her case on only one count alone.

M. 3:1

The first set of those to be flogged deals with sexual sins. Those named are subject to extirpation (M. Ket. 3:1); when warned by witnesses, however, they also are subjected to flogging. The connections listed at D are women who are not to marry the listed castes. The point of E, F, is that if a woman happens to be both a widow and a divorcee, a priest who has sexual relations with her is liable on two distinct counts, that is, to two sets of floggings of forty stripes. The woman, F, who is a divorcee and who also has performed the rite of removing the shoe is liable only on one count, since these two matters – divorce, *halisah* – are equivalent to one another and so fall within a single category of prohibition. This gloss is important for the interests of M. 3:7-9, but it breaks the flow of the list, which continues immediately.

A. [Also subject to flogging are]: (1) an unclean person who ate food in the status of Holy Things; (2) he who enters the Temple unclean;

B. (3) he who eats forbidden fat, blood, remnant of a sacrifice left overnight, meat of a sacrifice rendered invalid by the improper intention of the officiating priest, or unclean [sacrificial meat];

C. (4) he who slaughters an animal and offers it up outside of the Temple;

D.  (5) he who eats leaven on Passover;

E.  (6) and he who eats or who does an act of labor on the Day of Atonement;

F.  (7) he who prepares anointing oil like the anointing oil of the Temple; (8) he who prepares incense like the incense of the Temple; or (9) he who anoints himself with anointing oil;

G.  (10) he who eats carrion or *terefah-meat*, forbidden things or creeping things.

H.  [If] one ate (1) food from which tithes had not been removed at all, (2) first tithe from which heave-offering had not been removed, (3) second tithe or consecrated food which had not been redeemed, [he is liable to flogging].

I.  How much food which had not been tithed at all does one eat so as to be liable?

J.  R. Simeon says, "Any amount at all."

K.  And sages say, "An olive's bulk."

L.  Said to them R. Simeon, "Do you not agree with me in the case of one who eats an ant, however small, that he is liable?"

M.  They said to him, "It is because that is how it has been created."

N.  He said to them, "Also a single grain of wheat is precisely in the form in which it has been created."

M. 3:2

A.  [Also subject to flogging are]: (1) he who eats first fruits over which one has not made the required declaration,

B.  (2) Most Holy Things outside the Temple veils, (3) Lesser Holy Things or second tithe outside the wall [of Jerusalem].

C.  He who breaks the bone of a Passover-offering which is in a state of cleanness – lo, this one is flogged with forty stripes.

D.  But he who leaves over meat of a clean Passover-offering or who breaks the bone in the case of an unclean one is not flogged with forty stripes.

M. 3:3

M. 3:2, the second segment of the list begun at M. 3:1A deals with cultic prohibitions, e.g., violating the laws the Temple and of the altar, A-C, F; the rules of the holy days, D-E; the dietary taboos, G; and the laws of correct tithing and related matters, H, glossed by I-N, as indicated. The difference of opinion is explained in the debate, L-N. M. 3:3A-B present another group and conclude the list. C refers to Ex. 12:46, which prohibits breaking the animal's bone. Ex. 12:10 forbids leaving the meat until morning, but there is no concrete deed to be done. In line with M. 3:4D, there is no flogging here.

A.  He who removes the dam with the offspring –

B.  R. Judah says, "He is flogged, and he does not have to send the dam away."

C. And sages say, "He sends the dam away, and he is not flogged."

D. This is the governing principle, In the case of any negative commandment which involves doing a positive deed, one is not liable.

M. 3:4

A. (1) He who makes a baldness on his head [Deut. 14:1], (2) he who rounds the corners of his head and (3) mars the corners of his beard [Lev. 19:27], (4) or he who makes a single cutting for the dead [Lev. 19:28] is liable.

B. [If] he made a single cutting on account of five different corpses,

C. or five cuttings on account of one corpse,

D. he is liable for each and every one of them.

E. For [cutting off the hair of] the head, he is liable on two conts, one for each side of the head.

F. For cutting off the beard, he is liable on two counts for one side, two conts for the other side, and one count for the lower part.

G. R. Eliezer says, "if he removed all of it at once, he is liable only on one count."

H. And he is liable only if he will remove it with a razor.

I. R. Eliezer says, "Even if he removed it with pincers or with an adze, he is liable."

M. 3:5

A. He who tattoos his skin –

B. [If] he made a mark but did not tattoo it in,

C. tattooed it in but did not make a mark,

D. he is not liable –

E. unless he makes a mark and tattoos with ink or with eye-paint or with anything which lasts.

F. R. Simeon b. Judah says in the name of R. Simeon, "He is liable only if he will write the name ]of a god],

G. "as it is written, *Nor will you tattoo any marks on you, I am the Lord* (Lev. 19:28)."

M. 3:6

So much for the earthly court. What is left for Heaven to do? It too imposes the death penalty, and, since everyone dies anyhow, what this can only means is that Heaven shortens the life-span ordinarily accorded to a person, so that a felon punished by Heaven dies young or perishes in an extraordinary way. The Hebrew word for this penalty is translated "extirpation."

### Mishnah-tractate Keritot 1:1-2

A. Thirty-six transgression subject to extirpation are in the Torah:

B. He who has sexual relations with (1) his mother, and (2) with his father's wife, and (3) with his daughter-in-law;

C.  he who has sexual relations (4) with a male, and (5) with a beast; and (6) the woman who has sexual relations with a beast;

D.  he who has sexual relations (7) with a woman and with her daughter, and (8) with a married woman;

E.  he who has sexual relations (9) with his sister, and (10) with his father's sister, and (11) with his mother's sister, and (12) with his wife's sister, and (13) with his brother's wife, and (14) with his father's brother's wife, and (15) with a menstruating woman (Lev. 18:6ff.);

F.  (16) he who blasphemes (Num, 15:30), and (17) he who performs an act of blasphemous worship (Num 15:31), and (18) he who gives his seed to Molekh (Lev. 18:21), and (19) one who has a familiar spirit (Lev. 20:6);

G.  (20) he who profanes the Sabbath-day (Ex. 31:14);

H.  and (21) an unclean person who ate a Holy Thing (Lev. 22:3), and (22) he who comes to the sanctuary when unclean (Num. 19:20);

I.  he who eats (23) forbidden fat (Lev. 7:25), and (24) blood (Lev. 17:14), and (25) remnant (Lev. 19:6-8), and (26) refuse (Lev. 19:7-8);

J.  he who (27) slaughters and who (28) offers up [a sacrifice] outside [the Temple court] (Lev. 17:9);

K.  (29) he who eats leaven on Passover (Ex. 12:19); and he who (30) eats and he who (31) works on the Day of Atonement (Lev. 23:29-30);

L.  he who (32) compounds anointing oil [like that made in the Temple (Ex. 30:23-33)], and he who (33) compounds incense [like that made in the Temple], and he who (34) anoints himself with anointing oil (Ex. 30-32);

M.  [he who transgresses the laws of] (35) Passover (Num. 9:13) and (36) circumcision (Gen. 17:14), among the positive commandments.

M. 1:1

A.  For those [transgressions] are people liable, for deliberately doing them, to the punishment of extirpation,

B.  and for accidentally doing them, to the bringing of a sin-offering,

C.  and for not being certain of whether or not one has done them, to a suspensive guilt-offering [Lev. 5:17] –

D.  "except for the one who imparts uncleanness to the sanctuary and its Holy Things,

E.  "because he is subject to bringing a sliding-scale offering (Lev. 5:6-7, 11)," the words of R. Meir.

F.  And sages say, "Also: [except for] the one who blasphemes, as it is said, 'You shall have one law for him that does anything unwittingly' (Num 15:29) – excluding the blasphemer, who does no concrete deed."

M. 1:2

The list announced and carried through at M. 1:1 is then tied to M. 1:2A-C.  But only M. 1:2A is relevant to the foregoing, since M. 1:2B and C refer no to extirpation but to animal-offerings.  Scripture refers, M.

claims, to thirty-six sorts of transgressions subject to the penalty of extirpation. If one deliberately does any of these transgressions, he is liable to extirpation, M. 1:2B-C add that if he does them inadvertently, he brings a sin-offering, and if he is not sure whether or not he has done them, he brings a suspensive guilt-offering, as noted above. I am inclined to see M. 1:1A as somewhat misleading, because of M. 1:2A-C, all of which are served by the same list. But this is a quibble. M. 1:2 lists exception to M. 1:2B-C, and D-E and F. Meir refers to M. 1:1K (22), though he does not explicitly refer to its language. If a person is in doubt about whether or not he has accidentally entered the Temple while in a state of uncleanness, or whether or not he has eaten Holy Things in a state of uncleanness, he brings a sliding-scale offering (Lev. 5:2). It follows that in this case we do not invoke M. 1:2C. And it further follows that what serves Meir is not the superscription, M. 1:1A, but the subscription, M. 1:2A-C. Sages, M. 1:2F, refer to the language of M. 1:1F(16); this one does not do an actual deed but only says things he should not say, so is excluded. But they too refer not to M. 1:1A, 1:2A, but to M. 1:2B, C: such a one does not bring a sin-offering if he is certain he has done the deed or a suspensive guilt-offering if he is not certain.

What about penalties imposed by the Temple? These take the form of sanctions assessed against property. The Temple does not take an active role in imposing such sanctions. Rules apply, and the consequence of the rules in some instances is that the Temple is owed, and collects, property and passes it on to Heaven. The reason I regard the present sanction as distinct from those imposed by the Heavenly and the earthly courts is simple. Legitimate violence against the person or life of a felon, such as the earthly and Heavenly courts exercise, is precipitated by the consideration of a particular case, under appropriate rules, in the earthly court, and, I assume, counterpart procedures involving the individual miscreant in the Heavenly venue as well. But in the case of the penalties administered by the Temple, there is no court action that a particular sinner or felon faces. The rules apply in general and no need to investigate particular cases is suggested in the systemic document. The penalty of loss of property means that one is required *ex opere operato* to present to Heaven, through the Temple, something of value. The wealth to be given up must of course be given the form that the Temple can receive and transmit to Heaven, that is, an appropriate animal or vegetable product. There are no long lists of those subject to this sanction. Rather, we have classifications of sins or crimes to which the sanction applies. These are persons subject to a rite of atonement, rather than a life-threatening penalty, as in the following:

**Mishnah-tractate  Keritot  2:1-2**

A.  [There are] four whose atonement is not complete [until they bring an offering].

B.  And bring [an offering] for [a transgression done] deliberately as for [one done] inadvertently.

C.  These are those whose atonement is not complete [until they bring an offering]:
    (1) The *Zab*, and (2) the *Zabah*, and (3) the woman who has given birth, and (4) the *mesora'*.

D.  R. Eliezer b. Jacob says, "A proselyte is one whose atonement is not complete until the blood will be sprinkled on his behalf."

E.  And the Nazir as to [observing prohibition against] wine, shaving, and uncleanness [has not completed atonement until he has brought his offering].

M. 2:1

A.  These bring [an offering for a transgression done] deliberately as for [one done] inadvertently:

B.  (1) He who has sexual relations with a bondwoman; and (2) a Nazirite who was made unclean;

C.  and (3) for [him who utters a false] oath of testimony, and (4) for [him who utters a false] deposit-oath.

M. 2:2

The lists, M. 2:1A-B, are joined solely because of the common number, four (followed at M. 2:3 by five). B is clear as given. Even though those listed have immersed, they cannot eat Holy Things until they bring their animal in atonement. Eliezer, D, has a fifth item, and E yet another. A proselyte brings a burnt-offering and cannot eat Holy Things before its blood is tossed; the Nazir brings offerings (Num. 6:14), before which time his vow remains in affect. M. 2:2B and C are distinguished in form, in that C's items are expressed as 'L + verb. A Nazir who is made unclean by a corpse brings an offering, Num. 6:9-12. The oath of C3 is a false oath that one does not have a bailment left in his keeping, when in fact he does and admits it thereafter (M. Shabu. 5:1-2). The general rule is that for the inadvertent commission of a prohibited action, one brings a sacrifice, while for the deliberate commission of that same action, one suffers a penalty to life or body.

This brings us to the fourth and final category of sanctions, which are those involved in excommunication, shunning, or merely expressing disapproval. These closely related penalties prove not at all adventitious, even though applications of the sanctions of negative (or positive) attitude and opinion occur in scattered places and are not set forth in any one passage. While we have no catalogue of those penalized by disrepute, we do have sufficient examples to permit us to generalize on where, how, and by whom the sanction of public opinion is imposed. We review concrete instances in which appeal to consensus will allow us to identify the rule that dictates where consensus prevails and what actions are penalized by it. Set side by side, the following two entries yield a single proposition, which is that the classification of sages, distinct from any other political or institutional category, appeals to the sanction of shame or honor, and shunning or public approbation. First comes the positive sanction of sages' approval:

### Mishnah-tractate Shebiit 10:9

A. One who repays a debt cancelled by the Sabbatical year – the sages are pleased with him.

B. One who borrows money from a convert whose children converted with him need not repay the debt to his children . But if the debtor repaid the children the debt owing to their father after the father's death, the sages are pleased with him.

C. All chattels are acquired through drawing them into one's possession. But anyone who stands by his word and does not withdraw from the transaction before the chattels have changed hands – the sages are pleased with him.

M. Shebiit 10:9

Of greater consequence, of course, is the obverse of enjoying sages' approbation, which is suffering their disapproval. The specification of what that disapproval means is not detailed, but clearly this-worldly emblems marked the person who suffered sages' criticism. Excommunication or banning bears more concrete effects. What happens to one who is banned, and on what account is someone subjected to the consensus of the community in such wise as to be banished? The following contains answers that question:

### Mishnah-tractate Middot 2:2

A. All those who enter the Temple mount enter at the right, go around, and leave at the left, except for him to whom something happened, who goes around to the left.

B. "What ails you, that you go around to the left?"...For I am excommunicated."

C. "'May he who dwells in this house put it into their heart that they draw you near again,'" the words of R. Meir.

D. Said to him R. Yosé, "You have treated the matter as if they have transgressed the law on his account. Rather: 'May he who dwells in this house put it into your heart that you listen to the opinion of your fellows, and they draw you nigh again.'"

M. Mid. 2:2

The premise is that banning forms a sanction particular to sages' politics. The excommunication here seems to accord with the one imposed on Aqabiah, spelled out in the following, and therefore forms a detail of the system of sanctions pertinent in the politics of the sages' community in particular.

### Mishnah-tractate Eduyyot 5:5-7

A.   Aqabia b. Mahalalel gave testimony in four matters....
B.   They said to him, "Aqabia, retract the four rulings which you laid down, and we shall make you patriarch of the court of Israel."
C.   He said to them, "It is better for me to be called a fool my whole life but not be deemed a wicked person before the Omnipresent for even one moment, so that people should not say, 'Because he craved after high office, he retracted.'"

M. Ed. 5:6

A.   He would say, "They do not administer bitter water in the case of a proselyte woman or in the case of a freed slave girl."
B.   And sages say, "They do administer the test."
C.   They said to him, "There was the case of Karkemit, a freed slave girl who was in Jerusalem, and Shemaiah and Abtalion administered the bitter water to her."
D.   He said to them, "They administered it to her to make her into an example."
E.   They excommunicated him, and he died while he was subject to the excommunication, so the court stoned his bier....
F.   When he was dying, he said to his son, "My son, retract in the four rulings which I had laid down."
G.   He said to him, "And why do you retract now?"
G.   He said to them, "I heard the rulings in the name of the majority, and they heard them in the name of the majority, so I stood my ground on the tradition which I had heard, and they stood their ground on the tradition that they had heard. But you have heard the matter both in the name of an individual and in the name of the majority. It is better to abandon the opinion of the individual and to hold with the opinion of the majority."
H.   He said to him, 'Father, give instructions concerning me to your colleagues."
I.   He said to him, "I will give no instructions."
J.   He said to him, "Is it possible that you 'have found some fault with me?"

    K.  He said to him, "No, it is your deeds which will bring you near or your deeds which will put you off from the others."

M. Ed. 5:6-7

We see clearly that shame or honor are sanctions subject to the administration of sages, and they apply either where the earthly and Heavenly courts do not exercise jurisdiction or where sages govern their own affairs. References to conformity to the opinion of sages abound, as in the following: "The cow of R. Eleazar b. Azariah would go out with a strap between its horns – not with the approval of the sages" (M. Shab. 5:4J-K). Sages expressed their opinions: "Six rules did the men of Jericho make. For three sages reproved them, and for three they did not reprove them" (M. Pes. 4:8). The assumption is that sages' reproof would make a difference to the Jericho population.

The power of banning within sages' domain finds its counterpart in the crimes or sins for which banning forms the appropriate sanction. They represent breaches in the disciplines of sages' political structures, for example, disobedience, however well founded, of the ruling of the acknowledged authority of sages' institution. Since, as a matter of fact, the systemic document represents that same authority as a head of state and government, banning seems to form a sanction particular to, and distinctively effective within, what we should call the civil service or bureaucracy. The following story provides a striking instance of how banning did it work and in due course allows us access to the political myth that sustained excommunication as a sanction:

**Mishnah-tractate Rosh Hashshanah 2:8-9**

    A.  A picture of the shapes of the moon did Rabban Gamaliel have on a tablet and on the wall of his upper room, which he would show ordinary folk, saying, "Did you see it like this or like that?"

    B.  Two witnesses came and said, "We saw it at dawn [on the morning of the twenty-ninth] in the east and at eve in the west."

    C.  Said R. Yohanan b. Nuri, "They are false witnesses."

    D.  Now when they came to Yabneh, Rabban Gamaliel accepted their testimony [assuming they erred at dawn].

    E.  And furthermore: two came along and said, "We saw it at its proper time, but on the night of the added day it did not appear [ to the court]."

    F.  Then Rabban Gamaliel accepted their testimony.

    G.  Said R. Dosa b. Harkinas, "They are false witnesses.

    H.  "How can they testify that a woman has given birth, when, on the very next day, her stomach is still up there between her teats [for there was no new moon!]?"

I.    Said to him R. Joshua, "I can see your position."

M. 2:8

A.    Said to him Rabban Gamaliel, "I decree that you come to me with you staff and purse on the Day of Atonement which is determined in accord with your reckoning."

B.    R. Aqiba went and found him troubled.

C.    He said to him, "I can provide grounds for showing that everything that Rabban Gamaliel has done is validly done, since it says, *These are the set feasts of the Lord, even holy convocations, which you shall proclaim* (Lev. 23:4). Whether they are in their proper time or not in their proper time, I have no set feasts but these [which you shall proclaim] [vs. M. 2:7D]."

D.    He came along to R. Dosa b. Harkinas.

E.    He [Dosa] said to him, "Now if we're going to take issue with the court of Rabban Gamaliel, we have to take issue with every single court which has come into being from the time of Moses to the present day,

F.    "since it says, *Then went up Moses and Aaron, Nadab and Abihu, and seventy of the elders of Israel* (Ex 24:9).

G.    "Now why have the names fo the elders not been given? To teach that every group of three [elders] who came into being as a court of Israel – lo, they are equivalent to the court of Moses himself."

H.    [Joshua] took his staff with his purse in his hand and went along to Yabneh, to Rabban Gamaliel, on the Day of Atonement which is determined in accord with his [Gamaliel's] reckoning.

I.    Rabban Gamaliel stood up and kissed him on his head and said to him, "Come in peace, my master and my disciple –

J.    "my master in wisdom, and my disciple in accepting my rulings."

M. 2:9

What was at stake in the sanction imposed by the public opinion of sages was the discipline of the community, which meant obedience to the sage. That consideration, and, in Judaism, that alone, warranted ignoring the law in favor of establishing the precedent, and the precedent that validated ignoring the facts was the authority of sages' rule through the patriarch in the present example. Given the stakes, we cannot find surprising Gamaliel's insistence that Joshua violate the holiest day of the year.

It remains to ask, whose opinion matters in the consideration of the sanctions of shame and honor? In light of the stories just now reviewed, we may hardly find surprising that it is not appeal to public opinion at large, which is treated as null when the law intervenes. Only the attitude of sages, which is presumed to be shaped by the law, forms the medium for the sanctions of public opinion as distinct from court action against the person or property of an offended person. That is clear in the following, which shows that it is the opinion of sages forms the consensus that operates, and this is underlined by the rule that follows:

**Mishnah-tractate Peah 4:1**

    A.    Even if ninety-nine poor people say that the householder should distribute the produce and only one poor person says that the poor should take the produce on their own, leaving the householder out of the distribution process],

    B.    they listen to the latter [who said that the poor should take the produce themselves],

    C.    for he has spoken according to the law.

M. Peah 4:1

Accordingly, we cannot confuse mere opinion with the effective opinion of sages, who stand for the law. Any conception that appeal to the sanction of consensus implies a democratic system falls away in stories such as this. Dominion does not flow from popular opinion, and the opinions that do form the consensus are not everyone's.

This is the point at which, in a general way, Scriptures takes up its paramount position in our inquiry. Given the authority of Scripture and the character of the Pentateuch as a design of a holy state, on holy land, made up of holy people, living a holy life, we should not be surprised by silence, on the surface at least, about the reason why. People everywhere acknowledge and confess God's rule and the politics of the Torah, in its written form as the Pentateuch, claiming legitimacy attained through conformity to the law and politics. At some point, and in some way, therefore, our authorship should represent the entire system as the realization of God's dominion over Israel. The following lists the number of law violations that one commits by making a profit, which is to say, collecting interest:

> Those who participate in a loan on interest violate a negative commandment: these are the lender, borrower, guarantor, and witnesses.
>
> Sages say, "Also the scribe."
>
> They violate the negative commandment, "You will not give him your money upon usury" (Lev. 25:37); "You will not take usury from him" (Lev. 25:36); "You shall not be a creditor to him" (Ex. 22:25); "Nor shall you lay upon him usury" (Ex. 22:25); and they violate the negative command, "You shall not put a stumbling block before the blind, but you shall fear your God. I am the Lord" (Lev. 19:14)

M. Baba Mesia 5:11

Accordingly, we appeal to the Torah to justify law-obedience and to impose sanction for disobedience. But where is the myth that sustains obedience? Let me explain this question, which is critical to all that follows. On the basis of the passage just cited, we do not know, for example, what happens to me if I do participate in a loan on interest and so violate various rules of the Torah. More to the point, the generalized appeal to the law of the Torah and the assumed premise that one should obey that law and not violate it – these hardly tell me the morphology of the political myth at hand. They assume a myth that is not set forth, and they conceal those details in which the myth gains its sustaining vitality and power.

The consequence cannot be missed. Knowing that everything is in accord with the Torah and that God wants Israel to keep the laws of the Torah does not tell us the systemically active component of the political myth. The propositions themselves are too general – and also insufficient. That self-evident premise that [1] God revealed the Torah, [2] the political institutions and rules carry out the Torah, and therefore [3] people should conform, hardly sustains a concrete theory of *just* where and how God's authority serves the systemic construction at hand. A mere allegation that, in general, what the political authorities tell people to do is what God wants them to do illuminates not at all. For example, we find references here and there to "the kingdom of Heaven,"[4] and that suggests appeal to God's rule in an everyday framework. So at M. Ber. 2:5, to Gamaliel is attributed the statement, "I cannot heed you to suspend from myself the kingdom of Heaven even for one hour." Now as a matter of fact that is not a political context[5] – there is no threat of legitimate violence, for

---

[4]In line with the Mishnah's usage, I refer to God and God's heavenly court with the euphemism of "Heaven," and the capital H expresses the simple fact that "Heaven" always refers to God and God's court on high. The Mishnah is not clear on whether its authorship thinks God personally intervenes throughout, but there is a well-established belief in divine agents, e.g., angels or messengers, so in speaking of Heaven or Heaven's intervention, we take account of the possibility that God's agents are meant.

[5]I am puzzled by the fact that in the Mishnah "kingdom of Heaven" never occurs in what we should call a political context but always in the setting of personal piety. My sense is that this usage should help illuminate the Gospels' presentation of sayings assigned to Jesus concerning "the kingdom," "my kingdom," "the kingdom of God," and the like. Since the Mishnah presents a highly specific politics, the selection of vocabulary bears systemic weight and meaning (something I have shown in virtually every analytical study I have carried on); these are in context technical usages. But their meaning in their own context awaits the kind of systemic analysis conducted here on the political vocabulary of Judaism, treated systemically and contextually and not just lexicographically.

instance – for the saying has to do with reciting the *shema*, and no political conclusions are drawn from that allegation. Quite to the contrary, Gamaliel, head of the collegium of sages, is not thereby represented as relinquishing power to Heaven, only as expressing his obedience to divine rule even when he does not have to. "The kingdom of Heaven" does not form a political category, even though, as we shall see, in the politics of Judaism, all power flows from God's will and law, expressed in the Torah. In Judaism the manipulation and application of power, allowing the impositions of drastic sanctions in support of the law for instance, invariably flow through institutions, on earth and in Heaven, of a quite concrete and material character. "The kingdom of Heaven" may be within, but violate the law deliberately and wantonly and God will kill you sooner than you should otherwise have had to die. And, as a matter of fact, the Mishnah's framers rarely appeal in the context of politics and the legitimate exercise of violence to "the kingdom of Heaven," which, in this setting, does not form a political institution at all.

Not only so, but, on the basis of the pentateuchal writings, we can hardly construct the *particular* politics, including the mythic component thereof, that operates in this (or any other) Judaism. For, first of all, the Pentateuch does not prepare us to make sense of the institutions that the politics of Judaism for its part designs – government by king and high priest, rather than, as in the Pentateuch, prophet, and, second and concomitantly, the pentateuchal myth to legitimate coercion – rule by God's prophet, governance through explicitly revealed laws that God has dictated – plays no active and systemic role whatsoever in the formulation and presentation of the politics of Judaism. Indeed, among the types of political authority contained within the scriptural repertoire, the one that the Mishnah's philosophers reject is the prophetic and charismatic, and the one that they deem critical is the disciple of the sage, carefully nurtured through learning of rules, not through cultivation of gifts of the spirit. The authority of sages in the politics of Judaism does not derive from charisma, e.g., revelation by God to the sage who makes a ruling in a given case, or even general access to God for the sage. The myth we shall presently explore in no way falls into the classification of a charismatic myth of politics.

True, everybody knows and believes that God has dictated the Torah to Moses. But the Mishnah's framers do not then satisfy themselves with a paraphrase of what God has said to Moses in the Torah. The following allows us to see how matters might have been – but never were – phrased:

**M. Rosh Hashshanah 3:8**

A. *Now it happened that when Moses held up his hand, Israel provided, and when he let his hand fall, Amalek prevailed* (Ex.

B. Now do Moses's hands make war or stop it?

C. But the purpose is to say this to you:

D. So long as the Israelites would set their eyes upward and submit their hears to their Father in Heaven, they would grow stronger. And if not, they fell.

E. In like wise, you may say the following:

F. *Make yourself a fiery serpent and set it on a standard, and it shall come to pass that every one who is bitten, when he sees it, shall live* (Num. 21:8).

G. Now does that serpent [on the standard] kill or give life? [Obviously not.]

H. But: So long as the Israelites would set their eyes upward and submit to their Father in Heaven, they would be healed. And if not, they would pine away.

M. Rosh Hashshanah 3:8

The silence now becomes eloquent. We look in vain in the pages of our systemic writing for a *single* example in which authorities ask people to raise their eyes on high and so to obey what said authorities command. Such a political myth however may be implicit, But when made explicit and systemically active, not left in its inert condition, the myth we seek by definition precipitates concrete decision-making processes, inclusive of obedience to those decisions once made. And we shall know the reason why.

More to the point, we must ask the evidence before us this question: is God's direct intervention a preferred or even available sanction? Yes and no, but mostly no. For in our system what is important is that the myth of God's intervention on an ad hoc and episodic basis in the life of the community hardly serves to explain obedience to the law in the here and now. What sort of evidence would indicate that God intervenes in such wise as to explain the obedience to the law on an everyday basis? Invoking God's immediate presence, a word said, a miracle performed, would suffice. But in the entirety of the more than five hundred chapters of the Mishnah, no one ever prays to have God supply a decision in a particular case. More to the point, no judge appeals to God to put to death a convicted felon. If the judge wants the felon killed, he kills him. When God intervenes, it is on the jurisdiction assigned to God, not the court. And then the penalty is a different one from execution just now. It follows that an undifferentiated myth explaining the working of undifferentiated power by appeal to God's will, while relevant, is not exact and does not explain this system in its rich detail. The modes of differentiation among the available mythic materials now require attention. These must, we now realize, both specify and also generalize. That is to say, while the court orders and carries out the execution, the politics works in such a way that all three political institutions, God and the court and the Temple, the three agencies with the power to bestow or take away life and property and to inflict physical pain and suffering, work together in a single continuum and in important ways so cooperate as to deal with the same crimes or sins.

So we work our way through sanctions to recover the mythic premises thereof, beginning with God's place in the execution of legitimate violence and its institutionalization. The repertoire of sanctions encompasses God's direct intervention. True, that is hardly a preferred alternative or a common one. But it is commonplace in the case of violating oaths, which are held to be issues between the person who invokes God's name and God. Not only so, but when faced with an insufficiency of valid evidence under strict rules of testimony, the earthly court cannot penalize serious crime, the Heavenly court can and does do so. Hence, God serves to justify the politics and account for its origin. While God is never asked to join in making specific decisions and effecting policy in the everyday politics of the state, still, deliberate violation of certain rules provokes God's or the Heavenly court's direct intervention. Obedience to the law clearly represents submission to God in Heaven. Accordingly, forms of Heavenly coercion through other than prayer, such as we shall presently survey, suggests a complex mythic situation, with more subtle nuance than the claim that, overall, God rules, would suggest to us. A politics of rules and regulations cannot admit God's anecdotal participation, and this system did not do so. God joined in the system in a regular and routine way, and the rules took for granted God's part in the politics of Judaism.

Precisely how does the intervention of God into the system come to concrete expression? Understandably, origin of rules at Sinai forms one court of appeal, as in the story about R. Simeon of Mispah, who sowed his field with two types of wheat. The issue is involved in this action is as follows: does that act violate the law against sowing mixed seeds in a single patch? The matter came before Rabban Gamaliel. The passage goes on, with the important language in italics:

C. They went up to the Chamber of Hewn Stone and asked about the law regarding sowing two types of wheat in one field.

D. Said Nahum the Scribe, "I have received the following ruling from R. Miasha, who received it from his father, who received it from the

pairs, who received it from the prophets, who received the law given
to Moses on Sinai, regarding one who sows his field with two types of
wheat...."

M. Peah 2:6

Here is clear evidence that the legitimacy of the law is held to derive
from the chain of tradition from Sinai.  But that general principle was
invoked only rarely, and then – more to the point – for minor details.[6]
Nothing important requires so drastic a claim to be made explicit.  That
is to say, it is a mere commonplace that the system appeals to Sinai.
But this is not a politics of revelation.

For a politics of revelation consistently and immediately appeals
to the myth that God works in the here and now, all the time, in
concrete cases.  That appeal is not common in the Mishnah's statement
of its system, and, consequently, that appeal to the myth of revelation
does not bear important political tasks and is not implicit here.  Indeed
I do not think it was present at all, except where Scripture made it so,
e.g., with the ordeal inflicted on the wife accused of adultery.  Why
the persistent interest in legitimation other than through the
revelation of the Torah for the immediate case?  The answer to that
question draws upon the traits of philosophers, interested in the
prevailing rule governing all cases and the explanation for the
exceptions, rather than those of historian-prophets, engaged by the
exceptional case, represented then as paradigmatic.[7]  Our philosophers
appeal to a myth to explain what is routine and orderly, and what
they wish to explain is what is ordinary and everyday: institutions
and rules, not cases and ad hoc decisions yielding no rule at all.

The traits of the politics of Judaism then emerge in the silences as
much as in the acts of speech: in the characteristics of the myth, as
much as in the contents thereof.  The politics of Judaism appeals to not a
charismatic but a routine myth, in which is explained the orderly life
of institutions and an administration, and by which are validated the
rules and the workings of a political structure and system.  True, as I
have repeatedly emphasized, all of them are deemed to have been
founded on revelation.  But what kind of revelation and when did its
unsettling impact take place?  The answer derives from the fact that
none of the political institutions appealed in the here and the now to
God's irregular ("miraculous") intervention.   Treatment of the

---

[6]Another mode of establishing the law is sages' debate; but there too the form
or convention requires the confirmation that sages have in the end reached a
decision that, in accord with other sources, in fact has come from Sinai.
[7]A fine distinction, perhaps, but a critical one, and the distinction between
charisma and routine is not a fine one at all.

rebellious elder and the false prophet as we shall see tells us quite the opposite. The political institutions not only did not invoke miraculous intervention to account for the imposition of sanctions, they would not and did not tolerate the claim that such could take place.

It is the regularity and order of God's participation in the politics that the character of the myth of the politics of Judaism maintains we have to understand and account for. Mere allegations in general that the law originates with God's revelation to Moses at Sinai do not serve to identify the middle-range myth that accounts for the structure and the system. If God is not sitting at the shoulder of the judge and telling the judge what to do (as the writers of Exodus 21ff. seem to suppose), then what legitimacy attaches to the judge's decision to give Mr. Smith's field over, or back, to Mr. Jones? And why (within the imaginary state at hand) should people support, sustain, and submit to authority? Sages' abstract language contains no answers to these questions. And yet sages' system presupposes routine and everyday obedience to power, not merely the utilization of legitimate violence to secure conformity. That is partly because the systemic statement to begin with tells very few stories. Matters that the pentateuchal writers expressed through narrating a very specific story about how God said thus and so to Moses in this particular case, rewarding the ones who obeyed and punishing those who did not, in the Mishnah come to expression in language of an allusive and philosophical, generalizing character.

Once more we discern the character of the myth, even before determining its contents. The document's authorship to begin with found little use for narrative and the myth that narrative sets forth, preferring, instead the language of philosophy and accessible proposition. By this point we scarcely expect that that sort of writing is apt to spell out a myth, even though a myth infused the system. But we certainly can identify the components of the philosophical and theological explanation of the state that can have taken mythic form. Even here, to be sure, the evidence proves sparse. But it is, at least, articulated and explicit, in the following, which deals with oaths:

**M. Shabuot 3:6**

    A. [If] someone took an oath to nullify a commandment but he did not nullify it, he is exempt [from penalty for violating the oath].

    B. [And if he took an oath to] carry out [a commandment] and did not carry it out, he is exempt.

    C. It is logical that he should be liable, in accord with the words of R. Judah b. Betera.

D.   Said R. Judah b. Betera, "Now if concerning matters of free choice, about which one has not been subjected to an oath at Mount Sinai, lo, one is liable on that account [if he swore to do but did not do] —

E.   "matters concerning a religious duty, about which one has been subjected to an oath at Mount Sinai – is it not logical that one should be liable on its account?"

F.   They said to him, "No. If you have stated that rule in regard to an oath concerning a matter of free choice, in which *no* is treated as no different from *yes*, will you say the same concerning an oath involving a religious duty, in which a *no* is assuredly not treated as no different from a *yes!*

G.   "For if one has taken an oath to nullify [a religious duty] but did not nullify the religious duty, he is exempt."

To explain what is at stake for our inquiry, I have to specify the following facts: if one took an oath either not to keep or to keep a religious commandment, he is not liable should he fail to keep the oath. Why not? Because the oath is null to begin with. One cannot make a choice as to whether or not one will carry out one's religious duties, imposed as they are by God's commandment. Accordingly, an oath by God's name to do what God has forbidden or not to do what God has required is null.

The mythic fundament is then self-evident: individual Israelites are subject to God's rules. Then, it must follow, the state, the instrument for the exercise of power, cannot be framed other than in accord with God's rules; it further follows that the politics originates in Heaven. Judah b. Betera does not differ in principle. But he thinks that, logically, the rule for B should be that one is liable. His reasoning, D-E, is that if one swears to do something not involving a religious duty and does not do it, he is liable. He already is subject to the religious duties because of the oath imposed on the Israelites at Mount Sinai. It follows that if he vows to do such a duty and does not do so, all the more reason that he should be liable for not doing it!

Sages then have to distinguish religious duties from optional matters. Sages' reply is that if one swears *to do evil* or swears *to do good* (Lev. 5:4), he is liable for not doing what he swears to do. But Scripture has not treated religious duties in the same way. If one swears to do evil – namely, to nullify a commandment – he is exempt. It will then follow that if one swears to do good – namely, to keep a commandment – he also will be exempt if he does not do it. If there is no penalty for not fulfilling the negative oath, there is none for not carrying out the positive one either. This entire construction serves as an introduction to M.'s treatment of diverse kinds of oaths. The first is the rash oath, which is the one we have before us: *Or if any one utters with his lips a rash oath to do evil or to do good, any sort of rash oath that men swear...*(Lev. 5:4). The upshot of the passage is in the subterranean consensus that coercive action rests upon the (written) Torah's authority, and, it follows, Israel, the people, is ruled by a government that legitimates itself by appeal to that Torah. In that way, as we noted at the outset, Scripture supplies the political myth. But we also observe that, when the myth is invoked, it is by inference and allusion, rather than by a fully exposed statement of what is at stake and why.

Now to the details of the myth. First, of course, in the mythic structure comes God, who commands and creates, laying out what humanity is to do, exercising the power to form the social world in which humanity is to obey. God then takes care of God's[8] particular concerns, and these focus upon *deliberate* violation of God's wishes. If a sin or crime is inadvertent, the penalties are of one order, if deliberate, of a different order. The most serious infraction of the law of the Torah is identified not by what is done but by the attitude of the sinner or criminal.[9] If one has deliberately violated God's rule, then God intervenes. If the violation is inadvertent, then the Temple imposes the sanction. And the difference is considerable. In the former case, God through the Heavenly court ends the felon's or sinner's life. Then a person who defies the laws as these concern one's sexual conduct, attitude toward God, relationships within the family, will be penalized either (if necessary) by God or (if possible) by the earthly court. That means that the earthly court exercises God's power, and the myth of the system as a whole, so far as the earthly court forms the principal institutional form of the system, emerges not merely in a generality but in all its specificity. These particular judges, here and now, stand for God and exercise the power of God. In the latter case, the Temple takes over jurisdiction; a particular offering is called for, as the book of Leviticus specifies. But there is no need for God or the earthly court in God's name to take a position.

We may divide the sanctions just as the authorship of the Mishnah did, therefore, by simply reviewing the range of penalties for law-infraction as they occur. These penalties fall into four classifications: what Heaven does, what political institutions do, what religious institutions do, and what is left to the coercion of public opinion, that

---

[8]I cannot refer to "God" as "he" or as "she," hence the recurrent circumlocution, which is, admittedly, not ideal.

[9]The distinction between secular felony and religion sin obviously bears no meaning in the system, useful as it is to us. I generally will speak of "felon or sinner," so as not to take a position on a matter unimportant in my inquiry.

is, consensus, with special attention to the definition of that "public" that has effective opinion to begin with. That final realm of power, conferring or withholding approval, proves constricted and, in this context, not very consequential.

Let us begin with the familiar: sanctions exercised by the earthly court and its activities, fully described in Mishnah-tractates Sanhedrin and Makkot. We shall now undertake a protracted review of the representation of the imposition of sanctions by successive authorities, the earthly court, the Temple, the heavenly court, the sages. This review allows us to identify the actors in the system of politics: those with power to impose sanctions, the sanctions they can inflict. Only in that way will the initial statement of Judaism, in its own odd idiom, be permitted to make its points in the way its authorship has chosen. When we take up the myth to which that statement implicitly appeals, we shall have a clear notion of the character of the evidence, in rich detail, on which our judgment of the mythic substrate of the system has been composed.[10]

The most impressive mode of legitimate violence is killing; it certainly does focus our attention. The earthly court may kill a sinner or felon, and that is not murder but justice. The priority accorded to the earthly court derives from the character of the power entrusted to that court. It has full power to dispose of the property and life of all subject to its authority. In the context imagined by Judaism, that means all residents of territory under the control of the state. Imposing the death penalty is described in the following way:

**Mishnah-tractate Sanhedrin 7:1-3**

> A.  Four modes of execution were given over to the court [in order of severity]:
> B.  (1) stoning, (2) burning, (3) decapitation, and (4) strangulation.
> C.  R Simeon says, "(2) Burning, (1) stoning, (4) strangulation, and (3) decapitation."

M. 7:1

---

[10]All of these many details given above are necessary to sustain the judgment I shall propose at the end, when I show how the power exercised by the several foci of politics – Heavenly, earthly, and intermediary – intersects, and how in important ways each focus of power exercises responsibility for its own jurisdiction as well: Heaven, earth, the space between. Then we shall easily reconstruct the political myth, not as a set of generalities, but as a statement, through inarticulate detail, of a few overriding propositions. The survey to follow does lead to a single important point about the myth, even though, in the interim, the reader may wonder where it is all heading.

The passage leaves no doubt that the court could put people to death. At stake in the dispute is the severity of suffering imposed by each mode of execution. Simeon's order, C, differs from that of B, in the degradation and suffering inflicted on the felon. The manner of executing the convicted felon is described in detail, this being an account of a practical order indeed. The forms of legitimate violence are four, that is to say, the modes of execution. The sources on these are set forth in the appendix. In the account, the following is of special interest, with the key words in italics:

A. The religious requirement of decapitation [is carried out as follows]:
B. They would cut off his head with a sword,
C. just as the government does.
D. *R Judah says, "This is disgusting.*
E. "But they put the head on a block and chop it off with an ax."
F. *They said to him, "There is no form of death more disgusting than this one."*
G. The religious requirement of strangulation [is carried out as follows:]
H. They would bury him in manure up to his armpits, and put a towel of hard material inside one of soft material, and wrap it around his neck.
I. This [witness] pulls it to him from one side, and that witness pulls it to him at the other side, until he perishes.

M. 7:3

Judah's intervention leaves no doubt that in carrying out the law ("way of life") a world view was meant to come to realization. In the language he uses is implicit the conviction that the felon remained a human being, in God's image, and hence, in the theoretical discussions at hand, at stake was how to put someone to death in a manner appropriate to his or her standing after the likeness of God. It must follow that the court that puts the felon to death does so in a manner wholly in conformity to God's will, and the political myth of a dominion belonging to God and carrying out God's plan and program certainly stands behind the materials at hand.

But that observation still leaves us struggling with a mere commonplace. For on the strength of knowing that God stands behind the politics and that the consideration that human beings are in God's image and after God's likeness applies even in inflicting the death penalty, we cannot identify the diverse media by which power is carried out. More to the point, we hardly distinguish one media of power from another, such as, I maintain, we must do if we are to gain access to the myth that sustains what we shall soon see is the fully-differentiated political structure before us. For that purpose, the reader may now wish to review in the appendix the catalogue of those who are put to death by the earthly court through the four modes of execution introduced just now. We do well at this turning point to remember the theoretical basis for this entire inquiry. A politics is a theory of the on-going exercise of the power of coercion, including legitimate violence. Weber defines a state, we remember, as a political association with access to the use of physical force:

> ...a human community that (successfully) claims the monopoly of the legitimate use of physical force within a given territory.[11]

A political question, then, means "that interests in the distribution, maintenance, or transfer of power are decisive for answering the questions and determining the decision." And, as I have made the center of my argument, it is the fact that sanctions form the naked exercise of raw power – hence will require the protection and disguise of a heavy cloak of myth.

How to proceed? It is, as is clear, by close attention to the facts of power and by sorting out the implications of those facts. A protracted journey through details of the law of sanctions leads us to classify the sanctions and the sins or crimes to which they apply. What precisely do I think requires classification? It is to see who does what to whom, and, on the basis of the consequent perception, to propose an explanation for that composition. For from these sanctions of state, that is, legitimate exercise of coercion, including violence, we may work our way back to the reasons adduced for the legitimacy of the exercise of coercion, which is to say, the political myth. The reason is that such a classification will permit us to see how in detail the foci of power are supposed to intersect or to relate: autonomous powers, connected and related ones, or utterly continuous ones, joining Heaven to earth, for instance, in the person of this institutional representative or that one. What we shall see is a system that treats Heaven, earth, and the intermediating institution, the Temple, as interrelated, thus, connected, but that insists, in vast detail, upon the distinct responsibilities and jurisdiction accorded to each. Once we have perceived that fundamental fact, we may compose for ourselves the myth, or, at least, the point and propositions of the myth, that accounted for the political structures of Judaism and persuaded people to obey or conform even when there was no immediate threat of penalty.

A survey of [1] types of sanctions, [2] the classifications of crimes or sins to which they apply, and [3] who imposes them, now yields these results. First come the death penalty on earth and extirpation in Heaven:

---

[11]Pp. 77, 78.

| HEAVEN | EARTH | TEMPLE | COMMUNITY |
|---|---|---|---|
| *EXTIRPATION* | *DEATH PENALTY* | *DEATH PENALTY* | |

*for deliberate actions*

| | | |
|---|---|---|
| *sexual crimes:* | *sexual crimes:* | |
| incest | in improper relationships: | |
| violating sex taboos (bestiality, homosexuality) | incest | |
| *religious crimes against God:* | *religious crimes against God:* | |
| blasphemy | blasphemy | |
| idolatry | idolatry | |
| magic | magic | |
| sorcery profaning Sabbath | sorcery profaning Sabbath | |
| | *religious sins against family:* | |
| | cursing parents | |
| | *social crimes:* | |
| | murder | |
| | communal apostasy | |
| | kidnapping | |
| | *social sins:* | |
| | public defiance of the court | |
| | false prophecy | |
| *religious sins, deliberately committed, against God:* | | |
| unclean person who ate a Holy Thing | | |
| uncleanness in sanctuary | | |
| violating food taboos | | |

making offering
outside of Temple

violating taboos
of holy seasons

replicating Temple
incense or oil outside

Next we deal with court-inflicted sanctions carried out against property or person (e.g., fines against property, flogging or other social or physical violence short of death of the felon or sinner):

| HEAVEN | EARTH | TEMPLE | COMMUNITY |
|---|---|---|---|
| | *flogging* | *obligatory* | *shunning* |
| | *exile* | *offering* | *or approbation* |
| | | *and/or flogging* | |
| | | *for inadvertent* | |
| | | *action* | |
| | manslaughter | uncleanness | repay moral |
| | | | obligation |
| | incest | eating Temple | (debt |
| | | food in | cancelled |
| | violation of | violation | by sabbatical |
| | menstrual taboo | of the law | year) |
| | marriage in | replicating | stubbornly |
| | violation | Temple oil, | rejecting |
| | of caste rules | incense outside | majority view |
| | violating food | violating | opposing |
| | taboos | Temple food | majority will |
| | | taboos | |
| | removing dam | | opposing |
| | with offspring | violating | patriarch |
| | | taboos | |
| | violating | of holy days | obedience to |
| | negative | (Passover) | majority |
| | commandments | | or patriarch |
| | | atonement | |
| | | uncleanness | |
| | | (Zab, mesora, etc.) | |
| | | Nazirite | |
| | | sex with bondwoman | |
| | | unclean Nazirite | |
| | | false oath of testimony | |
| | | false oath of deposit | |

The operative distinction between the inflicting of a flogging and the requirement of a sacrifice (Temple sanctions against person or property) and the sanction of extirpation (Heavenly death penalty) is made explicit as follows: "For those [transgressions] are people liable, for deliberately doing them, to the punishment of extirpation, and for accidentally doing them, to the bringing of a sin-offering, and for not being certain of whether or not one has done them, to a suspensive guilt-offering." That distinction is suspended in a few instances, as indicated at M. Ker. 2:1-2.

This summary yields a simple and clear fact, and on the basis of that simple fact we may now reconstruct the entire political myth on which the politics of Judaism rested. Let me state the fact with appropriate emphasis: *some of the same crimes or sins for which the Heavenly court imposes the penalty of extirpation are those that, under appropriate circumstances (e. g., sufficient evidence admissible in court) the earthly court imposes the death penalty.* What follows is that the Heavenly court and the earthly court impose precisely the same sanctions for the same crimes or sins. The earthly court therefore forms down here the exact replica and counterpart, within a single system of power, of the Heavenly court up there. This no longer looms as an empty generalization; it is a concrete and systemically active and indicative detail, and the system speaks through its details.

But that is not the entire story. There is a second fact, equally indicative in our recovery of the substrate of myth. We note that there are crimes for which the earthly court imposes penalties, but for which the Heavenly court does not, as well as the opposite. The earthly and Heavenly courts share jurisdiction over sexual crimes and over what I classify as serious religious crimes against God. The Heavenly court penalizes with its form of the death penalty religious sins against God, in which instances a person deliberately violates the taboos of sanctification.

And that fact calls our attention to a third partner in the distribution and application of power, which is the Temple and its system of sanctions for precisely the same acts subject to the jurisdiction of the Heavenly and earthly courts. The counterpart on earth is now not the earthly court but the Temple, which automatically receives from the person who inadvertently violates these same taboos of sanctification the appropriate offering. The earthly court, for its part, penalizes social crimes against the community that the Heavenly court, on the one side, and the Temple rites, on the other, do not take into account at all. These are murder, apostasy, kidnapping, public defiance of the court, and false prophecy. The earthly court further imposes sanctions on matters of particular concern to the Heavenly court, with special reference to taboos of sanctification (e.g., negative commandments). These three institutions, therefore, exercise concrete and material power, utilizing legitimate violence to kill someone, exacting penalties against property, and inflicting pain. The sages' modes of power, by contrast, stand quite apart, apply mainly to their own circle, and work through the intangible, though no less effective, means of inflicting shame or paying honor.

The facts we have in hand draw us back to the analysis of the differentiation of applied and practical power, and that differentiation is what the systemic myth will have, in the nature of the facts, to account for. Power flows through three distinct but intersecting dominions, each with its own concern, all sharing some interests in common. The Heavenly court attends to deliberate defiance of Heaven, the Temple to inadvertent defiance of Heaven. The earthly court attends to matters subject to its jurisdiction, by reason of sufficient evidence, proper witnesses, and the like, and these same matters will come under Heavenly jurisdiction when the earthly court finds itself unable to act. Accordingly, we have a tripartite system of sanctions: Heaven cooperating with the Temple in some matters, with the court in others, and, as noted, each bearing its own distinct media of enforcing the law as well. What then can we say concerning the systemic myth of politics? The forms of power and the modes of mediating legitimate violence draw our attention to a single political myth, one that we first confronted, if merely as a generality and commonplace to be sure, at the very outset.

It is the myth of God's authority's infusing the institutions of Heaven and earth alike, an authority diffused among three principle foci or circles of power, Heaven's court, the earthly court, and the Temple in-between. Each focus of power has its own jurisdiction and responsibility, Heaven above, earth beneath, the Temple in the position of mediation, transmitting as it does from earth to Heaven the penalties handed over as required. And all media of power in the matter of sanctions intersect at some points as well: a tripartite politics, a single myth drawing each component into relationship with a single source and origin of power: God's law set forth in the Torah. But the myth has not performed its task until it answers not only the question of why, but also the question of how. Specifically, the details of myth must address questions of the details of power. Who then tells whom to do what? And how are the relationships of dominion and dominance to compliance and obedience made permanent through myth? We did not require this sustained survey to ascertain that God through the Torah has set forth laws and concerns. That generality now may be made quite specific. For it is where power is differentiated and parceled out that we see the workings of the political myth. So we ask, how do we know who tells whom to do, or suffer, what sanction or penalty? It is the power of myth to differentiate (and, as a matter of fact, to hierarchize, a point that will become important only at the end), that defines the generative question. And the myth answers that question of hierarchization in particular. The key lies in the criterion by which each mode of power, earthly, mediating, and Heavenly, identifies the cases over which it exercises jurisdiction. The criterion lies in the attitude of the human being who has done what he or she should not: deliberate, unintentional.

I state the upshot with heavy emphasis: *the point of differentiation within the political structures, supernatural and natural alike, lies in the attitude and intention of a human being.* We differentiate among the application of power by reference to the attitude of the person who comes into relationship with that power. A person who deliberately comes into conflict with the system, rejecting the authority claimed by the powers that be, does so deliberately or inadvertently. The myth accounts in the end for the following hierarchization of action and penalty, infraction and sanction: [1] If the deed is deliberate, then one set of institutions exercises jurisdiction and utilizes supernatural power. [2] If the deed is inadvertent, another institution exercises jurisdiction and utilizes the power made available by that same supernatural being.

A sinner or criminal who has deliberately violated the law has by his or her action challenged the politics of Judaism and God or God's surrogate, extirpation by the court on high, death or other appropriate penalty by the court on earth, imposes sanctions. A sinner or criminal who has inadvertently violated the law is penalized by the imposition of Temple sanctions, losing valued goods as a result of the inadvertent violation of the law. People obey because God wants them to and has told them what to do, and when they do not obey, a differentiated political structure appeals to that single hierarchizing myth. The components of the myth are two: first, God's will, expressed in the law of the Torah, second, the human being's will, carried out in obedience to the law of the Torah or in defiance of that law.

Have we come so far and not yet told the story that the myth contains? I have now to explain and spell out the story that conveys the myth of politics in Judaism. It is not in the Mishnah at all. I find the mythic foundation in Scripture, which accounts for the uses and differentiation of power that the Mishnah's system portrays. Why do I now appeal to Scripture? Because, as we realize, the political myth of Judaism has to explain the differentiation of sins or crimes, with their associated penalties or punishments and so sanctions of power.

And I have to find a story of how the power of God conflicts with the power of humanity in such wise as to invoke the penalties and sanctions in the differentiated modes we have before us. Where do I find such a story of the conflict of wills, God's and humanity's? The story of power, differentiated by the will of the human being in communion or conflict with the word of the commanding God, comes to us from the Garden of Eden. We cannot too often encounter the astonishing words that follow:

> The Lord God took the man and placed him in the garden of Eden...and the Lord God commanded the man, saying, "Of every tree of the garden you are free to eat; but as for the tree of knowledge of good and bad, you must not eat of it; for as soon as you eat of it, you shall die."

> When the woman saw that the tree was good for eating and a delight to the eyes, and that the tree was desirable as a source of wisdom, she took of its fruit and ate; she also gave some to her husband, and he ate...

> The Lord God called out to the man and said to him, "Where are you?"

> He replied, "I heard the sound of You in the garden, and I was afraid, because I was naked, so I hid."

> Then He asked, "Who told you that you were naked? Did you eat of the tree from which I had forbidden you to eat?"

> And the Lord God said to the woman, "What is this you have done!"

> So the Lord God banished him from the garden of Eden...

Now a reprise of the exchange between God, Adam, and Eve, tells us that at stake was responsibility: who has violated the law, but who bears responsibility for deliberately violating the law:

> "The woman You put at my side – she gave me of the tree, and I ate."

> "The serpent duped me, and I ate."

> Then the Lord God said to the serpent, "because you did this...."

The ultimate responsibility lies with the one who acted deliberately, not under constraint or on account of deception. Then the sanction applies most severely to the one who by intention and an act of will have violated God's intention and will. The distinction that is critical to the entire systemic differentiation comes to mythic expression in the story of the fall from grace.[12]

---

[12]That is not to suggest that that distinction is important only in the myth of Eden. Quite to the contrary, the authorship of the laws of Leviticus and Deuteronomy repeatedly appeals to that same distinction. But our interest is

The political myth of Judaism now emerges in all of its tedious detail as a reprise, in now-consequential and necessary, stunning detail, of the story of God's commandment, humanity's disobedience, God's sanction for the sin or crime, and humanity's atonement and reconciliation. The Mishnah omits all explicit reference to the myth that explains power and sanctions but invokes in its rich corpus of details the absolute given of the story of the distinction between what is deliberate and what is mitigated by an attitude that is not culpable, a distinction first set forth in the tragedy of Adam and Eve. Then the Mishnah's is a politics of life after Eden and outside of Eden.

The upshot of the matter is that the political myth of Judaism sets forth the constraints of freedom, the human will brought to full and unfettered expression, imposed by the constraints of revelation, God's will made known. Since it is the freedom of humanity to make decisions and frame intentions that forms the point of differentiation among the political media of power, we are required, in my view, to return to the paradigmatic exercise of that same freedom, which is in Eden, when Adam and Eve exercise their own will and defy God. Since the operative criterion in the differentiation of sanction, that is, the exercise of legitimate violence by Heaven or by earth or by the Temple, is the human attitude and intention in carrying out a culpable action, we must recognize, the politics before us rehearses the myth of Adam and Eve in Eden. For it finds its dynamic in the correspondence between God's will and humanity's freedom to act in whatever way it chooses, but also, its freely incurring the risk of penalty or sanction for the wrong exercise of freedom.

The principal point of differentiation shared by the political myth before us and the myth of the fall from Eden is on the surface. In Eden God cares what Adam and Eve do. But the attitude that shaped their deed is taken into account. Now again, in the differentiations important in representing the sanctions that embody power in politics, at stake is what Adam and Eve intend, propose, plan, for that is the point at which the politics intervenes, making its points of differentiation between and among its sanctions and the authorities that impose those penalties. That power to explain difference, which

---

in myth, and I find in the myth of Eden the explanation for the point of differentiation that the political myth of Judaism invokes at every point. So, as I have said, the sanctions lead to the systemic question that requires mythic response, and once we know the question, we can turn to Scripture for the myth (as much as we can find in Scripture ample expansion, in law, of that same myth).

is to say, the capacity to represent and account for hierarchy, we are required, in my opinion, to turn to the story of the fall of Adam and Eve from Eden. The reason is that the political myth derives from that same myth of origins its points of differentiation and explains by reference to the principal components of that myth – God's will and power, humanity's – the dynamics of the political system at hand. God commands, but humanity does what it then chooses, and in the interplay of those two protean forces, each power in its own right, the sanctions and penalties of the system apply.

Power comes from two conflicting forces: the commanding will of God, the free will of the human being. Power expressed in immediate sanctions is mediated, so too, through these same forces: Heaven above, human beings below, with the Temple mediating between the two. Power works its way in the interplay between what God has set forth in the law of the Torah and what human beings do, whether intentionally, whether inadvertently, whether obediently, whether defiantly. That is why the politics of Judaism is a politics of Eden. But, as we shall now see, we listen in vain in the creation myth of Genesis for echoes resounding from the institutions such as those the politics of Judaism actually invents. But the points of differentiation of one political institution from another will serve constantly to remind us of what, in the end, serves to distinguish this from that, to set forth not a generalized claim that God rules through whoever is around with a sword (or the right, that is, Roman sponsorship).

The careful descriptions of, and distinctions among, institutions, through a vastly and richly nuanced account of concrete and enduring institutions, will once more emphasize the main point. It is how people know that power lies here, not there, is exercised by this bureau, not that, that we find our way back to the myth of differentiation and hierarchization. In what is to follow, we shall see how effectively the politics of Judaism distinguishes one institution from another, just as, in our survey of sanctions, we recognize the points of intersection and of separation. At every point we shall therefore be reminded of the most formidable source of power, short of God, in all. That always is the will of the human being. And he and she are never mentioned as paramount actors, even though, in this politics, humanity is what is at issue. Only at the end, in Chapter Twelve, shall we fully grasp what is at stake.

# 8

# Sources of the Politics of Judaism

A Repertoire Supplementing *The Politics of Judaism*

When we consider the local government and administration, we should take note of the one institution that is identified. It is a class of persons who serve, in the community, to form the counterpart to the priesthood in the Temple. That class of persons, called the *maamad* or delegation, exercises no political power at all. It is brought into being when, in the Temple, a priestly watch from a given district or village came up to Jerusalem. At home, the delegation of the caste of Israelites would undertake rites as the local counterpart for what the local delegation in the Temple was even then supposed to do.

### Mishnah-tractate Taanit 4:1-2

A. On three occasions in the year priests raise up their hands [in the priestly benediction] four times a day:

B. (1) at the dawn prayer, (2) the additional prayer, (3) the afternoon prayer, and (4) the closing of the gates:

C. on the occasion of fasts, on the occasions of [prayers of members of the] delegation [*ma'amad*] and on the Day of Atonement.

M. 4:1

A. Now what is the delegation [*ma'amad*]?

B. Since it is said, *Command the children of Israel and say to them, My obligation, my food [for my offerings made of fire, of a sweet savor to me, shall you observe to offer me in their due season]* (Num. 28:2) —

C. now how can a person's offering be made, while he is not standing by its side?

D. The early prophets made the rule of twenty-four watches, and for each watch there was a delegation [*ma'amad*] in Jerusalem, made up or priests, Levites, and Israelites.

E. When the time for a watch came to go up to Jerusalem, its priests and Levites go up with it to Jerusalem.

189

F.   And Israelites who belong to that watch gather together in their towns and study the story of the works of creation.

M. 4:2

We hardly find here a political institution; no power is imputed to the delegation within the local setting.   What we see are the correspondences between one institution (if we can call it that) and another, between the village and the Temple.   This is scarcely a political portrait in any terms, even though the Temple collects and disposes of what are public funds and represents the intrusion, in the political economy, of a distributive economics that rests upon political, rather than free-market, disposition of scarce resources.[1]

## Mishnah-tractate Ketubot 13:1-9

A    Two judges of civil law were in Jerusalem.   Admon and Hanan b. Abishalom.

B.   Hanan lays down two rulings.

C.   Admon lays down seven.

I

D.   He who went overseas, and his wife [left at home] claims maintenance –

E.   Hanan says, "Let her take an oath at the end, but let her not take and oath at the outset [that is, she takes an oath when she claims her marriage contract after her husband's death, or after he returns, that she has not held back any property of her husband]."

F.   Sons of high priests disputed with him and ruled, "Let her take an oath at the outset and at the end."

G.   Ruled R. Dosa b. Harkinas in accord with their opinion.

H.   Said R. Yohanan b. Zakkai, "Well did Hanan rule.   She should take an oath only at the end."

M. Ket. 13:1

II

A    He who went overseas, and someone went and supported his wife –

B.   Hanan says, "He [who did so] has lost his money."

C.   Sons of high priests disputed with him and ruled, "Let him take an oath for however much he has laid out [in support of the wife] and collect [the debt]."

D.   Ruled R. Dosa b. Harkinas in accord with their opinion.

E.   Said R. Yohanan b. Zakkai, "Well did Hanan rule.   He has put his money on the horn of a gazelle."

M. Ket. 13:2

A    Admon lays down seven.

III  B.   He who died and left sons and daughters,

---

[1]I have explained this matter in my *Economics of Judaism.   The Initial System* (Chicago: University of Chicago Press, 1989).

C. when the property is ample,

D. the sons inherit, and daughters receive support [from the estate].

E. [And when] the property is negligible, the daughters receive maintenance, and the sons go out begging at [other peoples'] doors.

F. Admon says, "Do I lose because I am male?"

G. Said Rabban Gamaliel, "I prefer Admon's opinion."

M. Ket. 13:3

IV A He claims that his fellow [owes him] jars of wine, and the other party admitted that he owes him [empty] jugs –

B. Admon says, "Since he has conceded part of the claim, let him take an oath."

C. And sages say, "This is not concession along the lines of the original claim."

D. Said Rabban Gamaliel, "I prefer Admon's opinion.

M. Ket. 13:4

V A He who agrees to give money to his son-in-law but then stretched out the leg [defaulted] –

B. let her sit until her head turns white.

C. Admon says, "She can claim, 'If I had made such an agreement in my own behalf, well might I set until my head grows white. Now that father has made an agreement concerning me, what can I do? Either marry me or let me go!'"

D. Said Rabban Gamaliel, "I prefer Admon's opinion."

M. Ket. 13:5

VI A He who contests [another's]ownership of a field, but he himself is a signatory on it [the documents of ownership] as a witness –

B. Admon says, "He can claim, 'The second [owner of the property] was easier for me, and the first was harder then he [for purposes of repossessing the field which in any case is mine].'"

C. And sages say, "He has lost every right."

D. [If] he made his filed a boundary mark for another person, he has lost every right.

M. Ket. 13:6

VII A He who sent overseas, and the right-of-way to his field was lost –

B. Admon says, "Let him go the shortest way."

C. And sages say, "Let him purchase a right-of-way with a hundred *manehs* [if need be],

D. "or let him fly through the air."

M. Ket.. 13:7

VIII A He who produces a bond of indebtedness against someone else, and the other brought forth [a deed of sale to show] that the other had sold him a field –

B.  Admon says, "He can claim, 'If I owed you money, you should have collected what was coming to you when you sold me the field.'"
C.  And sages say, "This [first] man was smart in selling him the field, since he can take it as a pledge."

M. Ket. 13:8

IX   A   Two who produced bonds of indebtedness against one another –
     B.  Admon says, "If I had owed *you* money, how is it possible that you borrowed from *me?*"
     C.  And sages say, "This one collects his bond of indebtedness, and that one collects his bond of indebtedness."

M. Ket. 13:9

Any picture of the court as a judicial agency should attend to the points of differentiation and account of the conduct of trials. The following provides a sizable portrait of just these matters.

### Mishnah-tractate Sanhedrin 3:1-2

      A   *Property-cases are [decided by] three [judges]* [M. 1:1A].
I     B.  This litigant chooses one [judge], and that litigant chooses one judge, and then the two of the [litigants] choose one more," the words of R. Meir.
      C   And sages say, "The two judges choose one more."
II    D.  "This party has the right to invalidate the judge chosen by this one," the words of R. Meir.
      E   and sages say, "Under what circumstances?
      F.  "When he brings evidence about them, that they are relatives or otherwise invalid.
      G.  "But if they are valid [judges] or experts, he has not got the power to invalidate them."
III   H.  "This party invalidates the witnesses brought by that one, and that party invalidates the witnesses brought by this one," the words of R. Meir.
      I.  And sages say, "Under what circumstances?
      J.  "When he brings evidence about them, that they are relatives or otherwise invalid.
      K.  "But if they are valid [to serve as witnesses], he has not got the power to invalidate them."

M. 3:1

IV    A   [If] he said to him, "If one litigant said to the other, "I accept my father as reliable," "I accept your father as reliable," "I accept as reliable three herdsman [to serve as judges]," –
      B.  R. Meir says, "He has the power to retract."
V     D.  [If] one owed an oath to this fellow, and his fellow said, "[Instead of an oath], take a vow to me by the life of your head,"
      E   R. Meir says, "He has the power to retract."

    F.   And sages say, "He has not got the power to retract."

M. 3:2

The first three disputes devolve upon a single point, as is clear. They are joined to A as a gloss, although they were originally formed for their own purpose. The fourth and fifth entries go on to their own point of interest. If a party has voluntarily conceded not to exercise his rights, he may always retract, in Meir's view. Sages at all five points allow the litigant less leeway in determining the conduct of the court-case. The appendix contains an account of the rules of testimony in these courts.

## Mishnah-tractate Sanhedrin 4:1-2

    A   All the same are property cases and capital cases as to examination and interrogation [of witnesses],

    B.   as it is said, *You will have one law* (Lev. 24:22).

    C   What is the difference between property cases and capital cases?

    D.   (1) Property cases [are tried] by three [judges], and capital cases by twenty-three.

    E   (2) In property cases they begin [argument] with the case either for acquittal or for conviction, while in capital cases they begin only with the case for acquittal, and not with the case for conviction.

    F.   (3) In property cases they decide by a majority of one, whether for acquittal or for conviction, while in capital cases they decide by a majority of one for acquittal, but only with a majority of two [judges] for conviction.

    G.   (4) In property cases they reverse the decision whether in favor of acquittal or in favor of conviction, while in capital cases they reverse the decision in favor of acquittal, but they do not reverse the decision in favor of conviction.

    H.   (5) In property cases all [judges and even disciples] argue either for acquittal or conviction. In capital cases all argue for acquittal, but all do not argue for conviction.

    I.   (6) In property cases one who argues for conviction may argue for acquittal, and one who argues for acquittal may also argue for conviction. In capital cases the one who argues for conviction may argue for acquittal, but the one who argues for acquittal has not got the power to retract and to argue for conviction.

    J.   (7) In property cases they try the case by day and complete it by night. In capital cases they try the case by day and complete it [the following] day.

    K.   (8) In property cases they come to a final decision on the same day [as the trial itself], whether it is for acquittal or conviction. In capital cases they come to a final decision for acquittal on the same day, but on the following day for conviction.

L.   (Therefore they do not judge [capital cases] either on the eve of the
     Sabbath or on the eve of a festival.)

M. 4:1

A.   (9) In cases involving question of uncleanness and cleanness they
     begin [voting] from the eldest. In capital cases they begin from the
     side [with the youngest].
B.   (10) All are valid to engage in the judgment of property cases, but all
     are not valid to engage in the judgment of capital cases,
C.   except for priests, Levites, and Israelites who are suitable to marry
     into the priesthood.

M. 4:2

The rules of testimony in the sages' courts are described in the
following:

### Mishnah-tractate Sanhedrin 3:3

A.   And these are those who are invalid [to serve as witnesses or judges]:
B.   (1) he who plays dice: (2) he who loans money on interest; (3) those
     who race pigeons; (4) and those who do business in the produce of
     the Seventh Year.
C.   Said R. Simeon, "In the beginning they called them, 'Those who
     gather Seventh Year produce.' When oppressors became many
     [who collected taxes in the Seventh Year], they reverted to call them,
     'Those who do business in the produce of the Seventh Year.'"
D.   Said R. Judah, "Under what circumstance? When [the aforenamed
     (B)] have only that as their profession. But if they have a profession
     other than that, they are valid [to serve as witnesses or judges]."

M. 3:3

C glosses B.4 and D, the whole of A-B. The whole carries forward the
secondary exposition of M. 1:1A=M. 3:1A.

### Mishnah-tractate Sanhedrin 3:4-5

A.   And these are relatives [prohibited from serving as one's witnesses
     or judges]: (1) one's father, (2) brother, (3) father's brother, (4)
     mother's brother, (5) sister's husband, (6) father's sister's husband,
     (7) mother's sister's husband, (8) mother's husband, (9) father-in-
     law, and (10) wife's sister's husband –
B.   they, their sons, and their sons-in-law;
C.   but the stepson only [but not the stepson's offspring].
D.   Said R. Yosé, "This is the version of R. 'Aqiba. But the earlier version
     [is as follows]:
E.   "His uncle, the son of his uncle [Lev. 25:49] and anyone who stands
     to inherit him [M. B.B. 8:1]."
F.   and anyone who is related to him at that time,

G. [if] one was a relative but ceased to be related, lo, that person is valid.

H. R. Judah says, "Even if his daughter died, if he has sons from her, lo, [the son-in-law] is deemed a relative.

M. 3:4

A. "One known to be a friend and one known to be an enemy –

B. "one known to be a friend – this is the one who served as his groomsman;

C. "one known to be an enemy – this is one who has not spoken with him for three days by reason of outrage."

D. They said to [Judah], "Israelites are not suspect for such a factor."

M. 3:5

The secondary exposition of M. 1:1A=3:1A now turns to exclusions by reason of family ties. The basic entry, M. 3:4A-C, is clear as given. The earlier version, E, simply excludes all male relatives who stand to inherit. the second clarification, after Yosé's, is at M. 3:4F-H. F-G take account of the possibility of one's ceasing to be related, e.g., if one's wife died. Judah does not differ, but merely qualifies the matter. M. 3:5 is generally understood to continue Judah's saying. He now adds two items to the original list, and his additions are rejected for the stated reason, but only after B-C, a rather fulsome exposition of their own.

## Mishnah-tractate Sanhedrin 3:6-7

A. How do they test the witnesses?

B. They bring them in and admonish them,

C. then they take all of them out and keep back the most important of the group.

D. And they say to him, "Explain: How do you know that this one is liable to that one."

E. If he said, "He told me, 'I owe him,' 'So-and-so told me that he owed him,'" he has said nothing whatsoever,

F. unless he says, "In our presence he admitted to him that he owes him two hundred *zuz*."

G. and afterward they bring in the second and test him in the same way.

H. If their testimony checks out, they discuss the matter.

I.   I. [If] two [judges] say, "He is innocent," and one says, "He is guilty," he is innocent.

II.  J. [If] two say, "He is guilty," and one says, "He is innocent," he is guilty.

III. K. [If] one says, "He is innocent," and one says, "He is guilty," –

L. of even if two declare him innocent and two declare him guilty –

M. but one of them says, "I don't know,"

N. they have to add to the judges.

M. 3:6

A. [When] they have competed the matter, they bring them back in.

B. The chief judge says, "Mr. So-and-so, you are innocent," "Mr. So-and-so, you are guilty."

C. Now how do we know that when one of the judges leaves [the court], he may not say, "I think he is innocent, but my colleagues think he is guilty, so what can I do? For my colleagues have the votes!"

D. Concerning such a person, it is said, *You shall not go up and down as a talebearer among you people* (Lev. 19:16).

E. and it is said, *He who goes about as a talebearer and reveals secrets, [but he that is faithful conceals the matter]* (Prov. 11:13).

M. 3:7

M. turns to narrative style, except for the triplet, interpolated at M. 3:6I-N, which interrupts the sequence of the tale, and except for the appended homily, M. 3:7C-E. The story is clear as given and makes its points forcefully, specifically, M. 3:6D-F. They insist that the defendant in fact have recognized the witnesses as such.

## Mishnah-tractate Sanhedrin 1:2-3

C. (6) [The decision to] intercalate the month is before three.

D. (7) "[The decision to] intercalate the year is before three," the words of R. Meir.

E. Rabban Simeon b. Gamaliel says, "With three do they begin, with five [more] they debate the matter, and they reach a final decision with seven [more] [ judges].

F. "But if they reached a decision [to intercalate the year] with three judges, [the year is] intercalated."

M. 1:2

A. (8) "The laying of hands [on a community sacrifice] by elders and the breaking of the heifer's neck [Deut. 21:1-9] are done by three judges," the words of R. Simeon.

B. R. Judah says, "By five."

C. (9) The rite of removal of the shoe [breaking the levirate bond] (Deut. 25:7-9) and the exercise of the right of refusal are done before three judges.

D. (10) [The evaluation of] fruit of fourth-year planting [which is to be redeemed (Lev. 19:23-25)] and of second tithe (Deut. 14:22-26) whose value is not known is done before three judges.

E. (11) Assessment of the value [for purposes of redemption] of things which have been consecrated is done before three judges.

F. (12) [Property pledged as security for] vows of valuation, in the case of movables, is evaluated by three [judges].

G. R. Judah says, "One of them must be a priest,"

H. And [evaluation of property pledged as security for vows for valuation] in the case of real estate is done by nine and a priest.

I.    And so for [the valuation-vow covering] men.

M. 1:3

The catalogue of twelve kinds of cases which are adjudicated by a court of three judges bears its own glosses, so explaining the disputed entries. M. 1:1D-F probably accounts for the dispute of M. 1:2A-B as well; the one subject to stripes may die. The context of M. 1:3A requires that the laying on of hands by elders refer to the communal sacrifice, not ordination. The set at M. 1:3E-I is familiar from M. Ar. When, M. 1:3E, one goes to redeem property he has consecrated to Heaven, the price is set by a court of three judges. If one has said, "My value," or "The value of so-and-so, be upon me," in line with Lev. 27:2ff., and he wishes to pay off the valuation in kind, the value of the goods is assessed by court of three, inclusive of a priest. Ten, including a priest, evaluate real property. I f a slave is offered in payment, M. 1:3I, he is evaluated by a court of ten. H-I are drawn in the wake of F-G.

### Mishnah-tractate Yadayim 4:2

II    A.    On that day they said:
      B.    All sacrifices which were slaughtered not for their own name are fit.
      C.    But they do not go to their owner's credit in fulfillment of a n obligation,
      D.    except for the Passover and the sin-offering,
      E.    the Passover at its season, and the sin-offering at all times.
      F.    R. Eliezer says, "Also the guilt-offering.
      G.    "The Passover at its season, and the sin-offering and guilt-offering at all times."
      H.    Said R. Simeon b. Azzai, "I have a tradition of the seventy-two elders on the day on which they seated R. Eleazar b. Azariah in session, that:
      I.    "All sacrifices which are eaten, which have been sacrificed not for their own, name, are suitable.
      J.    "But they do not go to their owner's credit in fulfillment of an obligation,
      K.    "except for the Passover and the sin-offering."
      L.    Ben Azzai added only the whole-offering.
      M.    But the sages did not agree with him.

Here we see the intervention of a tradition, which correlates with Aqiba's ruling and sustains it. But Ben Azzai's detail is rejected without appeal to tradition; yet implicit is the inconsistency with his detail and the cited tradition. Now comes an instance of a sustained debate, that is, an exchange of reasoned positions, meant to persuade, rather than an appeal to tradition:

**Mishnah-tractate Yadayim 4:3**

III    A    On that day they said:

B.    What of Ammon and Moab in the Sabbatical year?

C.    R. Tarfon decreed [that they give] poor man's tithe.

D.    And R. Eleazar b. Azariah decreed [that they give] second tithe.

E.    1. Said R. Ishmael, "Eleazar b. Azariah: You must bring forth proof, since you give a stringent ruling.
2. "For everyone who gives a stringent ruling must bring forth proof."

F.    Said to him R. Eleazar b. Azariah, "Ishmael, my brother: I have not changed the order of the years.
2. "Tarfon, my brother, changed it, and he must bring forth proof."

G.    R. Tarfon answered, "Egypt is outside the Land [of Israel], and Ammon and Moab are outside the Land. Therefore [just as in] Egypt, poor man's tithe [must be given] in the Sabbatical year, so [in] Ammon and Moab, poor man's tithe [must be given in the Sabbatical year]."

H.    R. Eleazar b. Azariah answer, "Babylonia is outside the Land, and Ammon and Moab are outside the Land. Therefore, [just as in] Babylonia, second tithe [must be given] in the Sabbatical year, so [in] Ammon and Moab second tithe [must be given] in the Sabbatical year."

I.    Said R. Tarfon, "Egypt, which is near [the Land], have they made liable for poor man's tithe, so that the poor of Israel may depend upon it in the Sabbatical year. So too Ammon and Moab, which are near [the Land] have they made liable for poor man's tithe, so that the poor of Israel may depend upon them in the Sabbatical year."

J.    R. Eleazar b. Azariah said to him, "Lo, you are like one who would bestow [on them] worldly gain, yet you are like one who would cause them to perish.
2. "You would close up the heavens so that they send down neither dew nor rain,
3. "for it is written, *'Will a man rob God? Yet you rob me.' But you say, 'Wherein have we robbed you?' 'In tithes and heave-offering'* (Mal. 3:8)."

K.    Responded R. Tarfon.

L.    1. Said R. Joshua,
2. "Lo, I am like one who will respond on behalf of Tarfon, my brother, but not according to his reasoning.
3. "[The rule concerning] Egypt is a new decision, and that concerning Babylonia is an old decision, and the issue before us is a new decision. Let that which involves a new decision be derived from that which involved a new decision, but let not that which involves a new decision be derived from that which involves an old decision.
4. "The rule concerning Egypt is the decision of the elders. But the rule concerning Babylonia is the decision of the prophets. And the

issue before us involves a decision of the elders. Let the rule concerning a decision of the elders be derived from the rule concerning a decision of the elders, and let not the rule concerning a decision of the elders be derived from a rule concerning a decision of the prophets."

In the end there is a weighing of traditions; there is no clear ruling, but traditions yield principles, which can be applied appropriately. On that basis, there is also the vote:

M. They voted and decided:
N. Ammon and Moab give poor man's tithe in the Sabbatical year.
O. And when R. Yosé the son of the Damascene came to R. Eliezer at Lud, he [Eliezer] said to him, "What new thing have you [learned] in the *bet hammidrash* today?"
P. 1. He said to him, "They voted and decided:
2. "Ammon and Moab give poor man's tithe in the Sabbatical year."
Q. R. Eliezer wept, saying, *"The secret of the Lord is with those that fear him, and he will show them his covenant* (Ps. 25:14).
R. "Go and tell them, 'Do not be anxious about your vote. I have received a tradition from Rabban Yohanan b. Zakkai, who heard it from his teacher, and his teacher from his teacher, a law given to Moses at Sinai,
S. "'that Ammon and Moab give poor man's tithe in the Sabbatical year.'"

As before, so now, the representation of sages' decision-making process yields the stunning claim that, whatever sages decided, tradition confirms and accords with their decision. So the process of debate about reasoned propositions in the end yields an appeal to the confirmation of Heaven. The blatant presence of the myth that sages' decisions accord with Heaven's rules, not in general but to the last detail, once more sustains sages' agency and hardly requires specification.

### Mishnah-tractate Yadayim 4:4

IV A On that day:
B. Judah an Ammonite proselyte came and stood before them in the *bet hammidrash.*
C. He said to them, "Am I allowed to enter the congregation?"
D. Rabban Gamaliel said to him, "You are forbidden [to enter the congregation]."
E. R. Joshua said to him, "You are permitted."
F. Rabban Gamaliel said to him, "Scripture says, *An Ammonite or a Moabite shall not enter into the assembly of the Lord, even to the tenth generation* (Dt. 23:4)."
G. R. Joshua said to him, "And are there Ammonites and Moabites in this place?

H.   "Already has Sennacherib, king of Assyria, come up and mixed up all the nations.

I.   "As it is said, *I have removed the bounds of the peoples and have robbed their treasures and have brought down as a valiant man them that sit on thrones* (Is. 10:13)."

J.   Rabban Gamaliel said to him, "Scripture says, *But afterward I will bring again the captivity of the children of Ammon* (Jer. 49:6).

K.   R. Joshua said to him, "Scripture says, *And I will return the captivity of my people Israel and Judah, says the Lord* (Amos 9:14).
"And as yet they have not returned."

L.   And they permitted him to enter into the congregation.

As to the utilization of the funds paid to the Temple, these are deposited in the Temple treasury, and then, at appropriate times, drawn for the purchase of offerings for which all Israelites equally bear responsibility.

### Mishnah-tractate Sheqalim 3:1

A   At three times in the year do they take up the heave-offering of the [coins collected in the] [*sheqel-*]chamber:

B.   half a month before Passover, half a month before 'Aseret [Pentecost], and half a month before the Festival [of Sukkot].

C   "And these are the 'threshing floors' [the times at which the obligation to tithe becomes operative] for tithing cattle," the words of R. 'Aqiba.

D.   Ben 'Azzai says, "On the twenty-ninth of Adar, on the first of Sivan, and on the twenty-ninth of Ab."

E   R. Eleazar and R. Simeon say, "On the first of Nisan, on the first of Sivan, and on the twenty-ninth of Elul."

F.   On what account did they rule, "On the twenty-ninth of Elul," instead of saying, "on the first of Tishré"?

G.   Because it is a festival day, and it is not possible to give tithe on a festival day.

H.   Therefore they set it a day earlier, on the twenty-ninth of Elul.

M. 3:1

The heave-offering of the chamber of *sheqels*, A, is the point at which the *sheqels* to be used for the coming season are taken up for the purchase of the public offerings. This is done before the festivals, at which point demands on the Temple treasury are greatest. Aqiba glosses by observing that at this same time cattle born during the preceding period become liable to the process of tithing. At this point they are tithed, and those which are left over from the procedure of the tithe of cattle become available for sale and use on the coming festival. The other authorities do not differ about B, but about C. Ben

Azzai sets variable dates, two weeks before Passover, less than a week before Pentecost, and a month and a half before Tabernacles.

### Mishnah-tractate Sheqalim 3:2-4

A. With three baskets, each holding three *seahs*, they take up the heave-offering of the [coins collected in the] [*sheqel-*]chamber.

B. And written on them are the Hebrew letters, *alef, bet gimel.*

C. R. Ishmael says, "Written on them were the Greek letters, *Alpha, Beta, Gamla.*"

D. He who takes up the heave-offering went in wearing neither a sleeved cloak, nor shoes, sandals, phylacteries, or an amulet –

E. lest [in the coming year] he lose all his money and people say [about him], "Because of a transgression against the [*sheqel-*]chamber did he lose his money."

F. Or lest he get rich, and people say about him, "From the heave-offering of the [*sheqel-*]chamber did he get rich."

G. For a person must give no cause for suspicion to the Omnipresent, just as he must give no cause for suspicion to the Omnipresent,

H. as it is said, *And be guiltless towards the Lord and towards Israel* (Num. 32:22).

I. And so it says, *So shall you find favor and good understanding in the sight of God and humanity* (Prov. 3:4).

M. 3:2

A. A member of the household of Rabban Gamaliel would go in and take his *sheqel* between his finger-tips and throw it in front of the one who takes up the heave-offering [of the *sheqels*, so as to make sure his coin would be used for the purchase of the public sacrifices].

B. And the one who takes up the heave-offering intentionally pushes it into the basket.

C. The one who takes up the heave-offering does not do so until he says to them, "Shall I take up the heave-offering?" And they say to him, "Take up heave-offering, take up heave-offering, take up heave-offering," three times.

M. 3:3

The procedure for appropriating the funds is described in standard narrative style. The glosses, M. 3:2G-I, 3:3A-B, do not spoil the flow.

A. He took up [heave-offering] the first time and covered [the residue] with covers.

B. [He took up the heave-offering] a second time and covered [the residue] with covers.

C. But the third time he did not cover [it up].

D.  [He covered the first two times], lest he forget nd take up heave-offering from those *sheqels* from which heave-offering already had been taken.

E.  He took up the heave-offering the first time in behalf of the Land of Israel, the second time in behalf of cities surrounding it, and the third time in behalf of Babylonia, Media, and the more distant communities.

M. 3:4

Now we are given the data on how these funds are used:

### Mishnah-tractate Sheqalim 4:1-2

I    A.   As to the heave-offering [of the *sheqel*-chamber]: What did they do with it?

B.  They purchase with it [animals for] daily whole-offerings, additional offerings, and their drink-offerings,

C.  [wheat for] the *'omer*, the Two Loaves, and the Show Bread,

D.  and all [other] offerings, made in behalf of the community.

E.  Those who guard the after-growths of the Seventh Year receive their salary from the heave-offering of the [*sheqel*-]chamber.

F.  R. Yosé says, "Also: He who wishes to volunteer [may serve as] an unpaid guardian [of the after-growths]."

G.  They said to him, "You too rule that they [The *'omer*, Two Loaves, and Show Bread] derive only from public funds."

M. 4:1

A.  The red cow [Num. 19:1ff.], the goat which is sent out, and the red thread [Lev. 16:5] derive from funds of the heave-offering of the [*sheqel*-]chamber.

B.  The [cost of building] a causeway for the red cow, the causeway for the scapegoat which is sent forth, the thread between its horns, the [cost of the upkeep of the] water channel, the wall of the city and its turrets, and all needs of the city [of Jerusalem] derive from the residue [of funds of the *sheqel*-]chamber [coins not taken up with the heave-offering thereof.].

C.  Abba Saul says, "The ramp of the red cow – the high priests make it at their own expense."

M. 4:2

The essay on the disposition of the funds deriving from the Temple-tax names four ways in which the money is used: M. 4:1B-D, E, M. 4:2A, a triplet, then M. 4:2B. The first three come from funds deriving from the appropriation, of the taking up of the heave-offering; the fourth then is from the funds left over. The main point, of course, is M. 4:1B-D: Offerings made in behalf of all the people must derive from funds contributed by then all. E-G is a secondary development of M. 4:1C.

The point of E is that, in the Seventh Year, when no crops may be sown, it is necessary to watch over the aftergrowth of wheat, so that there will be grain for the preparation for the '*omer*, the Two Loaves, and the Show Bread (C). Since in ordinary years the wheat itself is purchased with the heave-offering of the *sheqel*-chamber, in the Seventh Year the wheat is secured through an appropriation from that same budget. Guards are hired to see that neither human beings nor animals eat the specified fields' aftergrowth, which then is kept for use in the cult. Yosé's position is rejected, G, because if a person guards without pay, then the produce of the field guarded by him automatically becomes his possession, and this, M. 4:1C makes clear, is not possible  An individual cannot supply what the entire community must give. M. 4:2A completes the trilogy. M. 4:2B then specifies how excess funds are used, after the three acts of taking up the heave-offering have left over in the chamber sizable sums of money. The city and its needs are met from public funds.

## Tractate Avot

3:1.   A   Aqabiah b. Mehallalel says, "Reflect upon three things and you will not fall into the clutches of transgression: "Know (1) from whence you come, (2) whither you are going, and (3) before whom you are going to have to give a full account of yourself.

  B.   "From whence do you come? From a putrid drop. Whither are you going? To a place of dust, worms, and maggots.

  C   "And before whom are you are going to give a full account of yourself? Before the King of kings of kings, the Holy One, blessed be He."

3:2.   A   R. Hananiah, Prefect of the Priests, says, "Pray for the welfare of the government. For if it were not for fear of it, one man would swallow his fellow alive."

  B.   R. Hananiah b. Teradion says, "[If] two sit together and between them do not pass teachings of the Torah, lo, this is a seat of the scornful, as it is said, Nor sits in the seat of the scornful (Ps. 1:1). But two who are sitting, and words of the Torah do pass between them – the Presence is with them, as it is said, 'Then they that feared the Lord spoke with one another, and the Lord hearkened and heard, and a book of remembrance was written before him, for them that feared the Lord and gave thought to his name' (Mal 3:16)." I know that this applies to two. How do I know that even if a single person sits and works on the Torah, the Holy One, blessed be He, set aside a reward for him? As it is said, Let him sit alone and keep silent, because he has laid it upon him (Lam. 3:28).

3:3   R. Simeon says, "Three who ate at a single table and did not talk about teachings of the Torah while at that table are as though they ate from dead sacrifices (Ps. 106:28), as it is said, 'For all tables are full of vomit and filthiness [if they are] without God' (Ps. 106:28).  But three who ate at a single table and did talk about teachings of the Torah while at that table are as if they ate at the table of the Omnipresent, blessed is he, as it is said, 'And he said to me, This is the table that is before the Lord' (Ez. 41:22)."

3:5        R. Nehunia b. Haqqaneh says, "From whoever accepts upon himself the yoke of the Torah do they remove the yoke of the state and the yoke of hard labor.  And upon whoever removes from himself the yoke of the Torah do they lay the yoke of the state and the yoke of hard labor."

3:6        R. Halafta of Kefar Hananiah says, "Among ten who sit and work hard on the Torah the Presence comes to rest, as it is said, 'God stands in the congregation of God' (Ps. 82:1).  And how do we now that the same is so even of five?  For it is said, 'And he has founded his group upon the earth' (Am. 9:6).  And how do we know that this is so even of three?  Since it is said, 'And he judges among the judges' (Ps. 82:1).  And how do we know that this is so even of two?  Because it is said, 'Then they that feared the Lord spoke with one another, and the Lord hearkened and heard' (Mal. 3:16).  And how do we know that this is so even of one?  Since it is said, 'In every place where I record my name I will come to you and I will bless you' (Ex. 20:24)."

3:7   A   R. Eleazar of Bartota says, "Give him what is his, for you and yours are his.  For so does it say about David, 'For all things come of you, and of your own have we given you' (I Chron. 29:14)."

       B.  R. Simeon says, "He who is going along the way and repeating [his Torah-tradition] but interrupts his repetition and says, 'How beautiful is that tree!  How beautiful is that ploughed field!'" – Scripture reckons it to him as if he has become liable for his life."

3:8        R. Dosetai b. R. Yannai in the name of R. Meir says, "Whoever forgets a single thing from what he has learned – Scripture reckons it to him as it he has become liable for his life, as it is said, 'Only take heed to yourself and keep your soul diligently, lest you forget the words which your eyes saw' (Deut. 4:9).  Is it possible that this is so even if his learning became too much for him  Scripture says, 'Lest they depart from your heart all the days of your life.'  Thus he becomes liable for his life only when he will sit down and actually remove [his learning] from his own heart.

3:9        R. Haninah b. Dosa would say, "Anyone from whom people take pleasure – the Omnipresent takes pleasure.  And anyone from whom  people do not take pleasure, the Omnipresent does not take pleasure."

3:11       R. Eleazar the Modite says, "(1) He who treats Holy Things as secular, and (2) he who despises the appointed times, (3) he who humiliates his fellow in public, (4) he who removes the signs of the covenant of Abraham, our father, (may he rest in peace), and (5) he who exposes aspects of the Torah not in accord with the law, even though he has in hand learning in the Torah and good deeds, will have no share in the world to come."

3:12 R. Ishmael says, "(1) Be quick [in service] to a superior, (2) efficient in service [to the state], and (3) receive everybody with joy."

3:13 R. Aqiba says, "(1) Laughter and lightheartedness turn lewdness into a habit. (2) Tradition is a fence for the Torah. (3) Tithes are a fence for wealth. (4) Vows are a fence for abstinence. (5) A fence for wisdom is silence."

3:14 A He would say, "Precious is the human being, who was created in the image [of God]. It was an act of still greater love that it was made known to him that he was created in the image [of God]. as it is said, For in the image of God he made man (Gen. 9:6).

B. "Precious are Israelites, who are called children to the Omnipresent. It was an act of still greater love that it was made known to them that they were called children to the Omnipresent, as it is said, 'You are the children of the Lord your God' (Deut. 14:1).

C. "Precious are Israelites, to whom was given the precious thing. It was an act of still greater love that it was made known to them that to them was given that precious thing with which the world was made, as it is said, 'For I give you a good doctrine. Do not forsake my Torah' (Prov. 4:2)."

3:15 "Everything is foreseen, and free choice is given. In goodness the world is judged. And all is in accord with the abundance of deed[s]."

3:16 A He would say, "(1) All is handed over as a pledge, (2) And a net is cast over all the living. (3) The store is open, (4) the storekeeper gives credit, (5) the account-book is open, and (6) the hand is writing.

B. "(1) Whoever wants to borrow may come and borrow. (2) The charity-collectors go around every day and collect from man whether he knows it or not. (3) And they have grounds for what they do. (4) And the judgment is a true judgment. (5) And everything is ready for the meal."

3:18 R. Eleazar Hisma says, "The laws of bird-offerings and of the beginning of the menstrual period – they are indeed the essentials of the Torah. Calculation of the equinoxes and reckoning the numerical value of letters are the savories of wisdom."

## Tractate Avot Chapter Four

4:1. Ben Zoma says, "Who is a sage? He who learns from everybody, as it is said, From all my teachers I have gotten understanding (Ps. 119:99). Who is strong? He who overcomes his desire, as it is said, 'He who is slow to anger is better than the mighty, and he who rules his spirit than he who takes a city' (Prov. 16:32). Who is rich? He who is happy in what he has, as it is said, 'When you eat the labor of your hands, happy will you be, and it will go well with you' (Ps. 128:2). ("Happy will you be – in this world, and it will go well with you – in the world to come.") Who is honored? He who honors everybody, as it is said, 'For those who honor me I shall honor, and they who despise me will be treated as of no account' (I Sam. 2:30)."

4:2.      Ben Azzai says, "Run after the most minor religious duty as after the most important, and flee from transgression. For doing one religious duty draws in its wake doing yet another, and doing one transgression draws in its wake doing yet another. For the reward of doing a religious duty is a religious duty, and the reward of doing a transgression is a transgression."

4:3.      He would say, "Do not despise anybody and do not treat anything as unlikely. For you have no one who does not have his time, and you have nothing which does not have its place."

4:4.   B.   R. Yohanan b. Beroqa says, "Whoever secretly treats the Name of Heaven as profane publicly pays the price. All the same are the one who does so inadvertently and the one who does so deliberately, when it comes to treating the name of Heaven as profane."

4:5.   B.   R. Sadoq says, "Do not make [Torah-teachings] a crown in which to glorify yourself or a spade with which to dig. So did Hillel say, "He who uses the crown perishes. Thus have you learned: Whoever derives worldly benefit from teachings of the Torah takes his life out of this world."

4:6.      R. Yosé says, "Whoever honors the Torah himself is honored by people. And whoever disgraces the Torah himself is disgraced by people."

4:7.      R. Ishmael, his son, says, "He who avoids serving as a judge avoids the power of enmity, robbery, and false swearing. And he who is arrogant about making decisions is a fool, evil, and prideful."

4:8.      He would say, "Do not serve as a judge by yourself, for there is only One who serves as a judge all alone. And do not say, 'Accept my opinion,' for they have the choice in the matter, not you."

4:9.      R. Jonathan says, "Whoever keeps the Torah when poor will in the end keep it in wealth. And whoever treats the Torah as nothing when he is wealthy in the end will treat it as nothing in poverty."

4:10.     R. Meir says, "Keep your business to a minimum and make your business the Torah. And be humble before everybody. And if you treat the Torah as nothing, you will have many treating you as nothing. And if you have labored in the Torah, [the Torah] has a great reward to give you."

4:11.  B.   R. Yohanan Hassandelar says, "Any gathering which is for the sake of Heaven is going to endure. And any which is not for the sake of Heaven is not going to endure."

4:12.     R. Eleazar b. Shammua says, "The honor owing to your disciple should be as precious to you as yours. And the honor owing to your fellow should be like the reverence owing to your master. And the reverence owing to your master should be like the awe owing to Heaven."

4:13. A.  R. Judah says, "Be meticulous about learning, for error in learning leads to deliberate [violation of the Torah]."

4:13. B.  R. Simeon says, "There are three crowns: the crown of the Torah, the crown of priesthood, and the crown of sovereignty. But the crown of a good name is best of them all."

4:14.  R. Nehorai says, "Go into exile to a place of the Torah, and do not suppose that it will come to you. For your fellow disciples will make it solid in your hand. And on your own understanding do not rely."

4:15. A.  R. Yannai says, "We do not have in hand [an explanation] either for the prosperity of the wicked or for the suffering of the righteous."

4:15. B.  R. Matya b. Harash says, "Greet everybody first, and be a tail to lions. But do not be a head of foxes."

4:19.  Samuel the Small says, "Rejoice not when your enemy falls, and let not your heart be glad when he is overthrown, lest the Lord see it and it displease him, and he turn away his wrath from him (Prov. 24:17)."

4:22. A.  R. Eleazar Haqqappar says, "Jealousy, lust, and ambition drive a person out of this world."

4:22. B.  He would say, "Those who are born are [destined] to die, and those who die are [destined] for resurrection. And the living are [destined] to be judged – so as to know, to make known, and to confirm that (1) he is God, (2) he is the one who forms, (3) he is the one who creates, (4) he is the one who understands, (5) he is the one who judges, (6) he is the one who gives evidence, (7) he is the one who brings suit, (8) and he is the one who is going to make the ultimate judgment.

4:22. C.  "Blessed be he, for before him are no (1) guile, (2) forgetfulness, (3) respect for persons, or (4) bribe-taking, for everything is his. And know that everything is subject to reckoning. And do not let your evil impulse persuade you that Sheol is a place of refuge for you. For (1) despite your wishes were formed, (2) despite your wishes were you born, (3) despite your wishes do you live, (4) despite your wishes do you die, and (5) despite your wishes are you going to give a full accounting before the King of kings of kings, the Holy One blessed be He."

Aqabiah's opening saying sets the stage. The bureaucrat judges but is judged, and he is no different from any other man. The link to God is striking; God judges the judge. Hananiah's insistence that every random social encounter, even the eating of meals, must constitute a transaction involving Torah-teachings, carries forward the transformation of professional ideal to the norm for the male population as a whole.

## Supplementing: *The Politics of Judaism,* Chapter Six

### Mishnah-tractate Sanhedrin 10:4-6

A.    The townsfolk of an apostate town have no portion in the world to come,

B.    as it is said, *Certain base fellows have gone out from the midst of thee and have drawn away the inhabitants of their city* (Deut. 13:14).

C.    And they are not put to death unless (1) those who misled the [town] come from that same town and from that same tribe,

D.    and unless (2) the majority is misled,

E.    and unless (3) men did the misleading.

F.    [If] (1) women or children misled them,

G.    or if (2) a minority of the town was misled,

H.    or if (3) those who misled the town came from outside of it,

I.    lo, they are treated as individuals [and not as a whole town],

J.    and they [thus] require [testimony against them] by two witnesses, and a statement of warning, for each and every one of them.

K.    This rule is more strict for individuals than for the community:

L.    for individuals are put to death by stoning.

M.    Therefore their property is saved.

N.    But the community is put to death by the sword,

O.    Therefore their property is lost.

M. 10:4

A.    *And you shall surely smite the inhabitants of the city with the edge of the sword* (Deut. 13:15) –

B.    Ass-drivers, camel-drivers, and people passing from place to place – lo, these have the power to save it.

C.    *Destroying it utterly and all that is therein and the cattle thereof, with the edge of the sword* (Deut. 13:17) –

D.    On this basis they said, The property of righteous folk which happens to be located in it is lost. But that which is outside of it is saved.

E.    And as to that of evil folk, whether it is in the town or outside of it, lo, it is lost.

M. 10:5

A-B link M. 10:4ff. to the antecedent construction. In fact we now revert to M. 9:1E, those killed by a sword (decapitation). C-E are matched against F-H + I-J. Individuals must be tried one by one. since the individual who worships idles is punished by a severe mode of execution, L, his property is handed to his heirs. M. 10:5 presents related materials, C-E. Since the whole is a complete exegesis, it is given as a unit .

I      A.    [Delete: As it is said,} *And you shall gather all the spoil of it into the midst of the wide place thereof* (Deut. 17:13).

B. If is has no wide place, they make a wide place for it.

C. [If] its wide place is outside of it they bring it inside.

II  D. *And you will burn with fire the city and all the spoil thereof, (every whit, unto the Lords you God)* (Deut. 13:17).

E. *The spoil thereof* – but not the spoil which belongs to heaven.

F. On this basis they have said:

G. Things which had been consecrated which are in it are to be redeemed; heave-offering left therein is allowed to rot; second tithe and sacred scrolls are hidden away.

III  H. *Every whit unto the Lord your God* –

I. Said R. Simeon, "Said the Holy One blessed be He: "If you enter into judgment in the case of an apostate city, I give credit to you as if you had offered a whole burnt-offering before me.'"

IV  J. *And it shall be a heap for ever, it shall not be built again* –

K. "It should not be made even into vegetable-patches or orchards," the words of R. Yosé the Galilean.

L. R. 'Aqiba says, "*It shall not be built again* – as it was it may not be rebuilt, but it may be made into vegetable patches and orchards."

V  M. *And there shall cleave nought of the devoted thing to your hand [that the Lord may turn from the fierceness of his anger and show you mercy and have compassion upon you and multiply you]* (Deut. 13:18) –

N. for so long as evil people are in the world, fierce anger is in the world.

O. When the evil people have perished from the world, fierce anger departs from the world.

M. 10:6

M. systematically interprets the relevant verses in five exegetical construction. The market, B-C, must be encompassed by the town walls. F-G restate the principle of E. The rest is clear as given.

### Supplementing: *The Politics of Judaism,* Chapter Seven

In the text I refer to Martin Jaffee's interpretation of Mishnah-tractate Maaserot. Here I wish to present a more substantial account of his exposition. It is entirely in his own words. I have selected and arranged the materials to make the points important in my argument in *Politics of Judaism,* Chapter Seven.

### Will and Intentionality in Mishnah-Tractate Maaserot: The Heart as the Meetingplace of God and Humanity

Martin Jaffee
Selected and Edited by Jacob Neusner

Understanding what is at stake in Mishnaic discourse carries us from the surface, at which concrete and detailed issues are worked out, to the depths of conviction and commitment that animate the system. Mishnah-tractate Maaserot (Tithes) is a case in point. The tractate defines the class of produce which is subject to Scripture's diverse agricultural taxes, and determines when payment of these taxes is due. It thus amplifies, in rather predictable ways, those aspects of Scripture which are likely to interest Israelites concerned with the proper tithing of their food. That is, the tractate tells its audience what to tithe, and stipulates when they must remove the offerings from food they wish to eat. Where Scripture is clear on these matters, the Mishnah is content to repeat and highlight the obvious. Thus in regard to the kinds of produce which must be tithed, Mishnah-tractate Maaserot simply affirms Scripture's view that these gifts, the priestly dues and tithes, are to be offered from all produce grown in the fields of the Land of Israel (cf. Dt. 14:22). The tractate's questions are: When, in the course of a crop's growth, may it be used to satisfy the obligation to tithe? When, further, in the course of the harvest of the crop, must the tithes actually be paid?

It is in the answers to these questions that we uncover the relationship between the human being and God that the Mishnah's authorship sets forth. For the Mishnah's answer to this twofold question is generated by Scripture's assumption that the agricultural offerings of the Land of Israel are a sacred tax which Israelites owe to God for the property they take from his Land (Lv. 27:30). Accordingly, the tractate points out that produce *may* be tithed as soon as it ripens, for at this point the crop becomes valuable as property. Payment of the tithes is not due, however, until the farmer or householder actually claims his harvested produce as personal property. This occurs, in Mishnah-tractate Maaserot's view, whenever a person brings untithed produce from his field into his home, or when he prepares untithed produce for sale in the market. Produce appropriated in this fashion is forbidden for consumption until it is tithed. Having claimed the produce for his own personal use, the farmer must remove those portions which belong to God before he may use it himself. The tractate thus addresses a theological problem. That is to determine, and then to adjudicate, the respective claims of man and God to the produce of the Land of Israel.

The fundamental theological datum of Mishnah-tractate Maaserot, then, is that God acts and wills in response to human intentions, God's invisible action can be discerned by carefully studying the actions of human beings. This datum must now be assessed in the context of the time and place in which Tractate Mishnah-tractate Maaserot is constructed. With the The Mishnah as a whole, Mishnah-tractate Maaserot comes into being in second-century Palestine, at a time in which Israel's hopes for God's victory over his enemies have been abandoned, and in a place in which his Temple, the visible symbol of his presence, no longer stands. In such a time and place, both Mishnah-tractate Maaserot's loyalty to Scripture's ancient tithing law, and its distinctive innovations upon that law, are equally suggestive. Fundamentally, Mishnah-tractate Maaserot affirms an essential continuity of God's Lordship over the Land of Israel. It presents Scripture's command to tithe all the fruit of the field as an obligation which extends even to the present. God's ancient tax on the Land must still be offered in its proper season, as it was when the Temple still stood and its priestly officiants brought God's blessing from heaven into the Land. At a time in which God's inability to protect his Land or its inhabitants has long been clear, this is a bold claim indeed. Mishnah-tractate Maaserot asserts that historical catastrophe has left the sacred economy of Israel undisturbed. While Temple is gone, the Land remains holy and its fruit is still under the claim of God. Those remaining in the Land, it follows, remain bound by the ancient system of obligations which their ancestors accepted in covenant with God.

At stake, in other words, in the detailed laws of the tractate before us is the relationship of Israel to the Lord of its ancestral land. The theological agendum emerges most clearly if, from our present standpoint, we return to the key points which interest the Mishnah as produce passes from the field of the Israelite farmer to his table. We recall that produce first becomes subject to the law of tithes when it ripens in the field. God's claim to the tithes of the produce, that is, is made only when the produce itself becomes of value to the farmer. Only after produce has ripened may we expect the farmer to use it in his own meals, or sell it to others for use in theirs. Thus God's claim to it is first provoked, and must therefore be protected, from that point onward. As we have seen, the produce is permitted as food only if the farmer acknowledges God's prior claim, e.g., by refraining from eating it as he would his own produce. Should the farmer overreach his privilege, however, either by preparing to make a meal of the produce in his field or by claiming to be its sole owner, he loses his privilege to eat altogether, until he tithes. Once God's claim against the produce is satisfied by the removal of the tithes, the produce is released for use in all daily meals. It is now common food.

The very law which affirms the continuity of God's Lordship over Israel, however, reveals how much has truly changed, both in the Land and in the imagination of some of its inhabitants. Unlike the theologians of Scripture's priestly laws, Mishnah-tractate Maaserot's authorities can no longer turn to the visible evidence of God's presence, the Temple, in order to legitimate the collection of agricultural taxes. Rather, the framers Mishnah-tractate Maaserot must locate the play of God's power, and the foundation of his claims upon the Land, in an invisible realm immune from the hazards of history. This, as we have seen, is the realm of human appetite and intention, as they are aroused in the mundane course of daily affairs, and as they are directed toward the produce of God's Land. In Mishnah-tractate Maaserot's view, the law by which God's Lordship is affirmed is itself set in motion by those who continue to affirm that he is Lord.

The God of Israel acts and wills in Mishnah-tractate Maaserot only in reaction to the action and intention of his Israelite partner on the Land. Nowhere do the framers of Mishnah-tractate Maaserot expect – or allow for – unilateral or uncontrollable actions proceeding from the initiative of God. As in the time of the Temple, then, God remains Lord of the Land of Israel, and owner of its fruits. But when his Temple no longer stands and his Land has been defiled, his status as Lord depends upon the action of his remaining people. That is the whole point of linking God's claim upon the tithes to the social rhythms of the agricultural enterprise. Those who impose upon themselves the task of reconstructing the human and social fabric of Israelite life make effective the holiness of the Land and make real the claims of its God. This reciprocity between Israel and its God, the near parity between two partners in the task of re-creation, is what distinguishes the vision of Mishnah-tractate Maaserot's thinkers from that of the priestly theoreticians of Scripture, from whom  The Mishnah inherits and transforms the law of tithes.

The chapter that we now examine balances the farmer's right to consume the fruit of his labor against the right of God to a portion of the land's yield. This balance is defined and elaborated within the limits of two formulaically identical catalogues, M. Maaserot 1:2-3 and M. Maaserot 1:5-8, each of which answers an important question. M. Maaserot 1:2A asks at what point produce growing in the field becomes subject to the law, a question for which M. Maaserot 1:1D-H has already provided a general answer. The subsequent catalogue, M. Maaserot 1:2B-3P, now offers a detailed exemplification of the familiar principle. The catalogue provides information regarding the point at which twenty kinds of produce are deemed edible and, therefore, subject to the law. The point is that prior to ripening, the catalogued items may be eaten without the removal of tithes. After ripening, however, they may not be eaten unless they are tithed. Since God claims the produce in its ripeness, man must satisfy that claim before he consumes the produce. The redactor of the chapter has laid out his materials in the following pattern:

| M. 1:1D-F: | produce edible small or large | (a) |
| M. 1:1G-H: | produce edible after it ripens | (b) |
| M. 1:2-3: | examples of 1:1G-H | (b) |
| M. 1:4 | examples of 1:1D-F, large or small | (a) |

The whole is a single well-constructed redactional unit, introduced by M. 1:1A-B+C. Its theme, the point at which produce growing in the field becomes subject to the law of tithes, is exhaustively examined, both in terms of guiding principles and particular details.

1:1

 A A general principle they stated concerning tithes:

 B. anything (*kl s-*) that is
   (1) food (*'kl*),
   (2) cultivated (*nsmr*),
   (3) and which grows from the earth is subject to [the law of] tithes (*hyyb bm' srwt*).

 C And yet another general principle they stated:

 D. anything (*kl s-*) which at its first [stage of development] is food and which at its ultimate [stage of development] is food (e.g., greens: T. 1:1b) –

 E even though [the farmer] maintains [its growth] in order to increase the food [it will yield] –

 F. is subject [to the law of tithes whether it is] small or large (i.e., at all points in its development).

 G. But (*w-*) anything (*kl s-*) which at its first [stage of development] is not food, yet which at its ultimate [stage of development] is food (e.g., the fruit of trees: T. 1:1b)

 H. is not subject [to the laws of tithes] until it becomes edible.

M. Maaserot 1:1

The tractate begins with two rulings, B and D-H. The former concerns the range of produce to which the law of tithes applies, while the latter treats the moment in the growth of such produce at which the law actually takes effect. The rulings are formally and substantively autonomous, but the order of presentation and the superscriptions (A, C) transform them into a complementary pair, inviting us to read D-H in light of B.

The three criteria enumerated at B point out that all plants cultivated by man as food are subject to the law of tithes. When such agricultural produce is harvested, the householder must designate a fixed percentage of it as heave-offering and tithes. These offerings are deemed sanctified and are therefore set aside from the rest of the harvest for the use of priests and others to whom such offerings are due (M. Ter. 3:5-8). Only after the removal of these offerings is the remaining produce deemed "unconsecrated," and permitted for general consumption.

The subject of this process of sanctification and deconsecration is food (B1) that exhibits two distinguishing characteristics. As agricultural produce, it is the focus of the Israelite farmer's labor on his own land (B2), and as plant-life, it grows from land given to Israel by God (B3). According to B, then, the law of tithes applies only to food which man labors to produce from land leased from God. Sanctification, in other words, pertains only to produce which issues from land over which both God and man have legitimate claims. Man's claim is justified by his need and his labor, God's by his ultimate ownership of the land and all its fruits. Claims on both sides are satisfied by the separation of a portion of the produce for God. With God's portion removed, the remainder is deemed fit for human consumption. In The Mishnah's technical language, it is now *hulin metuqanin,* food which has been made suitable for common use by the removal of offerings.

The second unit of M., D-H, assumes the criterion of edibility stated at B1, but raises an independent issue. It points out that agricultural produce need be tithed only after it has *actually become* edible. While C identifies D-H as a single rule, the unit actually contains two well-balanced rulings, D+F and G-H. An interpolation at E upsets this balance, but provides important exegetical guidance.

We begin with D+F. The rule takes for granted that only produce grown for food is subject to the law. Its claim is that the law goes into effect only at the point in the growth of the produce at which it is deemed to be food. It follows, then, that produce which can be eaten as soon as the edible portion develops, such as leafy vegetables, is subject to the law when these portions appear. It remains subject to the law throughout its future growth, or as long as these portions remain edible. G-H adds the logical complement of D+F. If the produce remains inedible until a relatively advanced point in the development of the portion usually eaten, as is the case with most fruit, the produce is exempt from the law until the portion in question becomes edible. If for some reason the produce is eaten before it is normally deemed to be food, it need not be tithed at all.

E, inserted between D and F, adds a new consideration which will become central to later developments in the tractate. It points out that once produce is edible it is subject to the law even if the farmer does not deem it worthy of harvest until the yield is greater. At issue is the criterion for determining when a crop is deemed to be food. Such a criterion can be based upon either the actual condition of the produce, i.e., its edibility, or the actions of the farmer, i.e., his harvest of the crop for food. E rules that the edibility of the produce is the normative criterion, for its edible condition permits us to assume that the farmer deems the produce useful as food. The alternative criterion is that we deem the crop to be food only when it is harvested as such. This would permit the farmer to use the produce prior to the harvest without removing tithes. By rejecting this alternative, E stresses the fact that food is food whether man intends to harvest it as such or not. It is subject to the law when it is edible, regardless of human intentions. The problem of establishing when the objective condition of produce imposes upon it the strictures of the law, and when, on the other hand, the subjective intentions of the owner are determinative, is an established interest.

1:2-3

A.　From what time is fruit (*prwt*) subject to [the law of] tithes?

B.　(1) Figs – when they have begun to ripen (*msbhlw*);

C.　(2) grapes and (3) wild grapes (*'bsym*) – when their seeds have become visible inside them (*mshb 'ysw*);

D.　(4) sumac and (5) mulberry – when they have become red;

E.　and (6) all red [berries] – when they have become red;

F.　(7) pomegranates – when they have become soft;

G.　(8) dates – when they have begun to swell;

H.　(9) peaches – when they have developed red veins;

I.　(10) walnuts (S adds: "and almonds") – when they have developed a chamber.

J.　R. Judah says "Walnuts and almonds – when they develop a husk."

M. Maaserot 1:2

K.　(11) Carobs – when they have become speckled;

L.　(12) and all black [produce, e.g., myrtle berries: y.] – when it has become speckled;

M.　(13) pears, and (14) crustumenian pears, and (15) medlar, and (16) crab-apples – when they have become smooth;

N.　(17) and all white produce – when it has become smooth;

O.　(18) fenugreek – when the seeds are able to sprout;

P.　(19) grain and (20) olives – when they reach a third of their mature growth (*meyknysw slys*).

M. Maaserot 1:3

The superscription A introduces a catalogue of twenty kinds of produce and the point at which each is deemed ripe (B-P). The pericope, in its present redactional context, is a detailed explication of the rule at M. 1:1G-H, that produce which is inedible at its first stage of growth becomes subject to the law as soon as it is edible. As A announces, we are now given criteria for determining when various kinds of produce have indeed become edible and, therefore, may no longer be eaten freely unless they are tithed.

From a literary-critical perspective, the pericope is a unitary construction. Any sources upon which the pericope's redactor my have drawn have been totally reshaped for use in the present context. Fourteen separate stichs (B-I, K-P), incorporating twenty substantives, are cast into the identical formulary pattern (substantive + *ms-* + imperfect plural) and placed into context by A. Indication that the principle of redaction is the number of substantives, rather than the number of stichs, coms at J, where Judah's lemma breaks the catalogue into two units of ten items each. Further, items such as E, L, and N, which add little new information, seem to be included solely for the purpose of reaching the desired number of items in the catalogue. I cannot explain, however, why twenty items in particular are desired.

While the redactor has crafted his sources into a unified literary whole, certain inconsistencies in the pericope suggest that the sources do not entirely agree as to what the various signs of ripeness indicate. As we have already pointed out, A, in juxtaposition with M. Maaserot 1:1G, leads us to expect that the signs of B-P indicate the point at which produce is edible, and therefore subject to the law of tithes. This is most plausible for the items of B-H and K-N, for all point to a relatively advanced stage in the ripening of the respective kinds of produce, an appropriate point at which they may be deemed edible. This is not, however, the case at I-J. At issue in the dispute is the point at which the fruit itself is deemed to have been formed. I claims that the walnut has been formed when the nutmeat is distinguishable from the shell. Judah (J), on the other hand, holds that the separated nutmeat is not a piece of fruit in its own right until it forms a husk, i.e., its own individual skin, around the meat. It is only within the context established by A that the issue is understood to relate to the point at which the produce is edible. If I-J is originally formulated in response to a problem concerning the law of tithes, its claim is that produce becomes subject to the law when the fruit forms, some time earlier than the point at which the produce may be eaten.

We meet similar problems at O and P. Fenugreek seeds, used primarily for medicinal purposes, can meet these purposes as soon as the seeds form. O, however, states that they are not subject to the law until they have become fertile. Edibility, therefore, is hardly at issue. Rather, the seeds become subject to the law when they can reproduce, i.e., when they become recognizable representatives of their species. Interpretation of P depends upon the meaning of the *terminus technicus,* "reaching a third." M. Sheb. 4:9 indicates that, in reference to olives, the term defines the point in their growth at which one *se'ah* of young olives will yield a third of the oil they would yield if fully-grown (i.e., one *log* instead of three *logs*). At issue, then, is the yield, not edibility. The point is the same for grain, which becomes subject to the law only when it can yield a worthwhile, if smaller than average, harvest. According to P, then, at least one sort of produce becomes subject to the law when it becomes an economically feasible harvest.

It is clear, then, that while M. Maaserot's redactor certainly wants us to understand all the signs he has listed to indicate edibility, his sources reveal the existence of rather different opinions. I-J and O suggest that produce becomes subject to the law when the edible portion becomes an independent entity, while P indicates that produce must become economically useful before it becomes subject to the law.

1:4

A. And among green vegetables –
B. cucumbers, and gourds, and chatemelons, and muskmelons (Sirillo adds: "are subject [to the law of tithes whether they are] large or small" [= D]).
C. Apples and citrons
D. are subject [to the law of tithes whether they are] large or small.
E. R. Simeon exempts citrons which are immature.
F. That which is subject [to the law] among bitter almonds [i.e., the small ones] is exempt among sweet [almonds].
G. That which is subject [to the law] among sweet almonds [i.e., the large ones] is exempt among bitter [almonds].

M. Maaserot 1:4

M. supplements and concludes M. 1:2-3's catalogue. The pericope consists of two autonomous units, A-D+E and F-G. The items of B and C are subject to the law whether they are large or small. The problem with this unitary reading, however, is that A, which promises a list of green vegetables, now includes among these apples and citrons, which do not fall within M.'s category of *yrq*. C-D, glossed at E, presents no problems. Apples and citrons are subject to the law when the fruit is "small," i.e., at the beginning of its formation, and remains so throughout its later growth. The ruling is congruent with M. 1:2I-J which, as we have seen, claims that produce is subject to the law when the portion normally eaten is fully formed. It disagrees, however, with the dominant thesis of M. 1:1D-H and M. 1:2-3, that produce becomes subject to the law only when it is edible. Simeon (E), on the other hand, represents the opinion of M. 1:1G-H. He exempts small citrons from the law, presumably because they are not edible until a later point in their growth. I cannot explain why he does not exempt small apples as well.

A pair of perfectly balanced declarative sentences, F-G, is entirely autonomous of the foregoing. The ruling assumes we know that bitter almonds are edible only when small, while sweet almonds are edible only when large. The point is that when the small bitter almonds are subject to the law, the sweet counterparts, which are still inedible, remain exempt. By the time the almonds become large, the sweet ones are subject to the law while the bitter ones are now exempt. F-G is a rather elegant conclusion to M.'s first major thematic unit, for the ruling permits us to apply the criterion of edibility to a concrete problem in the growth of produce. Let us now generalize on these very concrete matters.

What is striking in all this is that the entire mechanism of restrictions and privileges, from the field to home or market, is set in motion solely by the intentions of the common farmer. Priests cannot claim their dues whenever they choose, and God himself plays no active role in establishing when the produce must be tithed. Indeed, the framers of Mishnah-tractate Maaserot assume a profound passivity on the part of God. For them, it is human actions and intentions which move God to affect the world. God's claims against the Land's produce, that is to say, are only reflexes of those very claims on the part of Israelite farmers. God's interest in his share of the harvest, as I said, is first provoked by the desire of the farmer for the ripened fruit of his labor. His claim to that fruit, furthermore, becomes binding only when the farmer makes ready to claim his own rights to its use, whether in the field or at home or market. At this point we see how the heart forms the Meetingplace of God and Humanity, and how will and intentionality define the common ground of encounter. That is because, in will and intentionality, the human being and God are the same.

### Supplementing: *The Politics of Judaism,* Chapter Eight

#### Mishnah-tractate Gittin 4:2-6

|     |     |     |
| --- | --- | --- |
|     | A   | At first [the husband] would set up a court in some other place and annul it. |
|     | B.  | Rabban Gamaliel ordained that people should not do so, |
| I   | C.  | for the good order of the world. |
|     | D.  | At first he used to change his name and her name, the name of his town and the name of her town [i.e., to give an adopted name]. |
|     | E.  | And Rabban Gamaliel ordained that one should write, "Mr. So-and-so, and whatever alias he has," "Mrs. So-and-so, and whatever alias she has," |
| II  | F.  | for the good order of the world. |

M. 4:2

A. A widow collects [her marriage contract] from the estate of the orphans only by means of an oath.

B. They held back from imposing the oath on her.

C. Rabban Gamaliel the Elder ordained that she should take any vow the heirs wanted and collect her marriage contract.

D. The witnesses sign the writ of divorce.

III  E. for the good order of the world.

F. Hillel the Elder ordained the *prosbol*,

IV  G. for the good order of the world.

M. 4:3

A. A slave who was taken captive, and they redeemed him –

B. if as a slave, he is to be kept as a slave;

C. if a freeman, he is not to be enslaved.

D. Rabban Simeon b. Gamaliel says, "One way or the other, he is to be enslaved."

E. A slave who was made over as security for a debt by his master to others and whom the master [then] freed –

F. legally, the slave is not liable for anything.

V  G. But for the good order of the world, they force his master to free him.

H. and he [the slave] writes a bond for his purchase price.

I. Rabban Simeon b. Gamaliel says, "Only he writes [a bond] who frees him."

M. 4:4

A. "He who is half-slave and half-free works for his master one day and for himself one day," the word of the House of Hillel.

B. Said to them the House of Shammai, "You have taken good care of his master, but of himself you have not taken care.

C. "To marry a slave girl is not possible, for half of him after all is free.

D. "[To marry] a free woman is not possible, for half of him after all is a slave.

E. "Shall he refrain?

F. "But was not the world made only for procreation, as it is said, *He created it not a waste, he formed it to be inhabited* (Is. 45:18).

VI  G. "But: For the good order of the world, "they force his master to free him.

H. "And he [the slave] writes him a bond covering half his value."

I. and the House of Hillel reverted to teach in accord with the opinion of the House of Shammai.

M. 4:5

A. He who sells his slaves to a gentile,

B. or to someone who lives abroad –

C. he [the slave] has gone forth a free man.

D. They do not redeem captives for more than they are worth.

VII    E.    for the good order of the world

F.    And they do not help captives to flee,

VIII    G.    for the good order of the world.

H.    Rabban Simeon b. Gamaliel says, "For the good order of captives."

I.    and they do not purchase scrolls, *tefillin,* or *mezuzot* from gentiles for more than they are worth,

IX    J.    for the good order of the world.

M. 4:6

## Mishnah-tractate Baba Mesia 4:3

A.    R. Tarfon gave instructions in Lud: "Fraud is an overcharge of eight pieces of silver to a sela, one third of the purchase price."

B.    So the merchants of Lud rejoiced.

C.    He said to them, "All day long it is permitted to retract."

D.    They said to him, "Let R. Tarfon leave us where we were."

E.    And they reverted to conduct themselves in accord with the ruling of sages.

M. B. M. 4:3

The sage thus supervises the market. He makes provision for fair exchange, in the theory that a true value inheres in an object, so if one pays more than that true value by a given proportion, the sale is null.

## Mishnah-tractate Rosh Hashshanah 4:1-3

A.    The festival day of the New Year which coincided with the Sabbath –

B.    in the Temple they would sound the *shofar.*

C.    But not in the provinces.

D.    When the Temple was destroyed, Rabban Yohanan ben Zakkai made the rule that they should sound the *shofar* in every locale in which there was a court.

E.    Said R. Eleazar, "Rabban Yohanan b. Zakkai made that rule only in the case of Yabneh alone."

F.    They said to him, "All the same are Yabneh and every locale in which there is a court."

M. 4:1

A.    And in this regard also was Jerusalem ahead of Yabneh:

B.    in every town which is within sight and sound [of Jerusalem], and nearby and able to come up to Jerusalem, they sound the *shofar.*

C.    But as to Yabneh, they sound the *shofar* only in the court alone.

M.4:2

A.    In olden times the *lulab* was taken up in the Temple for seven days, and in the provinces, for one day.

B. When the Temple was destroyed, Rabban Yohanan ben Zakkai made the rule that in the provinces the *lulab* should be taken up for seven days, as a memorial to the Temple;

C. and that the day [the sixteenth of Nisan] on which the *'omer* is waved should be wholly prohibited [in regard to eating of new produce].

M. 4:3

A. At first they would receive testimony about the new moon all day long.

B. One time the witnesses came late, and the Levites consequently were mixed up as to [what] song [they should sing].

C. They made the rule that they should receive testimony [about the new moon] only up to the afternoon offering.

D. Then, if witnesses came after the afternoon offering, they would treat that entire day as holy, and the next day as holy too.

E. When the Temple was destroyed, Rabban Yohanan b. Zakkai made the rule that they should [once more] receive testimony about the new moon all day long.

F. Said R. Joshua b. Qorha, "This rule too did Rabban Yohanan b. Zakkai make:

G. "Even if the head of the court is located somewhere else, the witnesses should come only to the location of the council [to give testimony, and not to the location of the head of the court]."

M. 4:4

The rules of sounding the *shofar* turn to the special of the New Year which coincides with the Sabbath, M. 4:1A-C. Clearly, we have some diverse materials here since M. 4:1A-D (+E-F), are formally different from M. 4:3. The point of difference, however, is clear, since M. 4:3A has no counterpart at M. 4:1A-C, and this is for redactional reasons. That is, to connect his materials with what has gone before, the redactor could not introduce the issue of M. 4:1A-C with the formulary, *In olden times...When the Temple was destroyed...* Consequently, he has used the more common, mild apocopation to announce his topic, and then reverted to the expected formulary pattern, which I think, characterized M. 4:1A-C as much as M. 4:3. The dispute on M. 4:1A-D at E-F is presumably Ushan. M. 4:2A assumes a different antecedent construction from the one we have, a formulary which lists points in which Jerusalem is ahead of Yabneh, and, perhaps, points in which Yabneh is ahead of Jerusalem. But M. 4:2 clearly responds to M. 4:1E's view. M. 4:4A-C +D form a complete unit. E is distinctly secondary. The long antecedent narrative, A-D is formally out of phase with M. 4:3. The appendix supplied at F-G is thematically appropriate.

In the matter of the expiation for unwitting sin, Lev. 4:13-21 speak of the entire congregation's doing so:

"If the whole congregation of Israel commits a sin unwittingly and the thing is hidden from the eyes of the assembly, and they do any one of the things which the Lord has commanded not to be done and are guilty; when the sin which they have committed becomes known, the assembly shall offer a young bull for a sin-offering and bring it before the tent of meeting; and the elders of the congregation shall lay their hands upon the head of the bull before the Lord, and the bull shall be killed before the Lord. Then the anointed priest shall bring some of the blood of the bull to the tent of meeting, and the priest shall dip his finger in the blood and sprinkle it seven times before the Lord in front of the veil. And he shall put some of the blood on the horns of the altar which is in the tent of meeting before the Lord; and the rest of the blood he shall pour out at the base of the altar of burnt-offering which is at the door of the tent of meeting. And all its fat he shall take from it and burn upon the altar. Thus shall he do with the bull; as he did with the bull of the sin-offering, so shall he do with this; and the priest shall make atonement for them, and they shall be forgiven. And he shall carry forth the bull outside the camp, and burn it as he burned the first bull; it is the sin-offering for the assembly."

Lev. 4:22-26 say the same for the unwitting sin of the ruler:

"When a ruler sins, doing unwittingly any one of all the things which the Lord his God has commanded not to be done, and is guilty, if the sin which he has committed is made known to him, he shall bring as his offering a goat, a male without blemish, and shall lay his hand upon the head of the goat, and kill it in the place where they kill the burnt-offering before the Lord; it is a sin-offering. Then the priest shall take some blood of the sin-offering with his finger and put it on the horns of the altar of burnt-offering, and pour out the rest of its blood at the base of the altar of burnt-offering. And all its fat he shall burn on the altar, like the fat of the sacrifice of peace-offerings; so the priest shall make atonement for him for his sin, and he shall be forgiven."

The last relevant set of Scriptural verses is at Number 15:22-29, which go over the ground of the unwitting sin of the community.

"But if you err, and do not observe all these commandments which the Lord has spoken to Moses, all that the Lord has commanded you by Moses, from the day that the Lord gave commandment, and onward throughout your generations, then if it was done unwittingly without the knowledge of the congregation, all the congregation shall offer one young bull for a burnt-offering, a pleasing odor to the Lord, with its cereal-offering and its drink-offering, according to the ordinance, and one male goat for a sin-offering. And the priest shall make atonement for all the congregation of the people of Israel, and they shall be forgiven; because it was an error, and they have brought their offering, an offering by fire to the Lord, and their sin-offering before the Lord, for their error. And all the congregation of the people of Israel shall be forgiven, and the stranger who sojourns among them, because the whole population was involved in the error.

The program of Mishnah-tractate Horayot as a whole demands attention. The following outlines the treatment of the crisis represented by political error, which is to say, the system's remissions of its own discipline and rules:

## I. *The offering brought because of an erroneous decision by a court.* 1:1-5

1:1     If the court gave a decision to transgress any of the commandments and an individual did what they said, he is exempt, since he relied on the court. If someone on the court knew that the decision was in error, lo, this one is liable, since he knew and did not rely on the court. He who relies on himself (and makes an error) is liable; he who relies on the court is exempt.

1:2     If the court realized its error but the decision did not reach an individual, who went and did in accord with their original instruction, Simeon declares him exempt. Eliezer: He is subject to doubt.

1:3     If a court gave a decision to uproot a whole principle of the Torah, lo, they are exempt under the rule of Lev. 4:14. If they gave an instruction to nullify part and carry out part of a rule of the Torah, then they are liable under the rule of Lev. 4:14.

1:4     If the court was somehow impaired, they are exempt from a public offering under the rule of Lev. 4:14.

1:5     If the court and the community carried out the decision, they bring the required bullock, so Meir. Judah: Twelve tribes bring twelve bullocks.

## II. *The offering brought by the high priest who has unwittingly done what is contrary to the commandments of the Torah. The ruler.* 2:1-2:5

2:1     If an anointed high priest made a decision for himself and carried it out, all inadvertently, he brings a bullock. If he made the erroneous decision inadvertently but deliberately carried it out, or deliberately made an erroneous decision but inadvertently carried it out, he is exempt.

2:2     If a high priest made and erroneous decision by himself and carried it out by himself, he effects atonement for himself by himself. If it was with the community, he effects atonement for himself with the community.

2:3     Continuation of the foregoing.

2:4     They are not liable on account of a decision inadvertently violating a positive commandment of a negative concerning the sanctuary, but they are with regard to one involving a menstruating woman.

2:5     The inadvertent violation of Lev. 5:1-4's provisions does not fall under the laws of this tractate.

### III. Individual, anointed priest, community. 2:6-3:8

2:6     In the case of all the commandments of the Torah, on account of which they are liable for deliberate violation to expirpation, and on account of inadvertent violation to a sin-offering, and individual brings a female lamb; a ruler brings a male goat; an anointed high priest and court bring a bullock.

2:7     As to a suspensive guilt-offering, an individual and a ruler may become liable, but the anointed high priest and court do not become liable.

3:1     An anointed high priest who sinned and afterward was removed from office.

3:2     An anointed high priest who passed from his office as high priest and then sinned.

3:3     If they sinned before they were appointed and then they were appointed.

3:3-5   Definition of the anointed high priest. Amplification of M. 3:1-3.

3:6-8   Whatever is offered more regularly than its fellow takes precedence: bullock of an anointed priest and bullock of the congregation, etc.

### Appendix

The order of Scripture is to deal with unwitting sins on the part of the anointed priest, Lev. 4:3, then the whole congregation, Lev. 4:13, finally the ruler, Lev. 4:22. The Mishnah revises the order and regards as prior the unwitting sin of the whole community, committed, as we know, because of an erroneous instruction on the part of the court; then come the anointed priest and the ruler, treated more or less together. What is said at Unit I about the sin caused by the court's error is said at Unit II about that involving the high priest. There is a simple logic governing Unit I, first, the definition of culpability, M. 1:1-2; second, the explanation of the character of the court which is under discussion, M. 1:3-4, and an appendix at M. 1:5. M. 2:1-3 go over the same program. M. 2:4-5 form an appendix to all that has gone before. The final unit organizes relevant information but in no way advances the exposition of the topic. So the tractate is still shorter than it appears to be, since the final unit merely defines and clarifies terms used earlier.

A review of how Mishnah-tractate Horayot Chapter One sets forth the tractate's main principle is in order, since we see in the system's idiom of detailed exposition of minor points the fundamental principle by which the politics as a whole lays forth its claim to function as the ultimate source of power and authority for Israel. The Mishnah's authorship's unstated assumption is that Lev. 4:13-23 refers to a decision by a *court* which erroneously contradicts the Torah. On that basis, we treat the matter at hand as a political sin or crime and interpret issues in the context of the misuse of power. M. 1:1 asks about the culpability of an individual. Through a huge and laborious exercise, it makes the simple point that, when an individual relies upon a court decision, he is exempt, but if he relies upon his own view, he is liable. M. 1:2 carries forward this same problem and exempts an individual who could not possibly have known that a court had retracted an erroneous decision. Here there are some formal problems, but they do not stand in the way of the interpretation of the simple point. I present the remainder of the chapter in the appendix. There, it will be seen, M. 1:3 returns to the formal mode of making the point, which now is that, if the members of a court give an erroneous decision against clearly stated principles of the Torah, they are exempt from the penalties of Lev. 4:13, but if the court errs in some detail of a principle of the Torah, they are liable. M. 1:4 contains two pericopae, the first of which defines the court under discussion, and the second of which deals with the distinction between court and community, deliberate and inadvertent actions. Finally, M. 1:5 presents two triplets on whether the court under discussion is that of all Israel, or only of the several tribes, and on the number of bullocks owing in the case of error on the part of the high courts of the several tribes.

### Mishnah-tractate Horayot 1:1

A. [If] the court gave a decision to transgress any of all of the commandments which are stated in the Torah,

B. and [an individual] went and did in accord with their instruction, [so transgressing] inadvertently,

C. (1) whether they carried out what they said and he carried out what they said right along with them,

D. (2) or whether they carried out what they said and he carried out what they said after they did,

E. (3) whether they did not carry out what they said, but he carried out what they said –

F. he is exempt,

G. since he relied on the court.

H. [If] the court gave a decision, and one of them knew that they had erred,

I. or a disciple who is worthy to give instruction,

J. and he [who knew of the error] went and carried out what they said,

K.  (1) whether they carried out what they said and he carried out what they said right along with them,

L.  (2) whether they carried out what they said and he carried out what they said after they did,

M.  (3) whether they did not carry out what they said, but he carried out what they said –

N.  lo, this one is liable,

O.  since he [who know the law] did not in point of fact rely upon the court.

P.  This is the governing principle:

Q.  He who relies on himself is liable, and he who relies on the court is exempt.

M. 1:1

The perfect balance of A-G, H-O, allows P-Q to stand with very little exegesis. The main point is introduced at that element of the construction which is formally jarring, I mean, I, which underlines the shift of H and provides the antecedent of N. The one who follows the incorrect instruction of a court and does not know better is exempt from having to bring a sin-offering, for the obvious consideration of G. But the one who knew law but followed the incorrect decision of the court is going to be liable. The one who acts on his own knowledge is liable, and the one who knows only what the court tells him is exempt.

**Mishnah-tractate Horayot 1:2**

A.  [If] the court gave a decision and realized that it had erred and retracted it,

B.  whether they brought their atonement-offering or did not bring their atonement-offering,

C.  and [an individual] went and did in accord with their instruction –

D.  R. Simeon declares him exempt.

E.  And R. Eliezer says, "It is subject to doubt."

F.  What is the doubt?

G.  [If] the person had stayed home, he is liable.

H.  [If] he had gone overseas, he is exempt.

I.  Said R. 'Aqiba, "I concede in this case that he is nigh unto being exempt from liability."

J.  Said to him Ben 'Azzai, "What is the difference between this one and one who stays home?"

K.  "For the one who stays home had the possibility of hearing [that the court had erred and retracted], but this one did not have the possibility of hearing [what had happened]."

M. 1:2

M.'s main point is that if the court erred and discovered and corrected its error, but an individual did not know about the retraction, he is not liable, but this point is expressed in rather difficult style, because the dispute between Simeon and Eliezer is out of phase with what appears to be a quite separate conclusion supplied by 'Aqiba and Ben 'Azzai. 'Aqiba should not use the word, *concede,* since he has not *disagreed* with anything in the antecedent construction. While this theoretical story of the formation of the pericope has its problems, they are not more formidable than a unitary picture of the statement, since as we have it, we still have no grounds for 'Aqiba's conceding anything. In any event, the formal problems do not stand in the way of recognizing a perfectly clear conception, running through the whole, which, happily, I states quite lucidly.

A. [If] a court gave a decision to uproot the whole principle [of the Torah] –

B. (1) [if] they said, "[The prohibition against having intercourse with] a menstruating woman is not in the Torah [Lev. 15:19]."

C. (2) "[The prohibition of labor on] the Sabbath is not in the Torah."

D. (3) "[The prohibition against] idolatry is not in the Torah." –

E. lo, these are exempt [from the requirement of Lev. 4:14].

F. [If] they gave instruction to nullify part and to carry out part [of a rule of the Torah], lo, they are liable.

G. How so?

H. (1) [If] they said, "The principle of prohibition of sexual relationships with a menstruating woman indeed is in the Torah, but he who has sexual relations with a woman awaiting day against day is exempt."

I. (2) "The principle of not working on the Sabbath is in the Torah, but he who takes out something from private domain to public domain is exempt."

J. (3) "The principle of not worshipping idols is in the Torah but he who bows down [to an idol] is exempt." –

K. lo, these are liable,

L. since it is said, *If something be hidden* (Lev. 4:13) –

M. something and not everything.

M. 1:3

Once more a formally perfect construction makes its point both by contrast and by an explicit generalization at the end. A-E, + H-K, set up the obvious contrast, and L-M then make the whole still clearer. H refers to a woman who has a flow during the eleven *zibah*-days, on which a flux is not deemed menstrual. She has to wait for a clean day, that is, one on which there is no flux, before resuming sexual relations; this is a woman who is awaiting "day against day." Since she may not have sexual relations, a court which ruled to the contrary is in error. The other matters are clear as given. I am inclined to see the prooftext is needless. For the main point is that when the Torah is explicit,

there is no excuse for error.  No one is exempt specifically by reason of
the error of the court.  Exemption, E, is from that offering specified at
Lev. 4:14, therefore, in which the community as a whole commits an
unwitting error.  Here, at A-E, every individual remains liable to a sin-
offering, that is, each is penalized as an individual who has
committed a sin inadvertently.  Lev. 4:13 invokes the rule of the
offering made for the community which has erred only in the stated
circumstances, that is, where there is a true possibility of communal
inadvertence, such as the facts of B-D rule out.  Mere reason, unassisted
by revelation, stands behind that conclusion.

### Mishnah-tractate Horayot 1:4

A. (1) [If] the court gave a decision, and one of the members of the
court realized that they had erred and said to them, "You are in
error,"

B. or (2) if the head of the court was not there,

C. or (3) if one of them was a proselyte, a *mamzer*, a *Netin*, or an elder
who did not have children –

D. lo, these are exempt [from a public offering under the provisions of
Lev. 4:14]

E. since *Congregation* is said here [Lev. 4:13], and *Congregation* is said
later on [Num. 15:24].

F. Just as *congregation* later on applies only in the case in which all of
them are suitable for making a decision,

G. so *congregation* stated here refers to a case in which all of them are
suitable for making a decision.

I  H. [If] the court gave an incorrect decision inadvertently, and the
community followed their instruction [and did the thing in error]
inadvertently,

K. they bring a lamb of a goat )Lev. 4:32,27).

III  L. [If the court gave incorrect instruction] inadvertently, and [the
community followed their instruction and did the thing in error]
deliberately, lo, these are exempt [under the provision of Lev. 4:43].

M. 1:4

The point of the first pericope, A-G, is that the rule is invoked only in
the case of a valid court, B, C, and not one containing inappropriate
people, who are not suitable for a court; as we know from M. 1:1, in the
case of genuine error, A, there is no valid case.  Clearly A and B are out
of place, since the prooftext, E-G, has no relationship to the conception
of A or the consideration of B.  The second pericope, H-L, is far
smoother, a tight triplet.  H invokes the bullock referred to at Lev. 4:13
to a case in which the court and the community act inadvertently,
which is the clear sense of the verse: *If the whole congregation of
Israel commits a sin unwittingly and the thing is hidden from the eyes*

*of the assembly..., when the sin which they have committed becomes known, the assembly shall offer a young bull for a sin-offering.* J then interprets Lev. 4:27: *If any one of the common people sins unwittingly..., when the sin which he has committed is made known to him, he shall bring for his offering a goat, a female without blemish,* or, further, *If he brings a lamb as his offering, he shall bring a female* (Lev. 4:32). Since the reference is to the unwitting sin of a member of the community, it (must) follow, J-K, that the *court* is not unwitting but has deliberately given an incorrect ruling. L then follows from these two considerations, since Scripture makes no provision for the third case, it is excluded – which is where we started.

### Mishnah-tractate Horayot 1:5

| | | |
|---|---|---|
| I | A. | "[If] the court made an [erroneous] decision, and the entire community, or the greater part of the community, carried out their decision, they bring a bullock. |
| | B. | "In the case of idolatry, they bring a bullock and a goat," the words of R. Meir. |
| II | C. | R. Judah says, "Twelve tribes bring twelve bullocks. |
| | D. | "And in the case of idolatry, they bring twelve bullocks and twelve goats." |
| III | E. | R. Simeon says, "Thirteen bullocks, and in the case of idolatry thirteen bullocks and thirteen goats: |
| | F. | "a bullock and a goat for each and every tribe, and [in addition] a bullock and a goat for the court." |
| I | G. | "[If] the court gave an [erroneous] decision, and seven tribes, or the greater part of seven tribes, carried out their decision, |
| | H. | "they bring a bullock. |
| | I. | "In the case of idolatry, they bring a bullock and a goat," the words of R. Meir. |
| II | J. | R. Judah says, "Seven tribes which committed a sin bring seven bullocks. |
| | K. | "And the other tribes, who committed no sin, bring a bullock in their behalf, |
| | L. | "for even those who did not sin bring an offering on account of the sinners." |
| III | M. | R. Simeon says, "Eight bullocks, and in the case of idolatry, eight bullocks and eight goats: |
| | N. | "a bullock and a goat for each and every tribe, and a bullock and a goat for the court." |
| | O. | "[If] the court of one of the tribes gave an [erroneous] decision, and that tribe [only] carried out their decision, |
| | P. | "that tribe is liable, and all the other tribes are exempt," the words of R. Judah. |

Q.   And sages say, "There are liable only by reason of an [erroneous] decision made by the high court alone,

R.   "as it is said, *And if the whole congregation of Israel shall err* (Lev. 4:13) – and not the congregation of that tribe alone."

M. 1:5

At issue in the two triplets, A-F, G-N, is the position of Meir *vis à vis* both Judah and Simeon. Meir's view is that Lev. 4:14's reference to the congregation means the entire community of Israel. That is why, in the case of an erroneous decision on the part of a court, followed by the community as a whole, a single bullock is required; in the case of idolatry, Num. 15:24, a bullock and a goat are offered. Judah understands by *congregation* of Lev. 4:14 all the tribes, viewed severally. Simeon's position is a variation on Judah's. The only thing added by the second version of the triplet is at K-L, since Meir still has the required majority of the community, A. Judah now maintains that the tribes bring a bullock, K, for the reason given at L. O-R are required to clarify the position of Judah. Now we have only a single tribe which has committed a sin in line with Lev. 4:14. Only that tribe is liable, and Judah now does not require the other tribes to bring an offering too. The specific position of Q-R is out of line with all that has gone before. Sages of Q disagree with each of the views just now outlined, since, so far as they are concerned, *no* tribal court has the status of the high court, and the erroneous decision of none of them is going to be punished in the way specified by Scripture.

### Supplementing: *The Politics of Judaism,* Chapter Eleven

It is worth nothing that sages in the Mishnah could not conceive of a sizable settlement – town or city – as ethnically uniform. While for Aristotle, the presence of aliens in the polis did not form a consequential political fact, for the sages of the Mishnah, as we shall now see, a basic and definitive trait of the social order was that Israel did not make up the entirety, or the bulk, of the population of sizable settlements. And that fact did matter in the inner sanctum of the decision-making processes imagined by those sages. Let me give a concrete case to show the difference in the mode of thought that separated Aristotle's from sages' consideration of social difference. When the framers of the Mishnah spoke of a larger social unit than a village the assumption is that is was not made up entirely or mostly of Jews. Let me give a single graphic illustration of that fact, which also permits us to assess just how much difference that fact made in the larger thought of the philosophers at hand. Our case derives from Mishnah-tractate Uqsin 3:1-3,9:[2]

K. Lo, these (items) are classified as food only if there is an intention [on the owner's part to use them for human consumption], and [they become susceptible to impurity even] if there is no preparation (i.e., moistening). [The framers cannot determine the status of these things without asking the Israelite his intention].

L. [The following are examples]: (1) the carcass of a forbidden species of animal [such as a camel] regardless of its location [whether in a village or market place], and (2) an improperly slaughtered bird of a permitted species [such as a pigeon that an Israelite has] in a village.

M. These [items at L are classified as food only] if there is an intention [on the owner's part to use them for human consumption], and [they become susceptible to impurity even] if there is no preparation (i.e., moistening). The Israelite is forbidden to eat these things because they are a forbidden species of animal or because they were slaughtered improperly. Accordingly, the status of these items is uncertain. Will the Israelite throw them away or sell them to a gentile? To resolve the ambiguity, we take account of his intention]

N. [The following are examples of category IV]: (1) an improperly slaughtered animal of a permitted species [such as a cow], regardless of its location [whether in a village or market place], and (2) an improperly slaughtered bird of a permitted species [such as a pigeon, that an Israelite has] in the market place; and (3) the fat [from an animal of a forbidden species that an Israelite is carrying] in the market place.

O. Lo, these [items at N. may become susceptible to uncleanness even] if there is no preparation (i.e., moistening), and [they are classified as food even] if there is no intention [on the owner's part to use them for human consumption. The expectation is that he will sell them to a gentile because in one case he is in the market place (2) and in the other case the animal is extremely valuable (1). They are classified as food, therefore, regardless of what the owner intends].

What is important for our inquiry is the fact that the Mishnah's framers take account, in particular, of whether food is located in a village or in a city. Eilberg-Schwartz explains as follows:

> When the framers of this Mishnah can classify a foodstuff according to its normal use, they ignore the owner's plan. In the following rules, the framers consider food substances whose status they cannot

---

[2]Translation and commentary in Howard Eilberg-Schwartz, *The Human Will in Judaism. The Mishnah's Philosophy of Intention* (Atlanta: Scholars Press for Brown Judaic Studies, 1987), pp. 133-7.

determine on the basis of Israelite norms. This difficulty arises
because Israelites put certain types of things to more than one use.
Even in resolving this ambiguity, the framers appeal to subjective
criteria only as a last resort. First, they invoke three objective criteria:
1) the location of the foodstuff (whether in a town's market place or a
village), 2) its value (can the Israelite afford to discard it?) and, 3) its
marketability (will gentiles buy it?).

Eilberg-Schwartz's comments:

The framers consider the object's location. If they see an Israelite
carrying a fish of a forbidden species in the town market place,
Mishnah's philosophers classify it as food. Why? Since the Israelite
stands not in the village [which is all Jewish] but the market place [of a
town, where there also are gentiles], they assume he will sell this fish
rather than throw it away. When the Israelite carries the same fish in
his village, however, we can no longer be sure what he will do. On the
one hand, he may decide to throw it away, [since he has no gentile
near at hand]. On the other hand, he may choose to look for a gentile
buyer [who may happen by]. Therefore, to determine what he will do,
the framers must ask him his plan.

Two assumptions of the law become clear. First of all, the framers
take for granted that the inhabitants of a village will be mainly Jews.
Second, they assume that some of the inhabitants of a town large
enough to support a market will *not* be Jews – and, furthermore, that
fact makes a difference in determining the law in the case at hand. It
follows that a trait of a town, all the more so of a city will be different
from a trait of a village; the former will be made up of Jews, the latter
will be large, mixed, and diverse. I have dwelt on this matter at some
length to show that the passage at hand contains assumptions about
the character of Israelite settlement, on the one side, and of cities and
villages, on the other. These assumptions seem to be to enjoy the status
of facts, simply because people may be assumed to know what they are
talking about when the facts do not serve a controverted or polemical
purpose and in no way contradict what we know from other evidence.

The assumption that we must distinguish, as to the Jews' condition,
between settlements that were small and wholly Jewish and those that
were large and mixed bears several important implications for the
problem at hand – how Jews thought about, or experienced, large-scale
metropolitan life in late antiquity. To sum up: a town constituted an
economic unit, composed of economic units: a group of households, made
up of individual households, a household being the irreducible
economic unit of the society known to (or imagined by) sages. So much
for the sages' imagination of the household, town, and city. The
difference between town and city was trivial. It consisted of the fact
that, while in a town, pretty much everyone was Jewish, in a city,

there were gentiles – hardly a political unit, but rather an undifferentiated mass of faceless people, all of them falling into the same classification of "non-Jews."

A further word about Jerusalem and the matter of locativity. The several institutions that the system invents, for their part, locate themselves in a particular place, but are not enlandized on that account. I refer to the monarchy, Temple, and court or administration. True, all three locate themselves in Jerusalem. Nonetheless, the division of power among the institutions of politics is not locative. Wherever situated, the king and the court in fact mark distinctions that make no difference; the differentiation is fictive, because king, court, and Temple alike, are run by the ubiquitous sage. That is to say, shared responsibility to administer power is illusory; in fact the institutions are distinguished but the distinctions make no difference, since sages everywhere run everything.

But what of the supreme location, Jerusalem? Does the identification of that one unique place not impose upon all places a relationship, hence a location? Not at all. On the contrary, the locative quality of Jerusalem does not then impose upon other components of the political system hierarchical relationships based upon locative ones. True, the king is resident in Jerusalem, the high court is there, and the one Temple is there. But all other places are undifferentiated in relationship to that one place; that is to say, the only components of the politics that are located are those in Jerusalem; all the others are utopian in that they are no place in particular. Wherever they are is nowhere. And that means the locative quality of Jerusalem bears no implications for the utopian, nondescript situation of everywhere else. In fact, there are no spatial relationships indicated by relationship to the locus, Jerusalem, because the really indicative relationship in space is the one between Heaven and earth. That is locative, for it is centered on Jerusalem below, with Heaven corresponding above.

But then locativity pertains solely to Jerusalem, and the politics of everywhere else takes place no where in particular. The reason is then clear and I have specified it in context. No political institutions in the village or town correspond to any in Jerusalem. There are institutions that (in theory at least) are meant to link every place to that one place, e.g., the *maamad*, which serves in the village to carry out liturgies corresponding to those done in the Temple by the village's priesthood. But these are not institutions of power. And that is the point. The correspondence between village or town and Jerusalem is null; Jerusalem is somewhere in particular, but nowhere else is anywhere at all.  On that basis, there can be not politics but sacred geography.

# Appendix

# Why No Science in Judaism?

The Judaism of the Dual Torah on its own produced little philosophy, both in general and also in the particular natural and social forms that flourished in Christianity and Islam in the same time and circumstance. That claim of mine is captured by the simple fact that Copernicus was a monk in Poland in the sixteenth century and that the Church for purposes of accurately calculating the calendar assigned him the task that he performed, with unanticipated results to be sure. In Poland in that same century flourished countless towering intellectual figures within the Judaism of the Dual Torah; none of them known to us pursued questions of a scientific character in a philosophical manner, in the way in which their countryman and contemporary, Copernicus, did. And, of course, Copernicus stood in a long line of tradition, extending backward to the origins of Christian philosophy in Greece and forward into the seventeenth century. Nor did the Christian impetus for science end there; Mendelev, founder of genetics, we recall, was an Orthodox Christian monk. And the role of Protestant Christian philosophers, including scientists, in both the Reformation Churches and the free churches, hardly requires a sizable repertoire of instances. I may therefore stipulate as fact that until the seventeenth century science, as a division of philosophy, formed an important component of the intellectual life of the principal systems of Christianity, east and west, Greek and Latin. I maintain that the Judaism of the Dual Torah did not yield science, while, in the same times and circumstances, diverse Christian systems did. And I want to know what characterized the mind of Judaism that made philosophy, including natural philosophy, an uncommon outcome of intellectual inquiry: why this, not that?

## I. The Question of Science in the Larger Setting of Thought: Making Connections and Drawing Conclusions

The Judaism of the Dual Torah has coped only with considerable difficulty with the three definitive components of modern life, specifically, fundamental changes of behavior and belief in politics, economics, and intellect. Democracy, capitalism, and science including technology emerged elsewhere than from within the mind and imagination of thinkers nurtured by the canonical writings of that Judaism. While Jews sustained by intellectual resources in addition to the Judaism of the Dual Torah, for example, in medieval times by the Western philosophical tradition of Greece mediated by Islam, or in modern times by a different Judaism, or by no Judaism at all, found in democracy, or capitalism, or, for medieval times, science, medicine, and technology, valued sources for right thinking and worthwhile living, the institutions and intellect of the Judaism of the Dual Torah did not. Decision-making, individual and institutional, referred to the authority of sages. Sustained, systematic, rational economic activity took a subordinate place, well behind study of the Torah, as the paramount activity of men's (but not women's) lives. Scientific learning, empirical testing and sustained experiment in the sorting out hypotheses and evaluating of propositions, systematic skepticism concerning received truths – all of these routine contemporary modes of thought were held to be matters of triviality, wasting time best spent only in Torah-study.

## II. The Logics of Cogent Discourse: How Two Facts [=Sentences] Join Together to Make a Cogent Statement [=to Make Sense]

I propose to explain why the normative modes of thought and intellect, which I call, "the mind," of the Judaism of the Dual Torah did not generate the kind of thinking that produced science, the division of philosophy known until nearly our own day as natural philosophy. By thought I mean, specifically, two things, first, how people connect one thing to something else, one fact to another, in literary terms, one sentence to another; and, second, how they draw conclusions from the particular connections that they make in their minds. These two stages – the perception of connection, the discernment of (self-evidently valid) conclusions based on the connection – characterize mind. They further allow us to explore the potentialities and also the limitations of intellect, what people are likely to see or to miss. In particular I show the range of choices available in the making of connections and the drawing of conclusions. I call them "logics," meaning, specifically, the modes of intelligible discourse. Specifically, how do I join one thought to another, therefore also one sentence to another, in such a way as to make a point that you can grasp. Let me give a simple example.

*It rained heavily today./A ship came up the Mississippi River.*

In our world of cogent thought, sentence one standing by itself bears no relationship to sentence two.

*It rained heavily today./No ship came up the Mississippi River.*

In our world of cogent thought, sentence one explains sentence two; because of the rain, joined with heavy winds, shipping in the Mississippi River ceased. We could make sense out of the first of the two instances also, e.g., by adding "despite the fact that...," and the like. But the point is clear. We have rules in our minds that permit us to link one fact to another and that prevent us from doing so as well. When we know those rules, that is, the logics of cogent discourse and therefore also of intelligible thought, we know how our minds work.

## III. The Four Logics [=Principles of Cogent Discourse, the Ands and the Equals] of Judaic Holy Books [=Canonical Writings] in the Definitive Documents of Judaism

We turn directly to a single text and survey the several answers its authorship gives to a simple question: how do one *and* one *equal* two? We want only to define the *and* and the *equal,* simple parts of speech, so to speak. For a sample document, I have chosen Sifré to Deuteronomy. It is of indeterminate origin in time, but certainly coming after the formation of the Mishnah, in ca. A.D. 200, and before the closure of the Talmud of Babylonia or Bavli, in ca. A.D. 600. In the document at hand I see four different logics by which two sentences are deemed to cohere and to constitute a statement of consequence and intelligibility.

### A. Propositional Cogency

While philosophers in the Greco-Roman tradition will have made their points concerning other topics entirely, modes of proof will surely have proved congruent to the systematic massing of probative facts, all of them pertinent, all of them appropriate, to the argument and the issue. Collecting data and classifying them by their indicative traits, permitting identification of unities and diversities – the genus and the species – form the definition of one kind of scientific thinking. Here we see that kind of thinking. In propositional logic, which is the one we know best, connection is shown in a conclusion, different from the established facts of two or more sentences, that we propose to draw when we set up as a sequence two or more facts we claim to be connected and further claim out of that sequence to propose a proposition different from, transcending, the facts at hand.

## B. *Narrative Cogency*

Narrative connects facts into propositions in ways that for us are equally familiar to the philosophical mode, because narrative connections are, in their way, as propositional as the connections of philosophical logic. In this mode of thought, we prove propositions by appeal to teleology – the direction or purpose of facts, e.g., events. A proposition (whether or not it is stated explicitly) may be set forth and demonstrated by showing through the telling of a tale that a sequence of events, real or imagined, shows the ineluctable truth of a given proposition. The logic of connection demonstrated through narrative, rather than philosophy, is simply stated. It is connection attained and explained by invoking some mode of narrative in which a sequence of events, first this, then that, is understood to yield a proposition, first this, then that – *because of this.* That manufactured sequence both states *and also establishes* a proposition in a way different from the philosophical and argumentative mode of propositional discourse. Whether or not the generalization is stated in so many words rarely matters, because the power of well-crafted narrative is to make unnecessary explicitly drawing of the moral.

## C. *Metapropositional Cogency*

The third logic is a sustained and highly cogent propositional discourse carried on at two levels, the immediate and the generalizing, in which one analytical method applies to many sentences, with the result that many discrete and diverse sentences are shown to constitute a single intellectual structure. This too is a highly scientific way of thinking, since it asks for unities in diversity, the rule that underlies diverse data, the regularity and order that explain the surface of things. A variety of explanations and amplifications, topically and propositionally unrelated, will be joined in such a way as to make a point beyond themselves and applicable to them all. Here we have a fixed way of connecting diverse things, so showing that many things really conform to a single pattern or structure. It is the promiscuous application to a range of discrete facts of a single mode of thought, that is, a cogent analytical method. Methodologically coherent analysis then imposes upon a variety of data a structure that is external to all of the data, yet that imposes connection between and among facts or sentences, a connection consisting in the order and balance and meaning of them all, seen in the aggregate. One of the most common modes of intelligible discourse is to ask the same question to many things and to produce a single result, wherever that question is asked: methodical analysis of many things showing pattern and therefore order where, on the surface, none exists.

## D. *Fixed Associative Cogency*

Fixed associative logic does not yield a proposition. But, on the positive side, that logic tightly links one fact to another. It does so not by joining the two through a proposition shared among them both, that is, through an intrinsic intersection, but through a property shared by them both and extrinsic to them both, namely, intersection with a common point of connection formed by an available set of associations, hence, fixed (or available) associations (or extrinsic connections). I underline the fact that the sense of the logical connection and sequence of things that links in one composition sentence 1, then sentence 2, then sentence 3, *though there is no propositional connection between* 1 and 2 or 2 and 3, rests upon principles of intelligibility hardly commonplace in our minds. Nothing links one sentence (completed thought or fact) to the ones fore or aft. Yet the compositors present us with sequences of episodic sentences that they represent side by side with sentences that do form large propositional compositions, that is, that are linked one to the next by connections that we can readily discern.

The logic of fixed associations rests upon the premise that *an established sequence of words joins whatever is attached to those words into a set of cogent statements, even though it does not form of those statements propositions of any kind, implicit or explicit.* The established sequence of words may be made up of names always associated with one another. It may be made up of a received text, with deep meanings of its own, e.g., a verse or a clause of Scripture. It may be made up of the sequence of holy days or synagogue lections, which are assumed to be known by everyone and so to connect on their own. The fixed association of these words, whether names, whether formula such as verses of Scripture, whether lists of facts, serves to link otherwise unrelated statements to one another and to form of them all not a proposition but, nonetheless, *an entirely intelligible sequence of connected or related sentences.* What is said. The *and* therefore derives from a fixed association among traits or formulas common to sequential sentences but external to them all. Some may suppose that we have nothing more than a fancy statement of the plain old (il)logic of free association. But that is far from the case. Free association means, "there is this, and, by the way, this reminds us of that." But the logic of fixed association invariably appeals to an available structure to form connections between otherwise unconnected sentences or facts. And we can always identify the source of the fixedness of association, e.g., in a sequence of verses of Scripture, or in an established order of sages' names, or in a known set of historical events, deemed always to fall in a given order, or in the synagogue lections, and the like.

## IV. The Two Paramount Logics of the Talmud of Babylonia [Bavli]: Propositional for Setting Forth Completed Units of Thought [=Paragraphs] and Fixed Associative for Joining Sequences of Completed Units of Thought ["Chapters" or Whole Books]

Among the four logics I have outlined, all documents of the Judaism of the Dual Torah find ample guidance for making cogent statements. But one of those documents, the Talmud of Babylonia or the Bavli, took paramount place and served, from the seventh century to the present, to define Judaism. Accordingly, if we want to know how the mind of Judaism works, we turn in particular to the Bavli. What we find there is that two of the logics predominate, each for its own purpose. One, the logic of propositional discourse, defines how completed units of thought, which we should call "paragraphs," are composed. That is, two or more facts join together to make a point, prove a proposition, comprise an argument. The other, the logic of fixed association, is paramount when it comes to joining completed units of thought to one another. The upshot is that the Bavli's authorships' completed compositions of thought – the propositions, whether philosophical, or teleological, or metapropositional, in logical cogency – are laid out like a commentary to the Mishnah. Each of its discussions, cogent in itself because of the inner relationships of sentences in making points or establishing propositions – is placed where it is located specifically to amplify in some way or another a statement of the Mishnah (or of Scripture). So the discussions one by one turn out, in the aggregate, to be highly propositional, to intend to say some one thing and to prove it. But the discussions are joined to one another not through proposition and argument, but rather, through a position assigned to them, without regard to continuous argument and sustained meaning, because of their pertinence to the sequence of sentences or paragraphs of the Mishnah or of Scripture.

What defines the *and*, and what defines the *equal*, of the sentence, *two and two equal four*? What I see here is a mixed mode of putting two and two together, one propositional, for the paragraphs or the whole units of completed thought, the other not, for the linkage of the paragraphs into a sustained composition or discourse. The one makes points through juxtaposing facts, that is to say, sentences, which are meant to bear an intrinsic relationship to one another because they point toward a common conclusion. The other puts two units of discussion side by side not because of an intrinsic relationship, established by a shared proposition, but because of an extrinsic relationship, imposed and imputed from the outside by the simple fact that the sentences of the Mishnah or of Scripture demand this relationship and order and not some other or no relationship and order at all. So much for the way in which the four available logics of discourse work within the Bavli. And that brings us to the question with which I commenced: why no science in Judaism?

**V. Why No Science in Judaism? [1] There were both philosophy and science, but the modes of thought derived from other than the Bavli and its related writings. Judaism in its canonical writings did not put things together in the way in which philosophy, including natural philosophy, did, because it mixed two logics: propositional and fixed associative, while philosophy, including natural philosophy, remained wholly propositional.**

Science as a mode of thought bears two distinct, though related meanings; it is not a subject matter alone; it is preeminently a mode of thought. As subject matter, science concerns natural phenomena. As a mode of thought, science involves orderly and systematic comprehension, description, and explanation of natural phenomena, which, in my terms, I should call the making of connections between one thing and another and the drawing of conclusions based on the making of connections. And the critical component of science is the making of connections in one way rather than in some other: this relates to that, but it does not relate to the other thing. These connections – and also rejection of connections – are discovered or intuited, then tested empirically, not supplied, not received, and not dictated by convention. It is science in the latter sense, as a mode of thought, but encompassing the former, an interest in natural phenomena, that I claim not to find in mind exhibited by the formative stages of the canon of the Judaism of the Dual Torah.

Any claim that the mind made by the Bavli could not do science because speculative thinking of a philosophical order was prevented by traditional thinking of an unsystematic character, incapable of either pursuing curiosity or generalizing, contradicts the character of the Bavli itself. The Bavli, viewed whole and at the end, is not a traditional document, but one deriving from that sort of systematic and orderly thinking that we associate with the philosophical mind: speculative, highly rigorous and propositional in purpose. In the sense that "traditional" teachings derive from a long process of a sedimentary order, accumulation and conglomeration, tradition is incompatible with the notion of system, and the Bavli states its ideas whole, complete, and systemically. That statement that the Bavli as a whole makes, specifically, bears many traits that point to cogent and systematic thought – system-building – but few literary or historical traits of that long-term agglutination and conglomeration, such as a sedimentary process yields.

The authorship of the Bavli taught not only *what* to think, but *how* to think. The authorship of the Bavli exhibited in public the reasoning behind its results. It would follow that generations nurtured on the study of the Bavli would be educated to find self-evident not only the propositions of the Bavli but also its processes of thought, specifically, of analysis, the making of connections, and of synthesis, the drawing of conclusions. Because the Bavli records an on-going conversation, a dialectic without a final stopping point, the conversation never ended, and later generations could locate for themselves a place within it. And making intelligible statements within the intellectual syntax and structure of the Bavli, age succeeding age carried forward those principles of cogency and argument that found initial definition in the pages of the Bavli itself. That is why process, not only proposition, imposed upon the intellect of succeeding generations that character that the shared mind of Judaism exhibited. And from our perspective, a particular aspect of that dialectic, which the Bavli's ebb and flow of argument conveys, takes on special importance.

**VI. Why No Science in Judaism? [2] Why the mixed logics of propositional discourse for completed units of thought and fixed associative discourse for composition of large-scale, sequential units of thought, served exceedingly well: The power of the Bavli and the pathos of the Bavli are one and the same.**

*What makes possible the very distinctive character of the Bavli's discourse, its moving, or dialectical, argument, which flows from point to point in an unbroken stream of conversation, is the sense of the connectedness of thought that animates the whole.* Even the brief snippets we examined show how the authorships have put together discrete sentences in such a way that the connections between one and the next, or between one set and the next, derive not from proposition – "let us prove this, by appealing to the following facts" – but from a shared, prior, and a priori program. The fundamental logic of the dialectical argument, the principle by which cogency is imputed to two or more sentences in succession, is that same logic of fixed association that joins the very largest units of thought into a single sustained document, a treatment of a Mishnah-paragraph, a treatise on a Mishnah-tractate, upward to the Bavli as a whole. Let me state the link I perceive between dialectic and the logic of fixed association very emphatically:

*Given the clear sense of the compositors that they have, in fact, composed a cogent document made up of cogent compositions themselves comprising connected sentences, we have to conclude that dialectical argument appeals in the end to that logic of fixed association. That is what makes it necessary to maintain and sustain the movement that defines dialectical argument. Moving from one thing to the next, and by the way, there is this also to consider, but then this leads to that – that characterization of the dialectical argument tells us what holds the whole together. And it is that sense of the givenness of connection that makes unnecessary the disciplined composition of a sustained and well-constructed argument, proposition, proof, argument, and the like.*

**VII. Why No Science in Judaism? [3] The impediment to philosophical, therefore also scientific, thinking presented by the logic of fixed association: The pathos and the power of the Bavli's mixed logics.**

The fixed association of one thing to the next is imputed or supplied, not discovered or achieved by the engaged participants to discourse. That trait of mind precludes inquiry into matters beyond the framework of the convention of fixed association (whatever it is), except within the limits of reason defined by that convention. So while scientific argument may move in a dialectical manner, talmudic argument would not yield science. That is why it is the very power of the Bavli, namely, its exposition of its modes of thought and the steps of argument, that also constitutes its pathos, its strength, its weakness. For the two absolutely necessary traits of mind of philosophy, including natural philosophy, require, first, systematically thinking about propositions in a philosophical manner, and, second, highly speculative pursuit of wherever curiosity leads. *Connection therefore cannot be imputed and must be discovered.*

By contrast, dialectical argument, which appeals for connection to extrinsic points of intersection, e.g., with a common third element, may or may not yield philosophical argument about propositions. But a logic of fixed association, which, I argue, to begin with makes possible the dialectical argument that distinguishes the Bavli, assuredly imposes limits upon the free run of curiosity hither and yon. For fixed association is just that: fixed, defined from without. The fixedness of association is what makes possible dialectical argument, without the danger of chaos and descent into caprice and irrationality. But it also is what makes unlikely the free pursuit of curiosity wherever it leads: why this, not that? Once more, power and pathos meet: the strength of dialectic rests upon fixed association, which protects the integrity of discourse; the weakness of dialectic is this same fixed association, limiting, as it does, the potentialities of inquiry to a preassigned program and predetermined limits.

So at the center of matters is not the issue of propositional thought, of which the Bavli presents an ample and sophisticated example. It is the manner of making connections and – consequently, inexorably and unavoidably – also the drawing of conclusions, that is, that very centerpiece of mind that I identified at the outset as characteristic of the writings of the Judaism of the Dual Torah. The mode of argument, and not the character of the propositions, is what made unlikely the development of science as part of the philosophical tradition. Once connections came from without, the making of connections and drawing of conclusions would derive from that same received program of inquiry. The received program of fixed associations hardly stimulated looking to the world beyond the Torah, whether the world of nature or the world of social history. It is not because people within the Bavli's intellectual framework avoided making generalizations or presenting conclusions in an orderly and systematic way. That is beside the point, and it also is not true. It is because people used to receiving associations within a fixed and available program found slight stimulus to observe associations on their own, to ask why this, not that in circumstances in which this and that join together not in fixed and available intersection but solely in the mind of an observer.

Nature and social history did not form realms in which people would anticipate associating facts and explaining the association by drawing conclusion. The received program of the Torah, written and oral, set forth those realms in which people would expect to associate two unrelated facts and explain their intersection, unity, difference or harmony. Let me state matters simply: why in the mind of the Judaism of the Dual Torah was there no science in particular, even when there could be philosophy?

*Because in a system of fixed texts, you need a fixed text to make connection, and nature provides no fixed texts. In forming the large world in which everything would be contained in some one thing, the Bavli's authorship relied for connection upon the received text, and necessarily drew conclusions resting upon connection solely within the dictates of an a priori and imputed system of making connections. These constitute connections supplied and not discovered, structures ultimately imputed through extrinsic processes of thought, and not nurtured through the proposal and testing of propositions intrinsic to the matter at hand.*

## VIII. The Torah Begins Where Philosophy Ends

Philosophy and therefore also natural philosophy demanded what the mind of the Judaism of the Dual Torah could not – and can never – concede. And that was the datum that the quest for unity in diversity, simplicity in complexity, order in disorder, and regularity in anomaly, engaged only humanity's mind, but not God's too. All Judaisms, including especially the normative one of the Dual Torah, knew to search for unity, simplicity, order, regularity, and therefore explanation, because to begin with God created the world as unified, simple, orderly, regular, and therefore subject and susceptible to explanation. The premise that one might go in quest for systematic knowledge derived for the Judaism of the Dual Torah from the Torah, which recorded, for humanity to know, God's work in making the world and in forming Israel for the sanctification of the here and now and the salvation of the world at the end of time. Philosophy began with not knowledge but search for knowledge, and the mind of Judaism began with a quest made possible, to begin with, by the character of the human mind, made, as it was, "in our image, after our likeness."

Judaism therefore could not, on its own, generate philosophy, not because issues of a propositional character intervened, or even because modes of thought vastly differed, but for one simple reason.

*It was, and is, that philosophy ended where Judaism began.*

The Judaism of the Dual Torah could not deny the knowledge that to begin with the mind of Judaism encompassed. The upshot is simple. What philosophy sought – unity, simplicity, order, regularity – is that very destination at which the quest of the mind of the Judaism of the Dual Torah commenced. What the one wanted the other knew it had. And in consequence what the mind of that Judaism was meant to make possible was therefore a different search altogether from the philosophical and the scientific, which for the Judaism of the Dual Torah which is Judaism was, and is, that search for God whose being formed the unity, the simplicity, the order, the regularity, to which, in the mythic language of faith, sanctification in the world and salvation at the end of time referred. For sanctification spoke of all things bearing each its rightful name, the correct ordering of all reality in the natural world, and salvation addressed the right and true ordering, thus ending of all reality in the world of society, therefore of history. The one can have yielded scientific proposition, the other teleological proposition, and, in the context of the Torah, each did. But the mind of Judaism accomplished its tasks in its way, using its language, in response to the logics self-evident in its circumstance and perception of the world.

For the task of a quest for the explanation of how things intersected and made sense drew the mind of Judaism into the Torah, record of God's plan and program for the world.  And that has made all the difference.  And, if I may conclude as a believing Jew, it still can make all the difference, *it still can.*

# Index

Cross, Frank M., Jr. 5

Cyrus 24

Damages 46, 47, 102

daughter 82, 148, 153, 154, 156, 162, 195

David 204

Davisson 64, 65, 67, 68, 71, 87, 92, 94-96, 98

Day of Atonement 160, 162, 168, 189

Dead Sea Scrolls 30

democracy 236

Deuteronomy (Dt., Deut.) 27, 29, 34, 49, 51, 97, 101, 102, 105-107, 110, 112, 118, 151, 154-158, 161, 186, 196, 199, 204, 205, 208, 209, 210, 237

distributive economics 61, 63-67, 69-75, 77, 78, 87, 88, 91-96, 98, 101, 105-108, 111, 115, 118, 119, 190

Dosa 167, 168, 190, 204

Dual Torah 4, 8, 10, 12, 25-30, 32, 61, 62, 64, 88, 235, 236, 240, 241, 244, 245

Dumont, Louis 105

Eden 186-188

Egypt 24, 68, 96, 107, 198

Eleazar 148, 167, 197, 198, 200, 204-207, 220

Eleazar b. Azariah 167, 197, 198

Eleazar Haqqappar 207

Eliezer 157, 161, 164, 197, 199, 223, 226, 227

Eliezer b. Jacob 164

eschatological 39

Essene 49

Essenes 23, 77, 78

Essenes of Qumran 78

Essner, Howard Scott 114

ethics 30, 32, 79, 83, 84, 132

ethnos 30, 32, 125

ethos 30, 32

exegesis 6, 7, 26, 27, 33, 55, 61, 62, 90, 110, 150, 157, 158, 208, 226

Exile 24, 25, 34-38, 85, 156-159, 182, 207

Exodus 27, 49, 50, 175

Ezra 29, 35, 36, 50

Five Books of Moses 23, 35, 36, 38

fixed association, logic of 239, 240, 242-244

Fox-Genovese, Elizabeth 60

free association 239

Genesis Rabbah 10, 27, 29

Genesis (Gen.) 10, 26, 27, 29, 35, 77, 112, 127, 162, 188, 205

Gentiles 33, 46, 109, 116, 117, 220, 232, 233

Gerth, H.H. 123, 132

God 5, 8, 11, 12, 16, 24, 25, 27, 29, 37, 39, 40, 43, 45, 54, 55, 68-70, 72-75, 78, 88-91, 95-102, 104, 106-108, 112, 118, 119, 131, 133, 144, 146, 150-152, 161, 169-177, 179, 181, 183-188, 198, 201, 205, 207, 209-212, 214, 218, 222, 245

Goldscheider, Francis K. 127

gospels 77

Greco-Roman tradition 237

Greek 77, 135, 201, 235

# DATE DUE

| | | | |
|---|---|---|---|
| | | | |
| | | | |
| | | | |
| | | | |
| | | | |
| | | | |
| | | | |
| | | | |
| | | | |
| | | | |
| | | | |
| | | | |
| | | | |
| | | | |
| | | | |
| | | | |

HIGHSMITH    #LO-45220